FROM WAR TO PEACE

WISDOM AND LEADERSHIP

Ex-Servicemen's Role in Good Governance and Rural Development

---

FROM WAR TO PEACE
WISDOM AND LEADERSHIP

Ex-Servicemen's Role in Good Governance and Rural Development

Lt Gen (Dr.) S. K. Gadeock, AVSM (Retd)

PENTAGON PRESS LLP

First published in 2023 by

PENTAGON PRESS LLP
206, Peacock Lane, Shahpur Jat
New Delhi-110049, India
Contact: 011-64706243

Typeset in Palatino, 10.5 Point
Printed by Aegean Offset Printers, Greater Noida, U.P.

ISBN: 978-93-90095-76-6 (HB)

www.pentagonpress.in

DEDICATION

This book is most affectionately dedicated to my beloved wife, Sonalika, my charming daughter Dr. Safina Gadeock Humphries, PhD, her dynamic husband Bradley Simon Humphries, my very adorable son Safeer Gadeock and his wonderful spouse Mrs Radhika Gadeock who have provided me bounteous joy and been endearing source of inspirational patronage in all these beautiful years of my life. They have undeniably been the quintessence of the charismatic spirit of the 'trials and triumphs' in my finely-chequered and honorable military career in the Indian Army, an 'Epos Non-Pareil', which defined the crimson path of crowning glory till the twilight years of my superannuation. I would be infringing on the sensibilities in the sibling domain, if I do not mention the endearments shared and encouragement received from my parents and sisters Neera, Meera and Priya all through the passage of time.

Contents

PROLOGUE

A military career is respectable and honourable, pursued by many who find it extremely satiating. It is a balanced life, which manifests dignity and self-pride in serving the country as custodians of peace and security. However, as in all professions, the concern of any individual would be in the twilight years of superannuation, as to what next. There must be cogent answers by the Government and the respective branches of the Armed Forces to take good care of the remaining years of soldiers, sailors and airmen. Their welfare would now come first, having served the nation with sterling attributes of loyalty, dedication, tenacity, and foremost, an unblemished character exemplified by 'blood and honour'.

There are approximately 60,000 personnel who retire every year from the defence forces. There would be about 44 per cent of pensioners in the age group of 40–50, with 33 per cent in the 35–40-year age group, while 12 per cent of the citizens who leave the Services are in the age group of 30–35 years. The optimal utilisation of this well trained and comparatively younger workforce exiting the Services can yield numerous profits. *Firstly, it will exponentially lift the morale of Indian soldiers and give better self-confidence and pleasure of potential job security. Secondly, both the public and private sectors can profit by engrossing skilled and regimented employees, and thirdly, employing ex-servicemen is cheaper for the government as compared to new recruitments,* since they are remunerated only the difference between their entitled emoluments of the work and the pension drawn by them.

About 80 per cent of ex-servicemen of the rank of JCOs and NCOs post retirement have settled in their villages. Investments incurred in the focused training of the ex-servicemen while in service should not be permitted togo unutilised. It requires some time and money to make a man culturally wealthy to enable him to recognise the importance of firmness, discipline, truthfulness to occupation, honesty in dealings, etc. Therefore, the training acquired in the Army, both technical and moral, should not be allowed to go waste to ensure a holistic growth from the grassroot level up to the highest level in Indian states. The same also finds a mention in the questionnaire as replied by Dr. P. Sankar, IAS, District Collector, in the Nilgiris, *"The archetypal services of the ex-servicemen can be utilized not only in the RAPID model but also in various Government sectors such as Highways & Road Transport, Ports & Shipping, Aviation, Health, Disaster Relief, Public Works and Infrastructure, Supply Chain Management, e-Governance & Transport, etc."*

Various measures for national rural socio-economic transformation have been taken. They are based on detailed critical analysis, comprehensive study and intensive interactions, which are recommended for holistic growth of our rural areas, where ex-servicemen leadership is paramount and could make a conspicuous difference. State governments must *encourage agro-industry based self-employment*. A study done by the Directorate-General of Resettlement, New Delhi, has revealed that most of the self-employed ex-servicemen in the villages are engaged in the agriculture sector. Villages should be by supported (including retired defence personnel) by setting up small industries like dairy farming, poultry, piggery, sheep and goat breeding, beekeeping, sericulture, etc. Anti-poverty strategies, like alleviation of poverty all the way through social mobilisation, training and capacity building have proved to be successful. Using science and disruptive technology for inclusive rural growth to include e-health care and distance education is very important along with promoting the popularity of e-governance in villages.

Infrastructure development through the gram panchayats is vital for growth and development with more industries to penetrate rural India. The growth story of Indian industry is that of success; though all their products do reach the rural areas and villages, the role of middlemen in the marketing of farm produce end up in making the products expensive for rural consumers. It is therefore imperative for the industry to develop distribution capabilities in the rural areas by meticulous 'Distribution Planning'. The physical distribution system in rural market includes transportation, storage, local delivery and sub-distribution. Companies need to develop a barefoot approach and train local talent to operate as 'barefoot salesmen'. Ex-servicemen from the logistics branches of the three services who are residing in these villages have the knack for distribution management. Private industry must tap this potential to penetrate the rural market in a more profitable and economical way.

Problems of warehousing and storage in the rural marketing context are well known. It is not possible to service the interior outlets efficiently with the existing warehouses. Hence, rural warehousing co-operatives should be established with warehousing facilities in each of the RAID (Rural Area Integrated Development) cluster headquarters. Technical knowledge and expertise of ex-servicemen from the Engineers and MES branches of the three services should be exploited to construct and man these warehouses. For holistic growth involving ex-servicemen in nation building, the government should ensure that a certain plausible percentage must be employed with the Ministry of Defence (MoD), which is a major employer of the civilian workforce. Organisations like defence public sector undertakings (PSUs), defence research & development organisations (DRDO), Directorate-General of êuality Assurance (DGêA), defence think-tanks, Canteen Stores Department and hospitals employ several hundred thousand civilians. Absorption of ex-servicemen in such organisations will increase the overall synergy, reduce defence expenditure and increase the satisfaction levels of ex-servicemen.

India Inc. can efficiently utilise our ex-servicemen across functions, be it security, HR or procurement. However, the heartbreaking reality is that the bottom-line matters even for the companies with a big heart. India should take a lesson from the tax credit system that was available in the USA for employers who hired veterans (ex-servicemen). For a US corporate employer, the tax credit can be as high as $ 9,660 for every qualified veteran hired. A parallel model might be adopted by our Finance Ministry to give tax concessions to companies that hire ex-servicemen based on their ability. It is time to have a more cerebral approach and understand business realities. Further, there is a need to institutionalise this and make it a mandatory (rather than obligatory) provision under Corporate Social Responsibility (CSR).

The Department of Ex-Servicemen's Welfare offers a host of self-employment schemes but the demand which exists is far more than the availability. The government needs to create a climate which brings together industry as the franchisor, ex-servicemen as franchisees and the MoD as the facilitator, with the ultimate aim of forging a win-win partnership which can boost the national economy. The raising of environmental battalions by the Indian Army to assist in the enhancement of vegetation and green cover in the country was a novel initiative for the preservation and conservation of the biodiversity and the ecosystems. The 'Swachh Bharat

Abhiyan' and 'Ganga Rejuvenation Plan' are today national missions which can be best implemented by employing eco- battalions staffed and manned by ex-servicemen. These monumental national programmes with productive outcomes form a part of the civil-military fusion process initiated in the country by the visionary Hon'ble Prime Minister of India.

The ex-servicemen are a vibrant breed component of trained human resource, who have intrinsically embodied the sterling attributes of proficient execution of responsibilities in multi- disciplinary assigned tasks. They are highly dependable as managers for good governance attributed to enduring high risk calamitous situations, resolving complex conflict of interest cases, surmounting impediments and encumbrances, accomplish objectives with focused resilience and pragmatism, abide by ethical and moral conduct for organisational excellence, ensure whistle blower protectionist measures, gaining of intelligence and being custodians of natural security, adopting a fundamentally balanced approach in management of progressive work dynamics conforming to the Constitution of India and above all undying belief in supreme sacrifice and service to the nation.

Perhaps one of the most important untapped advantages that ex-servicemen have is their presence across the country. Exploiting their pan-India presence and optimising the leadership potential of select empowered ex-servicemen personnel to conjointly work with the village panchayat system will accrue overall progressive functioning by a disciplined, determined, dedicated and conscientious task force system with better fruition of plans, ensuring improved audit, accountability, monitoring and enforcement of projects for a more prosperous society and a nation on its journey to being a 'developed country' after hundred years of its independence in 2047.

H.E. Lt Gen Gurmit Singh, PVSM, UYSM, AVSM, VSM (Retd)
Hon'ble Governor of Uttarakhand
and Former Deputy Chief of Army Staff (DCOAS) Indian Army

ACKNOWLEDGEMENTS

My overwhelming joy is natural when it comes to thanking my dear elders, friends, acquaintances, relatives and large number who have encouraged, enlightened and inspired me to publish my work. I certainly owe my accumulated gratitude to Dr Thennarassu, Dr Uttam Kumar, Dr Pandian, Dr Neduchezian, Dr Subramanian, H.E. Lord Karan Bilimoria, Mr Kaiwaan Patel, Dr W Selvamurthy, Dr Ritu Grover, Dr Rukmani Joshi, Dr Arundhati, Mr Shanker, Mr Sudarshan Motwani, Dr Rajeshwari Devadass, Brig Nishant Sharma and Col Abhinandan Roy (Retired).

My profound gratitude to Dr Ashok K. Chauhan, Hon'ble Founder President, Amity Education Group, Lt Gen KM Seth, PVSM, AVSM (Retired) former Governor Chhattisgarh, Madhya Pradesh & Tripura, Dr Atul Chauhan, Chancellor Amity University Uttar Pradesh (AUUP) and Prof Dr. Balvinder Shukla, Vice Chancellor AUUP, who have always honoured my consistency in contributing to literary work and pedagogic pursuits in the multispectral domains of education at the "Cradle of Learning and Leadership" at Amity University, providing me incessant opportunities to showcase the well embodied indomitable spirit of nurturing ideals propagating defence studies, nationalistic fervor, besides highlighting the veterans and ex-servicemen noble contribution to society and nation building in fine perspective.

I wish to thank Pentagon Press LLP for evincing keen interest and shepherding the book to its culmination prior to the publication. Kindly pardon me, if inadvertently some names remain obscured in anonymity, but assure that you will always be there in my heart and soul for the selfless services rendered in shaping my dreams towards the accomplishment of the primary aim.

LIST OF TABLES

List of Figures

INTRODUCTION

"Strength does not come from physical capacity; it comes from an indomitable will"

—Mahatma Gandhi

The contemporary world presents a transformed picture of a human civilisation undergoing a speedy changeover in terms of evolving roles and expectations. ***Governments are also trying to deal with the issue by changing, reforming or even reinventing themselves.***[1] The major task before them is to plan for and achieve rapid economic growth so that faster inclusive growth and quick eradication of poverty can be achieved. The aim is to build an economic and social order based on equality of opportunity, full employment and provision of ample means of livelihood. It is a multi-dimensional task covering a wide range of activities, for example, economic, social, technical and cultural. It is the task of building the nation as well as serving the ***common man so that he not only leads a comfortable and dignified life, but also feels socially empowered.***[2]

The fundamental ingredient in the evolution of happy, peaceful and prosperous societies and nations is laying the foundation for sustainable development. As a global society, particularly in developing and emerging nations, humanity stands at its defining moment in history, mandating critical evolutionary imperatives for amelioration[3] of poverty conditions, comprising ***prosperity with inclusion, development with equity and industrialisation with environmental concern.*** Large-scale disparity between rural and urban areas of the world has manifested in the income levels and the quality of human amenities. This is unequivocally a loss of opportunity and a matter of great concern and trepidation, as regards the sustenance of peace, progress and prosperity in an eternal dimension of time.

Overcoming certain prejudices of prosperity and fundamental issues related to human living standards is a significant national challenge as well as an international responsibility. Today, more than three billion people in the developed, the developing and some parts of the underdeveloped nations of the world live in villages, often in a condition of under-utilisation of talent and resources and of deprivation.

The inclusive approach of development with equity has been followed in India since Independence, like in many countries of the world. Actions of different institutions such as state, market and civil society organisations can fix on inclusion/exclusion of population in various actions. Norms, principles, spiritual, religious and cultural beliefs can also determine the level of inclusion or exclusion.[4] There has been a perception that globalisation and liberalisation policies which have given more weightage to market have excluded many sections of the population. In a way 'Inclusiveness' may be said to have two dimensions: one, in terms of sectors or segments of the economy which need to be brought into the fold of a vibrant economy; and two, in terms of enabling sections of the population, whom the growth process has bypassed, to fully engage themselves with the developing process.[5]

From Independence till the opening of the economy in 1991, the Government of India, both at the Union and State levels, was guided by the cornerstone policy of the socialist ideology of the Constitution, which played a significant role in orchestrating the funding and execution of all major development programmes and projects in many key areas of the economy. In terms of social stratification of the people, success could not be achieved. This was attributed to the deteriorating law and order situation, corruption, spiralling price index, criminalisation of politics, politicisation of administrative machinery, mega financial scams, scandals, falling morals, poor ethical and social norms, and a degenerate value system.

The policy of globalisation has brought numerous advantages to urban India, like increase in employment and compensation, enhancement of living standards and increased purchasing power and empowerment of Indian youth. However, the growth trajectory of India is likely to be constrained soon by a low level of socio-economic development in rural areas. While the rest of the country is experiencing an accelerated growth rate, the Indian countryside is relatively neglected with a slower growth rate, widespread poverty and increasing inequality. The latest Human Development Report released by the United Nations Development Programme has ranked India at number 135 in a list of 187 countries, with 21.9 per cent of 1.2 billion people living below the poverty line or having an income of less than $ 1.25 a day.[6] Therefore, it is an imperative necessity for a country aspiring to become a global superpower to have a cardinal focus on an overall comprehensive integrated development concept for both urban as well as rural areas.

Rural India has 638,588 villages in its 612 districts. With about 750 million rural population, India has the largest in the world. The 600,000 plus villages of India have 94.8 per cent of land area with 70 per cent of population and 50 per cent of the National Domestic Product (NDP) of India. They have 42 per cent of the services and industrial sectors, 40 per cent target for rural consumers in the mobile user segment, 20 per cent of all the professional colleges in the nation and nearly more than 500 million youth below thirty-five years.

There is evidence that the pattern of growth in rural areas exerts highly negative externalities on society and environment. This is found both in agriculture – in which social and economic backwardness and deprivation coexist with rapid capitalist change and pollution – and in rural non-farm activities in which competitiveness is pursued through low labour and resource costs. Because of this pattern of growth, the Indian rural economy is moving along the 'low road of destructive competition', that leads to the depletion of available resources and makes minimum standards of social protection for the population hardly possible in the medium to long term.

A typical household in any of the 600,000 villages in India or elsewhere in the world would present the image of a truly versatile and self-sufficient economic unit. Roughly half the world population lives in these rural areas, often relying on archaic technology, untapped resources, underdeveloped skills and assistance, even donation-oriented policies for their basic livelihood. There is a lack of specialisation from the perspective of both technology and capability. In an increasingly knowledge-oriented society, where science governs every area of our life, from the way our automobiles run to the way our plants grow, knowledge is a prerequisite to prosperity. This is manifested in the need for creating markets that are efficient, accessible and well connected. Economic empowerment has to lead to societal transformation and thus the final focal area has to be creation of facilities and amenities that are accessible by and affordable for the needy of the world, wherever they may be.

Official reports[7] and statistics indicate the level of diversification in rural livelihoods in the last decade in India. Rural enterprises and the rural non-agricultural sector are expanding more relatively than agricultural enterprises. The number of non-agricultural establishments is more in the rural areas. Thus, there exist vast resources to be tapped in our rural areas if we want to ensure inclusive growth and follow the path of rapid development in the near future.

In the short term, the best way to improve the lot of the rural poor might be to promote a second Green Revolution.[8] Unlike in manufacturing, India has a competitive advantage in agriculture, with plenty of arable land, water and sunshine. To achieve such a change, however, would need a shift in focus from peasant farming to agribusiness and encourage private capital to move from urban to rural areas. It would need to remove the onerous distribution controls, allow large retailers to contract directly with farmers, invest in irrigation, and permit the consolidation of the fragmented holdings. With a large exodus of rural youth towards the cities, the only credible and educated workforce available in the villages, apart from the uneducated farmers is the retired personnel of the armed forces, who can be the common link in this holistic transformation.

No single institution has come to disappoint Indians more than their bureaucracy. In the 1950s, Indians bought into the cruel myth, promulgated by Nehru, that India's bureaucracy was its 'Steel Frame', supposedly a means of guaranteeing stability and continuity after the British Raj. However, today, Indians believe that their bureaucracy has become a prime obstacle to development, blocking instead of shepherding economic reforms. The Indian bureaucracy is a haven of mental reforms.[9] It still attracts many of the brightest students in the country, who are admitted based on a difficult examination. However, despite their very high IQ, most bureaucrats fail as managers. Most Indian civil servants fail to plan their projects well, monitor them, or follow through on them; their performance failures mostly have to do with poor execution. This lack of 'transformational leadership' is evident in the fields of the public education system, health, water and electricity services, delayed infrastructure projects and, above all, governance.

Thus, during the 1980s, discussion on good governance and rural development became the buzz word. Be it policy making or academia (at national or international platforms), everywhere it became a debatable issue on how one should define good governance, what are the ways in which it can be achieved and how it will lead to rural development. Another significant debate during that time (which is still relevant) was to identify the meaning of development.

Many utilitarian steps were suggested that could be taken to improve governance, such as an evolved process of decentralisation, delegation and devolution. It is often said, 'Growth of the society will have to come from the society itself', but rarely implemented. Thus, this study suggests that "Focusing on outcomes rather than internal procedures would help", as would delegation of responsibilities. This study claims that "The retired officers of the Armed Forces are yet another highly experienced pool available in civil society, which if dovetailed into the planning and monitoring process of the various government schemes will undeniably pay rich dividends. The officers belonging to this clan because of their expertise in transformational leadership not only can perceive and plan things, but most importantly their ability to lead sustainably from the front can also be helpful in execution within a time-bound manner with consistency and qualitative productive outcomes".

This study undertakes a causative analyses towards discerning the impediments in the existing growth structure of the rural areas, examines the present administrative set up, identifies and recommends efficacious models/structures and incorporates select retired, but promising, uniformed personnel (ex-servicemen) from all domains of the military and paramilitary forces. These suitable lower-level leadership personnel with prodigious potential in the age bracket between 30 and 55, would be extremely well trained, educated and experienced, to ensure 'Holistic and Inclusive Growth' of rural areas in synergy with the elected panchayats, forming a part of the Panchayati Raj System. This endeavour would culminate towards well-embodied development and multifaceted progression, thereby contributing substantially to India's inexorable quest for its due status as a super power in the international comity of nations.

Transforming India into a 'developed nation' implies that every citizen of the country lives well above the poverty line; that education and health are of a high standard; national security is assured; and that core competences in certain major areas will enable the production of quality goods for home consumption and for export, competitively; and, above all, that there will be prosperity for all citizens. The Indian Armed Forces have won worldwide appreciation for their valour, dedication and devotion. The achievements of the Indian Armed Forces in varying roles since independence, that is, guarding our frontiers, rendering military assistance to neighbouring countries or other nations as part of United Nations forces, maintenance of internal security and aid to civil power in civil disturbances and in national calamities (emergency in the 'Seventies), has always been a matter of pride for all of us in the country. The late Prime Minister Mrs. Indira Gandhi made the following observation in the Lok Sabha on 09 April 1981: "Finding alternative occupation and incorporating them into the national mainstream is our national responsibility. These servicemen whose retirement age is between 35 and 40 years is a trained and motivated force available to transform our great nation". The same sentiments were reiterated by our Defence Minister, Mr. Arun Jaitley[10] on 19 August 2014 while addressing the Director-General Resettlement (DGR) Corporate Conclave 2014 in New Delhi, where he restated that the corporate sector should utilise the services of ex-servicemen to meet their requirements of trained and disciplined manpower. Thus, there exists a credible force, both at the grass root (retired jawans) as well as the highest level (retired defence officers) which can be a major contributor towards a holistic growth from village to state level.

NOTES

1. D. P. Osborne & Gaebler, T. *Reinventing Government*, New York: Plume, 1991; Peters, B. Guy, "Government Reorganization: A Theoretical Analysis." *International Political Social Review*, 13(2), April 1992, pp. 199-217.
2. *Empowering Society: An Analysis of Business, Government and Social Development Approaches to Empowerment*, New Delhi: Foundation Books, 2006, pp. 3-13.
3. Usha Jumani. "Government Reorganization: A Theoretical Analysis", Osborne, D.P. & Gaebler, T., *Reinventing Government*, New York: Plume, 1991; Peters, B. Guy. *International Political Social Review*, 13(2), April 1992, pp. 199-217.

4. Mahendra S. Dev. "Inclusive Growth in India", *Oxford Collected Essays*, pp. 1-2.
5. N.A. Majumdar. *Inclusive Growth Development Perspectives in Indian Economy*, Academic Foundation, New Delhi, 2004, pp. 11-12.
6. Mahendra S Dev. "Inclusive Growth in India", *Oxford Collected Essays*, p. 1-2.
7. Elisabetta Basile & Ishita Mukhopadhyay. *Changing Identity of Rural India: A Sociohistorical Analysis*, Anthem Press, 2009, pp. 21-23.
8. Gurcharan Das. "The Indian Model", *Foreign Affairs*, 85.4, Jul/Aug 2006, p. 5.
9. Ibid., pp. 7-16.
10. *Economic Times & Business Standard*, 20 April 2014.

1

GOOD GOVERNANCE AND RURAL DEVELOPMENT: A CONCEPTUAL FRAMEWORK

"Good governance in a democracy is impossible without fostering in our communities and the electorate, an appetite for leaders who are committed to respectful conduct."

—Diane Kalen-Sukra

Introduction

The World Bank in its *World Development Report*, 1997 states that "State-dominated development has failed. But so has stateless development". A minimalist state would do no harm, but neither could it do much good. Development requires an effective state, one that plays a catalytic, enabling role, inspiring and supplementing the accomplishments of private businesses and individuals.

In the paradigm change of the late 1990s, there was another element which became significant along with the notion of economic growth to reduce poverty. It was the notion of "governance" or an effective state. There is broad consensus in the international donor community that formal social development is connected with the precondition of economic growth which was declared to be able to be pursued under the framework of implementing good governance by effective states.[1]

In recent years, good governance and rural development have become vitally important topics of discussion for many countries (especially for the developing and underdeveloped ones). What exactly are these concepts, and what do they mean for rural communities? In this chapter, we will explore the definition of good governance and rural development. How are the two concepts inter-related? This chapter will discover the relationship between good governance and rural development. We will look at how it can help to improve the standard of living of rural communities.

Good Governance

"Good governance" is a term that has become a part of the vernacular of a large range of development institutions and other actors in the international arena in the late 1990s. Almost all major development institutions today claim that promoting good governance is an important part of their agendas. However, there is no single, universally accepted definition of good governance. The definition of good governance can vary depending on whom you ask, but in general, it refers to principles such as accountability, transparency, and integrity. These principles are aimed at ensuring that governments operate efficiently and effectively for the benefit of all citizens.

The definition of good governance generally comprises a wish list of reforms, practices, and outcomes, specifically aiming at developing countries. Every institute which is concerned with the idea of good governance seems to build its own wish list. Some of them emphasise political and legal institutions – participation, accountability, rule of law, and human rights. Others emphasise neoliberal economic reforms and better management of resources. Some institutions also focus on social structures and practices. Most of the wish lists concern the interactions of state and society. They focus on the rules, processes and behaviour that define the nature and limits of political authority. They try to ensure that political actors at all levels should be responsive and accountable to stakeholders. They also seek that states act impartially and fairly and restrict themselves to particular domains.

According to Leftwich,[2] the concept of good governance has three main components: first, from a broad systemic point of view, it refers to a loser and wider distribution of both internal and external political and economic power. Governance thus denotes the structures of political and economic relationships and rules by which the productive and distributive life of a society is governed. In short, it refers to a system of political and socioeconomic relations or, more loosely, a regime.

Second, in its political sense, good governance implies a state enjoying both legitimacy and authority, derived from a democratic mandate and built on the traditional liberal notion of a clear separation of legislative, executive and judicial powers. It would involve a pluralist polity with some kind of freely elected representative legislature, subject to regular elections, with the capacity at the very least to influence and check executive power and protect human rights.

Finally, from an administrative point of view, good governance means an efficient, open, accountable and audited public service which has the bureaucratic competence to help design and implement appropriate policies and manage whatever public sector there is.

There are various elements that make up good governance, including:

- Participation: All members of society should be able to participate in the decision-making process. This includes giving rural communities a voice in decisions that affect them.
- Transparency: Decisions made by government officials should be transparent and open to public scrutiny. This ensures that everyone trusts the governing body and knows that they are making decisions in the best interest of all. Accountability: Government officials must be accountable for their actions. They should be held responsible when things go wrong and should be praised when things go well. This helps ensure that they perform their duties effectively and efficiently.
- Rule of Law: The rule of law must be respected at all times. This means that everyone, including government officials, is subject to laws that apply equally to everyone else. It also ensures fairness and justice in society
- Efficiency and effectiveness: Government institutions should be effective at delivering goods and services to citizens while using minimal resources. They should also be efficient at implementing policies and legislation.

It has been argued that a government that adheres to good governance principles is more likely to be successful and sustainable. Good governance is critical for the success of any rural community. It ensures that all members of the community are treated equally and equitably, that resources are managed properly, and non-archaic decisions with a futuristic dimension are made in the best interests of the people. When a community has good governance in place, it is more likely to experience a cascade of positive social and economic changes. Good governance is considered essential for achieving rural development, which is defined as: "The sustainable improvement in the quality of life of people living in rural areas and their productive ecosystems".

Rural Development

The term 'rural' is certainly abstruse. There is no precise definition of the term, but rural areas are evidently recognisable. They comprise the space where human settlements and infrastructure occupy only small patches of the landscape, most of which are dominated by fields and pastures, woods and forests, water, mountains and deserts.[3] IFAD (2001) adds that rural people usually live in farmsteads or settlements of 5 to 10,000 persons, but also makes the point that 'national distinctions between rural and urban are arbitrary and varied'.[4]

Beyond these core features related to natural resources and population density, rural areas can be regarded in different ways: as places where most people spend most of their working time on farms (*ibid.*); by the abundance and relative cheapness of land (Wiggins and Proctor); by high transaction costs associated with long distances and poor infrastructure (Binswanger & Deininger, 1997, cited by Kydd & Dorward); and by geographical conditions that increase political transaction costs and magnify the possibility of elite capture or urban bias (Binswanger & Deininger, 1997, and Moore & Putzel (1999) cited by Johnson).[5]

Similarly, development is also a contested concept. Usually, development is considered as an aspect of mainstream economics where it denotes the process of economic growth in per capita income and fundamental changes in the economy to facilitate, generate and sustain that growth. However, economic growth is just one essential component of development; it is not the only one, as development is not a purely economic phenomenon. It is a multidimensional process, involving the reorganisation and reorientation of both economic and social systems. For the purpose of this study, development is defined as Human Development which puts the people back at centre stage.

Combining the understanding of these two terms, 'rural' and 'development', lead us to the notion of rural development which is a continuous and complex process that not only envisages the development of rural areas but also the development of the rural masses. It is the process of improving the living conditions and economic opportunities of people who live in rural areas. This can be done by creating new jobs, providing access to health care and education, and increasing investment in the region.

It aims at optimum utilisation of the growth potential of villages, ensuring equitable distribution of benefits of development to the disadvantaged sections of society, and creating gainful employment opportunities. These basics cannot be achieved unless the rural development administration extends wholehearted support in the creation of various infrastructure facilities and provision of extension services. Moreover, no dent can be made in rural poverty unless the development personnel and elected representatives of rural local bodies clearly understand their respective roles and make well-coordinated efforts.

Three groups can be made up of development functionaries. Those who are involved in policy making are at the top. They create budgetary allotments to carry out programmes, design projects and schemes, and provide the necessary guidance and directives. They also translate the planning objectives into action plans. People who direct operations within the parameters of established policies and who spread knowledge, information, and technology to boost the implementation process are at the intermediate level. The third group consists of those who are actively involved in carrying out various programmes and initiatives. They interact with the populace directly. In this context, there has been a general feeling that the existing structure and culture of bureaucracy is inadequate for the achievement of these objectives.[6]

The concept of rural development has changed significantly during the last three decades. Until the 1970s, rural development was synonymous with agricultural development and hence focused on increasing agricultural production. This focus seems to have been driven primarily by the interests of industrialisation to extract surpluses from the agriculture sector to reinforce industrialisation. The establishment of the Millennium Development Goals has significantly reinforced concerns about non-income poverty. With the paradigm shifts in economic development from growth to broadly-defined development, the concept of rural development has begun to be used in a broader sense. In more recent years, increased concerns on the environmental aspects of economic growth have also influenced the changes. Today's concept of rural development is fundamentally different from that in vogue about three or four decades ago. The concept now encompasses concerns that go well beyond improvements in growth, income and output. The concern includes an assessment of changes in the quality of life, broadly defined to include improvement in health and nutrition, education, environmentally safe living conditions and reduction in gender and income inequalities. Today, there seems to be a universal consensus that the ultimate objective of rural development is to improve the quality of life in rural areas.

Inclusive rural development is a more specific concept than the concept of rural development. In broader terms, inclusive rural development is about improving the quality of life of all members of rural society. More specifically, inclusive rural development covers three different dimensions of the economic, social and political domains. The economic domain pertains to upliftment of the economic status, social domain aims to enhance the social structure and alleviate social maladies and the political domain endeavours to provide political awareness to the masses and facilitating them to exercise their rights.

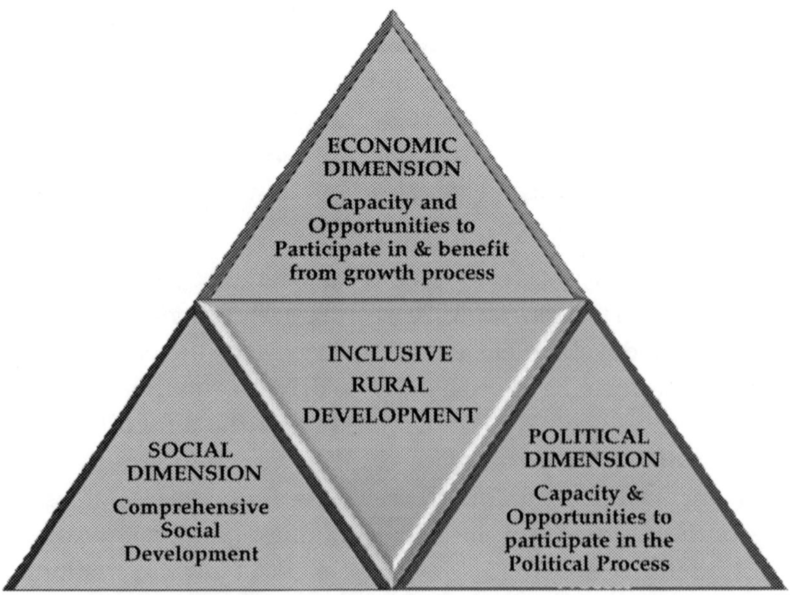

Figure 1.1. Three Dimensions of Inclusive Rural Development

Why Rural Development?

Development, in its essence, is a dynamic process that advances a society and economy from a relatively backward stage to one that is more advanced. Growth in production and income, structural changes in the economy and society, and institutional changes, shift in people's attitudes and values, and even change in traditions and social practices that are all part of the transition. The end result of the procedure is an enhancement of the general population's quality of life. In other words, a process of change will only be considered development if it improves people's quality of life, as evidenced by higher nutrition and health standards, more opportunities for education, and the removal of barriers to involvement in social and economic life.

The focus on rural development over and above the concern for overall economic development has arisen from two lines of reasoning. The first and the more obvious one, especially for a country like India, arises from the fact that a large majority of population, say around, 70 to 80 per cent for most states in India, live in rural areas among which the incidence and intensity of poverty is relatively higher. Interestingly, the widespread poverty and hunger in rural areas arise not so much from open unemployment as from the low intensity of employment and general low productivity of resources. Though in peak agricultural seasons, village communities often experience a shortage of labour, for the better part of the year agricultural workers find it hard to get paying work. The general deficiency of basic facilities such as roads, communications, power, education, health care and even sanitation and drinking water, not only contributes to and compounds low productivity and intensity of employment but also has a general depressing effect on the quality of life.[7] Obviously special attention is required to address the problem of development of rural areas and the people living there.

The other and somewhat less obvious line of reasoning, which calls for special focus on rural development, arises from disparities in the distribution of opportunities between urban and rural areas. With the concentration of industrial, commercial, financial and administrative set-ups in urban centres, in a modernising economy, socio-economic prospects and opportunities are usually disproportionately concentrated in towns and cities. This naturally pushes immigrants in pursuit of better opportunities. However, in most third world countries, the stagnancy in the neglected rural sector pushes far too many immigrants from villages to cities to be absorbed in the organised sector. While surplus immigrants wait in the informal sector swelling the ranks of the urban unemployed or semi-employed, the slums and squatter population expands. Urban poverty surfaces, civic facilities and basic infrastructure are strained and the urban environment is degraded. Thus, developing urban oriented islands of growth without concomitant improvement of opportunities in rural areas has landed many developing countries in a dualistic structure not conducive to sustainable overall progress of the economy and society. Hence, greater attention, efforts and resources for expediting rural development have become an imperative not only for improving the quality of the lives of people in the villages but also for ensuring that the metropolitan centres of industry, commerce and administration take long strides towards prosperity with less congestion and a better socio-economic and physical environment.

The growth of rural and urban areas is connected. These connections are significant because there are economic, financial, and social connections between rural and urban livelihoods. Most farmers in rural areas rely on metropolitan markets to support their livelihoods. For a variety of services (such as hospitals, banks, and government offices) and for the provision of many private and public products, rural households rely on urban centres or small towns. Moreover, the rural sector benefits from remittances sent by urban-based family members.[8]

Likewise, urban areas are linked to the rural sector through several channels. For example, various urban businesses and enterprises depend on rural demand for their goods and services. They also rely on rural areas for the supply of raw materials. Urban consumers, on the other hand, benefit from cheap and sustained food supply from rural areas. Furthermore, many poor urban households partly depend on rural activities (e.g., farming) for their livelihoods. The rural sector can also act as a buffer from the impact of macroeconomic shocks on the urban economy. Links between the rural and urban sectors include flows of information such as markets and employment opportunities, as well as flows of people moving between rural and urban centres on a temporary or permanent basis.[9]

Development strategies that support these rural-urban connections can boost the economy and fight poverty. How does this synergistic and balanced interaction function? According to economic theory, resources should be free to move around so that marginal returns are balanced across sectors and geographical areas. It is possible that an increase in agricultural production comes before urban settlement expansion. However, when new technologies emerge in the urban sector, urban labour productivity and earnings increase, luring more people to move to the city. Urbanisation may also increase access to money, spurring additional mechanisation or other developments that are helpful to agricultural production. Growing agricultural production causes the income and productivity inequalities between rural and urban areas to draw closer. The productivity and income disparity between the two sectors grows when innovations resume in the urban sector. Capital travels to rural areas as rural labour starts to migrate to the urban sector. Emerging modern trends are a new equilibrium.

The primary driver of economic growth and development is the process of transitioning from a state of disequilibrium to equilibrium as a result of technological advancements in both sectors. However, a lot of developing nations obstruct the normal course of economic growth. In an effort to accelerate or skip this process, governments frequently interfere in favour of the urban sector by distorting the capital and labour markets to favour urban over rural locations. As resources do not move to their "free-market" destinations where they would ordinarily receive the maximum rate of return, overall efficiency is lost. As a consequence, the rural-urban gap increases, and the natural growth that would occur in rural areas, as well as in urban areas, is circumvented.[10]

In fact, in developing countries, we typically observe the coexistence of a modern urban sector and a traditional rural sector. In these countries, the urban population is often better off than their rural counterparts. This rural-urban divide evolves when governments in developing countries give preference to the urban sector in their public policies. Price policies, public investments, and welfare transfers are a few examples of preferential practices that benefit urban populations over rural ones. In part, this urban bias may also occur because urban centres in developing countries may be better organised politically and thus have a greater influence on policy makers than the rural population.[11]

Reasons for the Rising of Urban Bias

Urban bias is seen in the disparity between urban and rural areas in terms of poverty rates, per capita income, and labour productivity. The bias is more pronounced and wider in the gaps between these measures. Naturally, changes in labour quality and living expenses between the two sectors must be taken into account when adjusting per capita income and productivity. For India and China, urban bias has usually arisen from a combination of following three different but related policies:

- The first and most prevalent one has to do with regulations impacting trading terms (i.e., price policies). Very often agricultural outputs are underpriced, with levels that are much lower than those that would result from a free-market situation or in the international market.[12]
- Second, the overvalued currency rates of most developing countries increase this tendency, having a negative impact on all traded items but typically especially agricultural ones. The urban or industrial sectors may attract labour and capital if the returns there are more attractive if they are fully mobile. Unfortunately, many countries like China have also heavily distorted factor markets by restricting the movement of labour and capital. Despite the fact that there was a significant labour shortage in the rural sector and a lower marginal return to work, farmers were not permitted to relocate to urban areas in China under the 'Household Registration' System, or Hukou. Farmers were permitted to move to cities after the reforms in 1978, but there are still many limitations on their ability to find jobs there.
- Third, the tendency of governments to favour urban centres are reflected in their spending policies. Public spending, like other government initiatives, aims to encourage more equal development and boost productivity by addressing market shortcomings. Governments may sometimes be forced to choose between equity and efficiency objectives. However, it is also crucial to understand that there are not always equity-efficiency trade-offs. The presence of so-called "win-win" possibilities, where government intervention results in both a more efficient and equitable allocation of resources, arises when market failures are more pervasive among the poor (i.e., the poor are poor because they are disproportionately

affected by market failures). For example, public investment in rural infrastructure has not only generated economic payoffs by correcting market failures but has also led to poverty reduction.

Consequences of Urban-Biased Policies

The consequences of this dangerous bias politics could be as under:

- First, these policies widen the disparities between rural and urban areas in a number of development metrics, including poverty, per capita income, health, and nutrition.
- Second, rising inequality may lead to tensions that constrain the prospects for future growth through a variety of social, political, and economic mechanisms.[13]

A Fundamentally Unbalanced Relationship

According to historians, towns grew as a result of economies of scale in the storing of the surplus and the necessity for its protection when agricultural improvement enabled farmers to produce a surplus. Comparative advantages prompted trading in agricultural goods between various places once there was a production surplus. Transfer nodes for agricultural products turned into trading posts and these in turn became trading towns.[14]

Towns could develop only if three conditions were met, namely, an agricultural surplus large enough to support the urban population, differences in productivity that generated comparative advantages, able to offset transport costs and the economics of scale in transportation that made large-scale trade and central marketplaces efficient.[15] Regardless of the precise order, urban regions grew to become the centres of wealth and power, supported by religion and reliant on agricultural surplus. The elite moved into towns and then to cities. Due to their connections with the monarch, the religious establishment and the military, the urban population made up a tiny but significant portion of the entire population. The vast majority of people were rural dwellers who worked in agriculture and provided labour and food to the city through the market towns. Traditional cities and towns distinguished themselves from the countryside as centres of power, religion, and wealth. Rural areas were places close to nature where the simple, hard-working people lived and laboured, whereas urban areas were hubs of civilisation. Urban dwellers developed a sense of superiority over the peasants in the countryside.[16]

With the elite in the urban areas and the masses in the rural areas, the distinction between urban and rural society also became an ideological and political one. The ideology emphasised the need for urban areas with rulers, traders and priests. The ruler ensured law and order so that the rural population could farm. The traders were prepared to leave their urban homes to buy the agricultural surplus from the farmers to sell in far-away places. Religious leaders gave meaning to life and sanctioned the status quo; they prayed for the well-being of the ruler and his people, so that all would prosper.[17]

The ideology dictated that the common people should live on and off the land, and that farming was the natural way of life. Urbanites would admit that they preferred to live in the country but that they could only do so when they had aged and retired. It was left to the rural people to feed them in the interim in a mutually beneficial relationship. The agricultural surplus may be purchased from farmers in urban areas at a fair price, but more frequently, urban regions would just take it from rural areas for free or with minimal profit to the farmers. Farmers simply felt it their responsibility to provide food and other products from the country to the urban regions because towns created a real political-commercial-religious complex. Rulers could tax the farmers for their land, their products and their income.[18]

The inherent advantages of urban settlements over rural ones are their economies of scale and agglomeration. The large size of the urban population creates a high demand for goods and services, and this promotes increased supply of goods and services at lower cost of production per unit. The presence of a large variety of resources in a constrained space encourages specialisation and creativity. When it comes to organisation and the expression of needs, goals, and preferences through political processes, the rural population is at a disadvantage due to the dispersed layout of rural settlements and the poor communications and transportation networks. The fact that officials in urban areas often take decisions on behalf of the rural population about their future and the use of their natural resources is an expression of this imbalance in political power between urban and rural areas.[19]

Steps Recommended to Reduce the Urban–Rural Divide

Urban-biased policies still prevail, particularly in terms of government investment priorities, which disproportionately favour urban areas in both countries. This impedes the efficient allocation of resources (such as labour and public investments), therefore contributing to unequal development between the rural and urban sectors. The following policies are recommended to help correct the urban bias and, strengthen the links between rural and urban sectors, and promote growth and poverty reduction:

- **Targeted Public Investment**. Governments in developing nations must target their investments better to meet economic and poverty alleviation goals due to the limited resources available, utilising the synergies provided by rural and urban linkages. In poor areas such as western China and eastern India, investments in rural infrastructure, agricultural research, and education have a larger poverty reduction impact than similar investments in more-favoured areas. The influence of rural investment in reducing poverty extends to urban poverty reduction through such channels as lower food prices, which is even more significant for rural-urban links. These findings overwhelmingly support the idea that investing in rural areas and underserved communities is a win-win strategy for reducing poverty in both urban and rural areas, and that more funding should now be directed to these regions.
- **Reduction of Migration Restrictions**. Rural-urban migration has the ability to assist rural communities through improved land/labour ratios in the agricultural sector as well as improved migrant well-being. In reality, previous research has shown that rural-to-urban migration in China and India has aided in the eradication of poverty. More specifically, remittances increase the per capita income of rural residents, diversify incomes and provide initial capital to develop the rural non-farm economy and small towns. However, formal and informal institutions and policy barriers still restrict the movement of population. Lack of education and access to information and poor infrastructure are the most critical constraints. In China, many jobs in the urban areas still require urban residence. Even if farmers are able to find employment, their rights are typically not upheld, and they frequently lack access to

many social services that urban inhabitants enjoy. Large-scale migration should be made possible (both permanently and seasonally) by eliminating these constraints and obstacles, with additional funding directed as necessary to support this movement and safeguard rural migrants.

- **Development of the Rural Non-Farm Sector**. The development of the rural economy and the eradication of poverty both depend on the rural non-farm sector. It also offers opportunities for low-income rural households to diversify their sources of income, with landless and nearly landless workers receiving between one third and two thirds of their income from sources outside the farm. Research has shown that the share of household non-agricultural income is inversely related to farm size. In India, the bulk of the poor are landless or live on small farms with inadequate land for their own food needs. Consequently, they depend heavily on earnings by supplying unskilled wage labour to other farms or to non-farm enterprises. Public investment in physical infrastructure (road, transportation, communication) as well as in education and health is crucial for small farms to establish their own businesses and access non-farm jobs in the rural non-farm sector.
- **Development of Small Rural Towns**. Small and medium-sized towns serve as crucial transitional areas between rural and urban areas and are also significant sources of social and economic services. Small and medium-sized towns and cities, in particular, serve as service delivery hubs for rural areas, connecting the rural economy with external input and output markets and lowering transaction costs. A study of small rural towns in Madhya Pradesh and Odisha, two poor states of India, found that such towns and their nearby villages are strongly linked through consumption, production, employment, and financial linkage. By absorbing some of the agricultural labour excess and reducing the pressure placed on already crowded metropolitan areas, small towns can also act as stepping-stones or an endpoint for people of rural areas while contributing to the expansion of the national economy. Small- and medium-sized towns face unique problems, which should be taken into account in development efforts. However, poverty cannot simply be transferred from the fields to these areas. The development of small rural towns requires better infrastructure (in

terms of quantity and quality), which in turn will facilitate access to markets and lower transportation costs.

Vision and Strategy for Rural Development

Starting at the present base, a realistic vision for rural development to be achieved, say by 2020, may include the following components as the vision:

- Deprivation of all rural households from the basic needs of drinking water, shelter and sanitation is eliminated.
- Access to primary health care is available to all.
- All children acquire functional literacy and get basic quality education to be able to access opportunities in the increasingly knowledge-based economy of the future.
- All villages are connected to communications network and remain accessible throughout the year.
- All villages are not only electrified but also get benefited from uninterrupted power supply in adequate voltage.
- Farm production takes place at near-potential levels. Rural employment not only expands in volume but also diversifies with agro processing, trading and catering various productive services to the modernised farm sector emerging as important economic activities.
- With widespread participation in the upswing of the rural economy, disparities across genders and groups, such as castes and tribes, get markedly reduced.[20]

Two-Pronged Approach Strategy. In essence the strategy for realisation of this vision can be a simple two-pronged approach comprising the following:

- Acceleration of income and employment growth through facilitation of fuller utilisation of production potential. The income and employment generation process will be spearheaded by farm sector growth which can rise from fuller exploitation of technical possibilities in combination with better use of a natural resource base. Apart from direct employment on farms, increased farm production will generate income and employment in related activities through backward and forward linkages. Backward linkages will force higher activity levels in provision of sectoral infrastructure like irrigation and services like input supply, extension and repair and maintenance of farm activities. Forward linkages will induce growth in storage, processing and trading of farm products. Thus, farm sector growth will lead to mutually reinforcing growth in income and employment in both farm and non-farm economic activities in rural areas. However, the farm sector-led growth strategy presupposes that rural markets are integrated with regional, national and global markets so that farmers need not produce only that which will be absorbed in their local markets but can specialise in such production activities for which their resource base is most suited and for which they are adequately rewarded.

- Elimination of deprivation of people from the basic facilities of drinking water, shelter, sanitation, elementary education and primary health care by directly providing these services.[21] Special delivery mechanisms will have to be designed for encompassing people in special problem sectors such as flood-prone areas, interior hills and also for such sections of the population as those internally displaced by violence and women and children in the fringes of society.

Conclusion

Good governance is the key to realising rights, leaving no one behind and achieving sustainability of rural development through collective wisdom of pragmatic reforms. Good governance as an approach to rural development is the engagement of government, private sector and civil society, based on active and effective participation, transparency, accountability, rule of law, justice, efficiency and effectiveness as well as human development.

In the following chapters of this book, while describing the case study of India will discuss the significance of good governance in attaining the myriad goals of rural development. This study describes how good governance pays special attention to institutionalising, enabling and empowering local people's participatory development. This study argues that realisation of the goal of good governance and rural development becomes more attainable if the leadership is given in the hands of strong, trained ex-servicemen, suitably selected and placed in their respective states, who along with the panchayat system, through their epitomized leadership traits ingrained in their bloodline can execute projects with a sense of abiding loyalty, commitment and vitality.

NOTES

1. Rukmani (2013) 'The Concept of Good Governance' in Tapan Biswal (ed) *Governance and Citizenship*, New Delhi: Viva Publications, Pp. 83.
2. Leftwich, A. (1993). 'Governance, Democracy and Development in the Third World'. *Third World Quarterly*, vol.14, no. 3, pp. 605-623.
3. Maxwell, S. & Heber-Percy, R. (2001) 'New Trends in Development Thinking and Implications for Agriculture', in K. G. Stamoulis (ed.), *Food, Agriculture and Rural Development: Current and Emerging Issues for Economic Analysis and Policy Research*. Rome: FAO.
4. IFAD (2001) *Rural Poverty Report 2001: The Challenge of Ending Rural Poverty*. Oxford: Oxford University Press for IFAD, pp. 17.
5. Ashley, Caroline & Simon Maxwell (2001) 'Rethinking Rural Development' *Development Policy Review*, 19 (4), pp. 395-425.
6. Surat Singh & Singh, Mohinder. *Rural Development Administration in the 21st Century: A Multi-Dimensional Study*, Deep & Deep Publications Pvt. Ltd., 2007.
7. Komol Singha. *Rural Development in India: Retrospect and Prospects*, Concept Publishing Company, 2010, pp. 22-24.
8. Micheal Bunce. *Rural Settlement in an Urban World*, Taylor & Francis Publishers, Cambridge, 1982, p. 5.
9. Bimalendu Bhattacharya. *Urban Development in India since Pre-Historic Times*, Shree Publication House, New Delhi, 2009, p. 10.
10. Retrieved from http://www.fig.net/pub/morocco/proceedings/PS1/PS1_1_okpala.pdf, at 21:00 on 02-04-2012.
11. Mahmoud Bah. *Rural-Urban Transformations*, IIED Publishers, New Delhi, 2003, p. 23.
12. Retrieved from http://lanic.utexas.edu/project/etext/llilas/cpa/spring06/welfare/corbridge.pdf, at 10:00 on 03-04-12.
13. Ashutosh Varshney. *Beyond Urban Bias*, Frank Class and Company Limited, London, 1993, p. 249.
14. Retrieved from, http://www.unescap.org/pdd/prs/ Project Activities/ Ongoing /Rural-Urban%20 Linkages/ Rural-Urban%20Linkages-policyimp.pdf, 04-4-2012.
15. R.B. Mandal and Ashok Kumar Mittal. *Introduction to Rural Settlements*, Concept Publishing Company, New Delhi, 2001, p. 328.
16. Ibid., p. 329.
17. Alister Scott, Alana Gibert & Ayele Gelan. *The Urban-Rural Divide: Myth or Reality*, Macaulay Land Use Research Institute, Macaulay, 2007, p. 27.
18. Ibid., p. 28.
19. Retrieved from, http://economics.ouls.ox.ac.uk/9480/, on 05-04-2012.
20. Komol Singha. *Rural Development in India: Retrospect and Prospects*, Concept Publishing Company, 2010, pp. 34-35.
21. Acharya Poromesh. 'Education: Panchayat and Decentralization, Myths & Reality', *Economic and Political Weekly*, February 2002, pp. 15-16.

2

ODYSSEY OF SOCIO-ECONOMIC GROWTH IN INDIA

"For as long as our people are held hostage by controllable socio-economic forces, we cannot afford to be indifferent to the ravages of poverty in all its dimensions and ramifications."

—**Ibrahim Babangida**

Introduction

Indian national projects have been indisputably more successful than predicted at the time of India's birth as a modern state. When India attained Independence in 1947, many sceptics doubted that such a country marked by crushing poverty, bewildering diversities and weak institutions could endure for long. Sir Winston Churchill spoke for the legions of cynics when he plainly declared–long before the British Raj ended in the subcontinent–that India was little other than "an abstraction...a geographical term. It is no more a united nation than the Equator."[1] Viewed seventy-five years after its founding, the Indian nation has indeed proved the pessimists wrong: not only has the country managed to preserve its national unity, its territorial integrity, and its political autonomy largely unscathed, it has done so through a historically unprecedented experiment centred on building, as Jawaharlal Nehru told Andre Malraux, "A just society by just a means".

This monumentally ambitious project was erected on a distinctive triadic foundation of liberal democracy, civic nationalism, and socialist economics. These three components were intended to be mutually reinforcing. Together they were meant to fulfil India's dream of becoming a great power in the most comprehensive sense envisioned by the modernists of India's founding generation. That India was a great civilisation was to them an evident and acknowledged fact.[2] Transforming this venerable entity into a great power in the contemporary sense – one that would possess the capacity to exert wide influence beyond its borders – would require India to become the paragon of a new political order. The success of this order would hinge fundamentally on its ability to produce rapid growth and meaningful development, which would eliminate mass poverty while bringing justice and dignity to millions of socially disenfranchised Indians. These citizens would continue to associate peacefully with their well-to-do countrymen, making decisions about their common future through a system of universal franchise, that, whatever the outcomes, would be sufficiently respectful of the identities and preferences of the diverse people who made up this new nation.

Socialism was beguilingly attractive for many reasons at the time of India's independence. In fact, ever since the Great Depression, socialist ideas increasingly came to be seen as a viable alternative to market capitalism. Furthermore, the visible success of the Soviet Union, which had transformed itself from a feudal society into an industrial economy within the space of a few decades, seemed to prove the superiority of centralised planning and state control over the means of production and distribution sufficiently enough that many newly- independent nations in the 1950s voluntarily adopted socialism as the ideology for organising their own economies.[3]

In early post-independent India, the urgent necessity of quickly overcoming vast poverty made the allure of socialism even more enticing. Its appeal for Nehru, however, was derived from more than purely instrumental calculations. He was a Fabian socialist from his early years, and as such his commitment to socialism was based on a deep suspicion of the profit motive that is central to capitalism and his perception of capitalism's intrinsic connection with inequality. He also had a strong conviction that capitalism, imperialism, and colonialism – the last of which he had spent his entire adult life up to that point opposing – were inextricably interlinked and were the fundamental causes of India's decline since the beginning of the modern era. If the material foundations of the new Indian nation were to be rapidly rebuilt in the aftermath of independence, a socialist reorganisation of the Indian economy was thus inevitable so long as Nehru – given his convictions – remained at the helm. Given his strong democratic temper, however, Indian socialism would involve neither a violent decapitation of the capitalist classes nor a systematic nationalisation of existing capital stocks. In fact, it permitted the existence of a private sector, but unfortunately one that would enjoy only restricted opportunities in an economy that would come to be dominated by the state. These imperatives that drove this domination were coloured greatly by the desire to make India a conventional great power. Indian socialism took the form of a state-dominated mixed economy oriented toward the acquisition of a heavy industrial base.

At its core lay a systematic effort at centralised planning that was intended not simply to provide strategic direction to the economy but also increase the share of public investments through the energetic mobilisation of national savings. These savings would be ploughed into vast public sector enterprises that would populate the "commanding heights" of the Indian economy. Furthermore, planning entailed systematically regulating the activities of private enterprise in the secondary sector of the economy through comprehensive licensing intended to control the levels and composition of industrial production and prevent the "excessive" concentration of wealth.

This endeavour unfortunately resulted in the suppression of competition in India's domestic markets with all its pernicious accompanying consequences: scarcity, compromised product quality and higher prices. Moreover, the explicit bias in Indian central planning towards self-reliance resulted in curtailing India's connectivity with international trade. Instead, strategies of "import substitution", aimed at generating increased investment and employment mainly through internal resources, ruled the day. The obsession with domesticating high technology and filling the "investment gap" through indigenous resource mobilisation, ended up in preventing the Indian state from emphasising on human capital investments through strengthened private property rights and other direct welfare expenditures that might have directly assisted the country's indigent population. Finally, the central planners' fixation with mopping up all available domestic resources to support the strategy of directed investment resulted in the creation of a high tax regime. That stifled whatever private initiative survived and, equally problematically, drove the taxable surpluses into the black market beyond the reach of the state. As a result, India's governments could not enjoy the revenue growth required to advance welfare objectives, and the phenomenon of pervasive tax evasion became a legacy with which the nation struggles to this day.[4]

Oddly, the obsession with creating a modern nation through state-dominated planning, investment and regulation resulted in a dreadful neglect of Indian agriculture and the informal sectors, where most of the Indian population found employment at the time of independence. Although Nehru's government in the First Five Year Plan focused on several elements pertaining to agriculture, such as land reforms, irrigation upgrades and cooperative farming, this focus was quickly displaced by industrialisation from the Second Five Year Plan onwards. The result is that Indian agriculture, which still employs close to half the population, contributes to exhibit a weak performance where productivity, innovation and output are concerned.

The transformation of Indian agriculture, that great base of national employment, especially immediately after independence, required the fruits of capitalism for lasting success. The institutionalisation of a well-ordered market system to bring agricultural products to the final consumer would have elicited increased private investments in mechanisation, biotechnology, irrigation and fertilisers. Instead, India embarked on tepid land reforms that served mainly to increase the fragmentation of land holdings.[5] Coupled with the state interventions in food pricing and procurement, these policies have served only to retard the larger transformation of the primary sector of the Indian economy. The Green Revolution of the 1960s, although making India self-sufficient in food grains, obscured Indian agriculture's larger problems. By masking the necessity for fundamental market reform, it resulted in the enthronement of unsustainable production ecology. Today, thanks to subsidies, freebies and highly regulated agricultural inputs, this production ecology dangerously threatens the public treasury. Furthermore, it has failed to produce the output and productivity gains that the agricultural sector would have otherwise enjoyed under an alternative institutional regime.[6]

Parenthetically, the dominance of the informal sector in India is also a consequence of the restrictions imposed on large enterprises through insidious labour laws. Whatever its causes, however, the low productivity in the informal sector, which is reflected in its pervasively low incomes, implies that the large number of individuals employed therein were unable to enjoy the fruits of India's deliberate effort to grow. The net result tragically was that Nehru's great ambition to "ensure justice and fullness of life to every man and woman" was undermined from the word go by the relative neglect of the most important sector affecting the lives of most Indians. This results in deteriorating conditions in our rural areas.

The 1960s, however, became a turning point when the commitment to socialism steadily mutated from idealism into a sclerotic instrument of power and patronage. These trends, unfortunately, gathered steam until at least the 1980s, when Nehru's daughter, Indira Gandhi, enthroned the "permit–licence raj" as the new face of the Indian political economy. She took intrusive control and political manipulation of the Indian economy to heights beyond Nehru's wildest imagination. With her brand of populist socialism came a singular focus on nationalisation, extortion from private enterprises for political ends and expansive promises of state-led redistribution. These endeavours did little to produce the economic transformation her father desired. Instead, they exacerbated the economic and social dividend within India and inaugurated the era of questionable entitlements with which the nation struggles to this day. By the end of Gandhi's life, she had achieved the distressing distinction of having managed to firmly enshrine political decrepitude and economic stagnation that became the hallmarks of Indian socialism, the third element of the defining triad that characterised New Delhi's post-independence project.

By 1980, the abysmal results of the Indian socialist experiment were visible for all to see. Many apologists for socialism in India would argue that the country's deplorable economic performance, the three per cent or so "Hindu rate of growth" chalked up between 1950 and 1980, was still an improvement over the previous one hundred years of British Raj. During these times, the Indian economy essentially remained stagnant, growing at roughly the same rate as India's population. If India's pre-1980 economic performance is measured relative to the growth chalked up during the Raj, India does appear to be a superlative performer.[7] Even so, it could not transform the lives of its people, whose explosive demographic growth after independence was attributed to the falling death rates produced by improved public health and sanitation. When measured against the economic accomplishments in the rest of the world, India's failures were stark and unforgiving. In 1950, the welfare of the average Indian was 29 per cent of that of the average world citizen. By 1979, it had reduced to 20 per cent, or one fifth of the average world citizen.

The Indian dalliance with socialism from the moment of its modern founding thus painfully corroborates the aphorism "The road to hell is paved with good intentions". Sadly, it was, and remains to this day, the fatal weakness of the post-independence project and one that the country has struggled to escape from since at least the 1980s.[8] In retrospect, Nehruvian socialism produced two contradictory effects. On one hand, it laid the foundations, however, inefficiently, for building a modern industrial state in India, a remarkable achievement. On the other hand, it simultaneously served to stifle native Indian entrepreneurship. The first element has undergone some change in recent times because resource limitations have constrained the Indian government's ability to pursue high-profile investment of different kinds. The second element, however, persists virulently. Although, Indian private enterprises are now freer than ever before, they still struggle in the face of an overbearing state. Instead of creating conditions for their success, the state seems overly focused on extracting societal resources in order to underwrite its populist handouts. More recently, the advocates of these giveaways have sought to legitimise their disbursal under the guise of creating a "rights-based welfare state", where the masses would have unprecedented constitutional claims to such rivalrous and excludable goods as food, education, health and housing.[9] Forgetting that such private goods can never be distributed as a matter of political right because their production is neither effortless nor can it be assured by a *dues ex machine,* the persistence of such ideational claims only highlights the entrenchment of a bankrupt statism in India and the colossal burdens it continues to impose on the nation's productive citizenry. At any event, all that the socialist experiment did was to prevent the country from reaching its economic potential. Even though that shortcoming was distressing enough, it might have been forgivable. However, its consequences were far more corrosive and sweeping.

The net result of socialism's intellectual and political dominance in India was that the nation careened toward the betrayal of its promises until it was confronted by a series of crises. Although, these debacles first manifested themselves in the 1960s, they reached a boiling point only in 1991. It was in that fateful year that India's non-alignment crumbled with the demise of the Soviet Union and its socialism came apart due to a devastating balance-of-payments crisis. Only then, under the then Finance Minister, Manmohan Singh, did India begin to take the first step towards undoing the economic damage that had been inflicted during the past forty-plus years.

In the modern era, it is almost impossible to build non-violence on a factory civilisation, but it is feasible and practical to do the same in self-contained villages. The soul of India lives in its villages. India is still predominantly rural; over 70 per cent of its people live in villages. As of 2021, of the total population of 1.2 billion, the urban population has increased to 377 million but an overwhelming majority of 833 million is still in villages, big and small. India, it has been said, lives in her mid-sized villages,[10] with as many as 485 million people living in them with a population ranging from 1,000 to 5,000. Additionally, 103 million people live in villages of 500-1,000 population, and 47 million people in villages of less than 500 people (refer to Figure 2.1 for the Urban–Rural Divide).

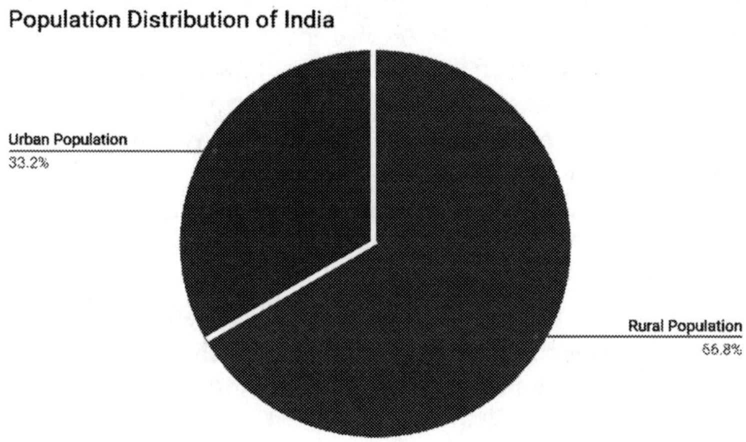

Figure 2.1. The Rural–Urban Population Divide

Due to the rapid pace of urbanisation, rural life is also being transformed. Villages are becoming fewer and bigger across the country. As cities become bigger, neighbouring villages are merging with them. All these factors lead to reduced land for cultivation and irrigation, encroachment of ponds and lakes and, ultimately, villages become congested like cities. At the same time, the village and municipal amenities are not being developed. Lack of quality infrastructure, lack of quality education, lack of quality healthcare facilities still make life difficult in many villages.

The first priority for the societal transformation of India is accelerated rural development. The key here is that all developmental actions have to be sustainable and should be activated in 600,000 villages that have missed both the Industrial Revolution and information technology revolution and in fact even the first Green Revolution in many of the states. The growth of the Indian state is likely to be constrained in the next future by the low level of socio-economic development experienced by the rural areas.[11] While the rest of the country is experiencing an increasing rate of growth, the Indian countryside is lagging behind with slower growth rate, widespread poverty and increasing inequality.

To access the pattern of growth in the Indian countryside and its impact on living standards, it is necessary to focus on three main traits that distinguish the economy and society in contemporary rural India. First, to be considered should be the complexity of the Indian rural economy, which is a composite system with each component presenting specific features in terms of productive and social structure, and of market integration. Second, it is necessary to consider the institutional embeddedness of the Indian rural economy, that is, the fact that the economy is embedded in rural society and rural change is the result of the interplay between institutions and individuals. Finally, it is necessary to assume the historical specificity and path dependency of change in rural India, that is, the fact that socio-economic dynamics are context-specific, influenced by historical trajectories and local culture.

Agriculture is no longer the unique centre of economic life in rural India. The advance of Capitalism has led to the emergence of industrial and service activities that have changed the spatial and inter-sectoral allocation of resources and production relations in the countryside, providing different forms of livelihood and creating a rural non-farm path to economic growth. The outcome is an integrated system,[12] in which non-farm activities are linked to agriculture, employing former agriculture resources – both labor and capital – and sharing infrastructure and institutions. Rural sectoral diversification is an 'anomaly' of Indian contemporary capitalism: a process substantially unpredicted by the conventional narrative on capitalist growth that establishes the economic supremacy of agriculture in rural areas and the shift to rural industry in urban centres.[13]

Sex	Year	India, all age groups			
		Agricultural workers			WPR
		Cultivators	Labour	Agri. workers % to total workers	
Male	2017–18	76.96	21.83	40.24	52.07
	2018–19	77.18	21.60	38.28	52.25
	2019–20	76.55	21.63	39.95	53.89
Female	2017–18	64.52	34.21	56.99	16.51
	2018–19	67.66	31.20	55.29	17.61
	2019–20	70.34	28.00	59.95	21.85
Persons	2017–18	73.23	25.55	44.13	34.69
	2018–19	74.15	24.66	42.49	35.29
	2019–20	74.25	23.99	45.57	38.17

Source: NITI Aayog Discussion Paper/2022 – Workforce Changes and Employment: Some Findings from PLFS Data Series[14]

Table 2.1. Per cent Distribution of Agricultural Workers among Cultivators and Labour Categories

An analysis of Table 2.1 shows that three-fourths of agriculture workers are self-employed as cultivators and this share has remained more or less stable in the last few years. In fact, the number of cultivators in India has increased quite considerably in perspective, from 147 million in 2017–18 to 173 million in 2019–20 while the number of agricultural labourers showed a decrease of only 4.6 million in two years.

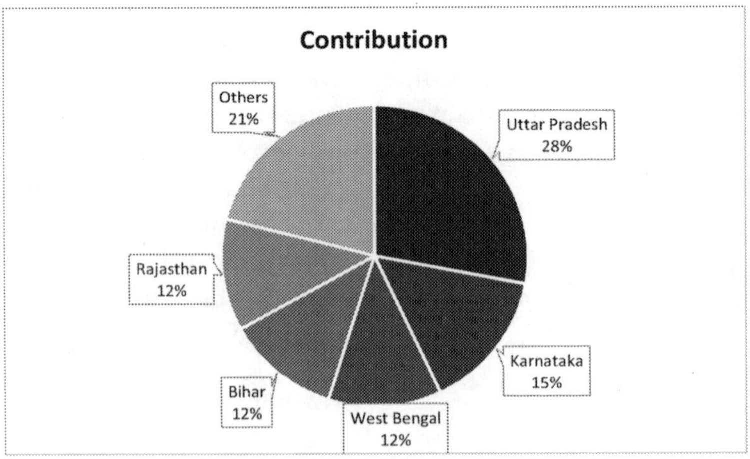

State	Agricultural Labour (Million)		Reduction (Million)
	2004-05	2011-12	
Uttar Pradesh	43.30	34.83	8.47
Karnataka	17.60	12.91	4.69
West Bengal	15.50	11.79	3.71
Bihar	21.30	17.67	3.63
Rajasthan	17.40	13.83	3.56
Others	143.83	137.31	6.52
Total	258.93	228.36	30.57

Figure 2.2. Contribution of States to Agriculture Labour Force Reduction, 2004-05 to 2011-12

An analysis across the states shows that for Kerala, Uttarakhand, etc., even though the absolute magnitude of reduction is not large, it forms a substantial share of the agricultural workforce these states had in 2004-05. The analysis clearly highlights that between the period 2004-05 and 2013-14, a large percentage of the agricultural workforce across states moved away from agriculture.

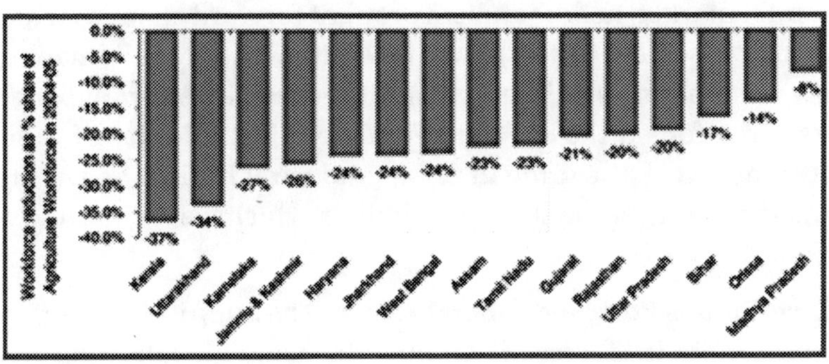

Figure 2.3. Changes in Agricultural Workforce between 2004-05 and 2013-14

Source: NSSO Report 61st and 68th Round Census of India, KPMG Analysis.

There are a few doubts that history and culture matter in India. Evidence and analysis show that in contemporary India, social structures and power relations inherited and developed from the colonial and pre-colonial past are intertwined in capitalist production relations. This intertwining is particularly significant in rural areas where social change lags behind economic change and individual and social behaviour is deeply embedded institutionally. A major consequence of this intertwining is that the capitalist nature of social production relations in rural areas is often hidden behind institutional residuals of the Indian colonial and pre-colonial past and it might be difficult to assess. As a consequence, it is difficult to focus on the mechanisms of work and change of the different social systems that appear to be deeply rooted in a tradition that may also be defined and invented on purpose.

Neo-Liberalism and Capital/Labour Transformation in India

India in a declared way adopted neo-liberalism in 1991. Although the declaration of the official policy was made in 1991, the Indian economy had showed signs of liberalisation earlier. The neo-liberal policy came as a package of liberalisation, globalisation and privatisation. This meant redefining capital labour relations in rural as well as in urban India. While this resulted in flexibility and informal labour and a simultaneous fluidity in the capital market, neo-liberalism brought forward changes which were alien to Indian society in the era of inception. The transformation of the economy is sometimes riddled with differences and complexities. Neo-Liberalism reinforced the differences in the other. Fluidity of capital and labour did not work the same in urban and rural India. The Urban–Rural divide has been one of the strongest divides which was reinforced by neo-liberalism.[15]

Rural Livelihoods Post Neo-Liberalisation: The question of changing rural livelihoods under the forces of neo-liberalism and globalisation arises due to complexity in the form of flexibility of the labour force and multiplicity of occupations. Official reports and statistics indicate the level of diversification in rural livelihoods in the last decade in India. Rural enterprises and the rural non-agricultural sector are expanding relatively more than agricultural enterprises. According to Economic Census 2013, rural India was far more enterprising than urban areas, as it accounted for 61.3 per cent of the country's industrial units compared to just 38.7 per cent in towns and cities. However, what is pertinent to note is that both in the rural and in the urban areas, part-time labour (unorganised) is employed in greater proportions than full-time labour.

There has been a clear indication of the rural livelihood diversification in favour of non-farm activities. Table 2.2 indicates the directions of the drift from agricultural activities. The drift is particularly observed in rural India. To understand rural employment, it is absolutely necessary to understand the nature of the drift from agricultural establishments. Although this initially started as a livelihood substitute for the people living on agriculture, it became a livelihood support for rural people. Table 2.2 reveals that in 17 of the major non-agricultural activities the proportion of establishments in rural areas exceeds that of urban areas in seven activities.

S. No.	Major Activity Group	Rural India	Urban India	India
1.	Mining & Quarrying	0.31	0.15	0.24
2.	Manufacturing	26.02	19.87	23.28
3.	Electricity, Gas & Water Supply	.21	0.14	0.18
4.	Construction	.86	0.94	0.90
5.	Sale, Repair, Maintenance of Motor Vehicles	1.20	3.01	2.00
6.	Wholesale Trade	1.86	3.04	2.38
7.	Retail Trade	39.28	45.00	41.38
8.	Hotels & Restaurants	4.01	4.37	4.17
9.	Transport, Storage	4.30	4.14	4.23
10.	Post & Telecommunications	1.55	2.45	1.95
11.	Financial Intermediation	0.65	1.03	0.82
12.	Real Estate, Renting	2.04	3.83	2.84
13.	Public Administration & Defence	1.97	1.152	1.60
14.	Education	5.43	2.30	4.03
15.	Health & Social Work	2.16	2.22	2.18
16.	Other Community, Social & Personal Service Activities	8.15	6.35	7.35
17.	Other Activities	.01	0.00	0.00

Table 2.2. Participation of Population in Non-Agricultural Activities in Rural and Urban Areas

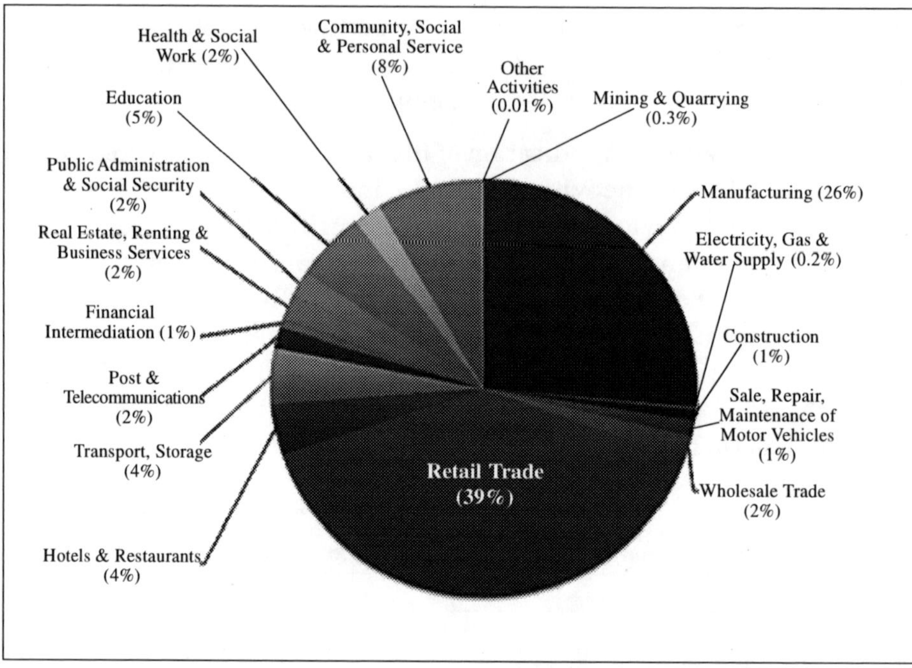

Figure 2.4. Distribution of Major Non-Agricultural Establishments in Rural India During 2005

Source: "Economic Census All-India Report (2005)", Govt. of India, Ministry of Statistics and Programme Implementation.

Trends of Non-Farm Employment and Income

The rural non-farm economy in recent times is being considered an effective strategy for decentralisation of economic practices in rural India and pausing the migration of people to urban centres. According to the Sixth Economic Census 2016, there are around 45.36 million non-agricultural establishments in India, of which 22.71 million are in rural areas and 22.65 million in urban areas. The Census report states that there are around 108.41 million persons who worked in non-agricultural establishments, constituting about 82.57 per cent of the total employment of which about 46.84 million (43.20%) of the total employment in the non-agricultural sector was in rural areas, whereas 61.57 million (56.80%) of the total employment in non-agricultural sector was in urban areas.[16]

The three key activity groups that drew the most own establishments were manufacturing, retail commerce, and other communal, social, and personal service activities. When compared to retail commerce and manufacturing, the percentage of other categories, such as social and personal service activities, was significantly lower. Retail commerce employed 7.5 million people, or 43.12 per cent of all people working in own enterprises in rural areas. Manufacturing employed 5.4 million people, or 31.01 per cent, while other social and personal service activities employed 1.3 million people, or 7.67 per cent. The percentage share trend is consistent with the pattern seen in businesses that employ people. Manufacturing, construction, trade, transportation, and business services were the non-agriculture sectors with positive and greater employment growth during the 1990s, whereas mining and quarrying, utilities, and community services experienced negative employment growth.

Non-farm employment can broadly be classified into three categories: regular employment, self-employment and casual employment. A trend in the employment status of rural labour in India is presented in Figure 2.5.

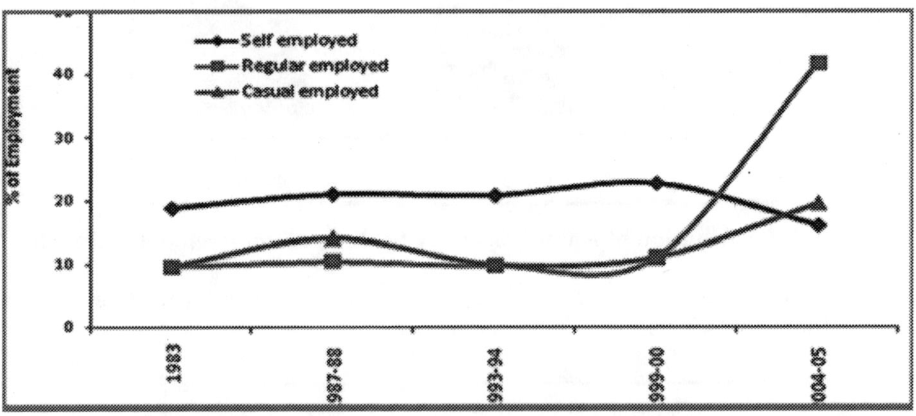

Figure 2.5. Trends in Employment Status in Rural Labour Force (Male + Female) by Sector

Source: NSS Report No. 522 (62/10/01) *Employment and unemployment situation in India, July, 2005* - June, 2006.

Nearly 27 million people were employed in the organised sector in 2003. Since 1998, when there were 28.1 million people working in this area, employment has been declining. According to estimates, 92 per cent of

Indian workers are employed in the unorganised sector, with the organised sector making up the remaining 8 per cent. Additionally, it should be mentioned that in India, 89 per cent of males and 95 per cent of women labour are in the unorganised sector. Non-agricultural activities in India appear to be incredibly disorganised, even though the informal nature of farm activities in rural areas has been somewhat documented. Distribution of workers in organised and unorganised sectors is shown in Figure 2.6.

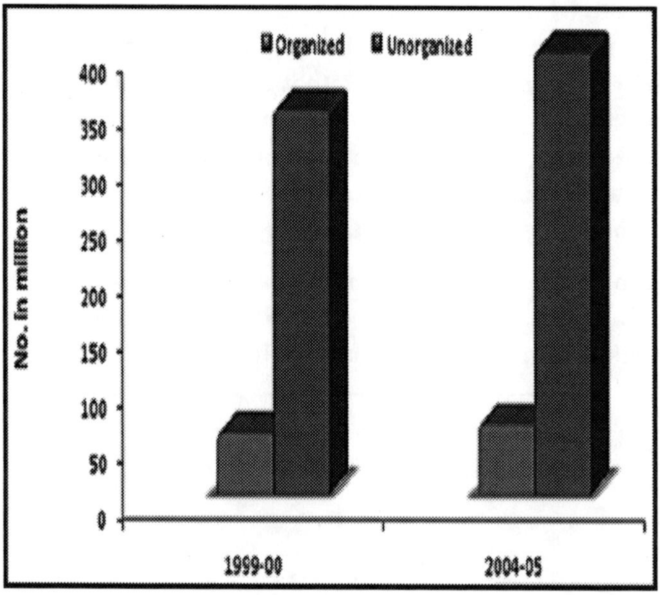

Figure 2.6. Distribution of Rural Workforce by Type of Employment and Sector

Source: NSS Report No. 522 (62/10/01) Employment and Unemployment Situation in India, July 2005, June 2006.

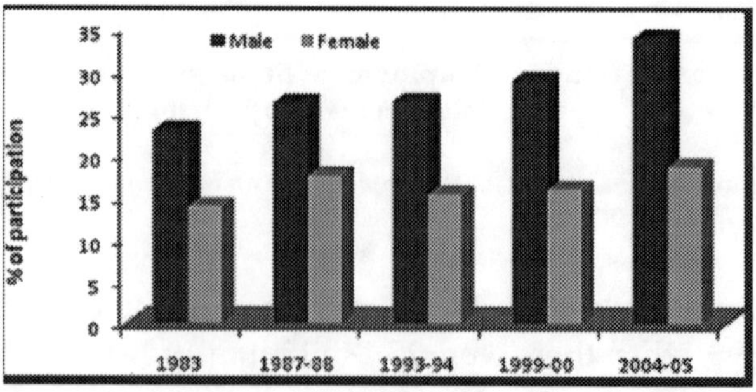

Figure 2.7. Distribution of Rural Workforce in Non-Farm-Activities

The process of livelihood diversification clearly indicates a story of agrarian transformation. The present-day transformation in rural India is not a story of capital transformation but reiterating the old bondage of semi-feudal-semi-capitalist production process in the form of an advanced neo-liberal bondage based on free markets, fluidity of capital and flexibility of labour.[17] Livelihood diversification is a reflection of this new kind of bondage. However, the expansion in self-employed enterprises and non-agricultural opportunities and introduction of new rural enterprises indicate the potential productive capacity of a huge pool of surplus resources and labour upon which an alternative rural development model can be built.

Strength and Weaknesses of Non-Farm Sector

Non-farm activities either prevent the poor from descending into deeper poverty or help the poor rise above it. Given this, it is crucial to pinpoint the non-farm sectors in India's strengths and limitations in order to concentrate efforts on reducing poverty. The next paragraphs go through the advantages and disadvantages of India's rural non-farm sector as identified by Mukherjee and Zhang (2005).

Strengths

- **Institutional Basis for Rural Non-Farm Sector**. The structures in India that support the growth of the rural non-farm economy are highly robust. The KVIC, State Khadi Board, NHHDC, Small Industries Development Bank of India (SIDBI), State industrial corporations, policies and programmes promoting linkages with agriculture, especially agro-industries, domestic marketing channels for rural non-farm production, as well as government support in export promotion, are a few examples. The institutional foundations for the rural non-farm sector's quick expansion are already in place.
- **Decentralisation Process**. State governments in India have had much more freedom to make decisions over the past 20 years than they did prior to 1980. Coalition governments at the Centre rely heavily on regional parties. In exchange, they have won economic independence in the creation of state-specific development strategies. Foreign direct investment (FDI) has also grown to have a significant role in the overall policy environment since the

economy was opened up in 1991. State governments are competing with one another to draw more FDI into infrastructure and manufacturing. Although the amount of FDI moving into India is less than 10 per cent of what is going into China, it is similar to the path taken by that country in several ways. On the plus side, though, this opens the door for future investment at greater levels.

Manifested Weaknesses

- **Infrastructure**. The most significant bottleneck in generating higher levels of rural non-farm activity in India is the quantity, quality and reliability of infrastructure. For example, the World Bank Investment Climate Survey for India indicates that power outages were one of the most serious obstacles in the development of the non-farm sector.[18] Although, corrective steps are now being taken, increased infrastructure remains the most important priority for the future. To achieve a sustained growth rate of 8-9 per cent, the investment rate must be stepped up from the current level of 24 per cent to nearly 35 per cent over the next decade, with investment directed at the rural sector.[19]
- **Regulatory Restrictions on Small-Scale Sector**. Regulation of the small-scale sector constitutes an important aspect of non-farm development policy in India. In the initial stages, capital investment restrictions were imposed to protect the small-scale sector, especially in rural areas, from predation by large industry. To develop a domestic market, the sector started reserving items, and quantitative constraints were put in place to shield it from import competition. However, as the 1990s ended, these very policies started to work against the small-scale sector's vitality, particularly in rural areas. Limits on capital investment have prevented economies of scale, and benefits given to small businesses have created disincentives to reinvest. Several official reports have recommended a substantial increase in the capital investment limit (from the present level of around $ 200,000) to make better use of technology and improve productivity.[20] However, no such policy announcement has been made as yet.
- **Importance of Product Reservations for the Small-Scale Industry.** This has increasingly decreased, yet it has led to rents in the system. All reserved items would be free to be imported at the current tariff

rate as a result of the government's decision to move them all into the open general licence category starting in April 2005. According to WTO standards, the latter is expected to gradually decline to roughly 20 per cent, effectively ending the protection to small-scale industry.

- **Quality of Manpower.** High levels of illiteracy in rural India have hampered the growth of the rural non-farm sector. Education has both intrinsic and instrumental value. Apart from having a positive correlation with wages, a minimum basic standard of education is necessary to apply for credit, to be aware of one's rights and responsibilities and to deal with instances of corruption and malpractices. Often, a lack of education is intrinsic to poverty, which seems to have been the case in India until recently.[21]
- **Lack of Knowledge**. It causes labour in rural areas to stagnate in agriculture or shift to temporary jobs in non-agricultural industries rather than take salaried jobs with better pay and benefits. Together with lack of technical skills, there is little incentive for rural firms to invest in technology, leading to low levels of labour productivity in the rural manufacturing sector compared to urban manufacturing.[22] The same can be said for the service sector, which has room to grow, given the urban economy's already solid foundation. Policymakers should prioritise increased spending to enhance both the quality and accessibility of education (primary, secondary, and above).
- **Forward and Backward Linkages**. Performance of non-farm operations in rural regions is significantly impacted by the absence of proper forward and backward integration. The RNF sector's forward links act as inputs for other industries. The RNF sector also requires outputs of other industries in backward linkages. Empirical studies show that where traditional agricultural technologies are used, forward links between RNF activities and agriculture (rural produced agricultural inputs) are especially important, while backward links between RNF activities and agriculture, particularly the links between rural agricultural processing and the agriculture sector and between rural transport and rural marketing activities, are quite significant for rural economic development. However, gaps in the integration of production linkages brought about by poor infrastructure, low

> accessibility of market, support service weaknesses and intervention of middlemen have constrained the development of non-farm enterprises in India.[23]

It is necessary to find suitable and efficient institutional vehicles for the creation of non-farm sector policy and interventions for job possibilities. In numerous nations, RNFE promotion strategies and programmes have been developed. The labour-intensive township and village businesses (TVEs) of China, which are sometimes cited as the "engine of growth" behind that nation's impressive expansion over the past few decades, serve as the forerunner in the country's new capitalism. It is also vital to improve the marketing links between village entrepreneurs and larger business firms in the towns/cities. Such strategic alliances or partnerships can contribute to the sustainability of small village and tiny enterprises in the rural areas. Other important considerations that need to be focused on may include human resource development, financial/credit facilities, research and development and women's participation to make the activities self-sustaining in the changing competitive environment.

Reality Check: Rural Areas

The present dismal situation and provisioning of essential facilities in the rural areas is indeed a cause of concern for us as a nation. From the time the government changed at the centre in 2014, many schemes for the growth of the rural areas have been initiated like Fasal Bima Yojana, Soil Health Card Scheme, and Kaushal Bharat-Kushal Bharat, etc. However, there is still a lot to be desired if we want to incorporate villages in the overall growth story of our nation. A quick reality check of a few of the aspects has been highlighted in the succeeding paragraphs.

Healthcare System. Access to health care is unusually challenging in India. Nearly 69 per cent of the country's 1.2 billion population lives in rural areas where distribution of health care products and services is difficult. Urban areas, particularly metros and tier-1 towns, have much better availability of doctors and hospital beds than rural areas. For instance, witness the wide disparity between the number of doctors per 1,000 persons in urban areas and that in rural areas (2 vs. 0.35, respectively), or the number of hospital beds per 1,000 persons in urban India vs. that in rural India (4 vs. less than 1 in rural). The infographic below examines a facet of this issue at the state level – the variation in the availability of hospital beds in government hospitals across states and the rural-urban disparity within each state. To understand the yawning chasm between availability of government hospital beds in rural and urban areas, just note that the scale of the bar chart is logarithmic. Then look again at the values against the bars. Among the states, the rural–urban gap is the widest in Maharashtra, which also has a relatively low number of people served per government hospital bed. Surprisingly, Rajasthan, Jharkhand, Assam, Arunachal and Mizoram stand out for having a greater number of beds in government hospitals in rural areas than in urban.[24]

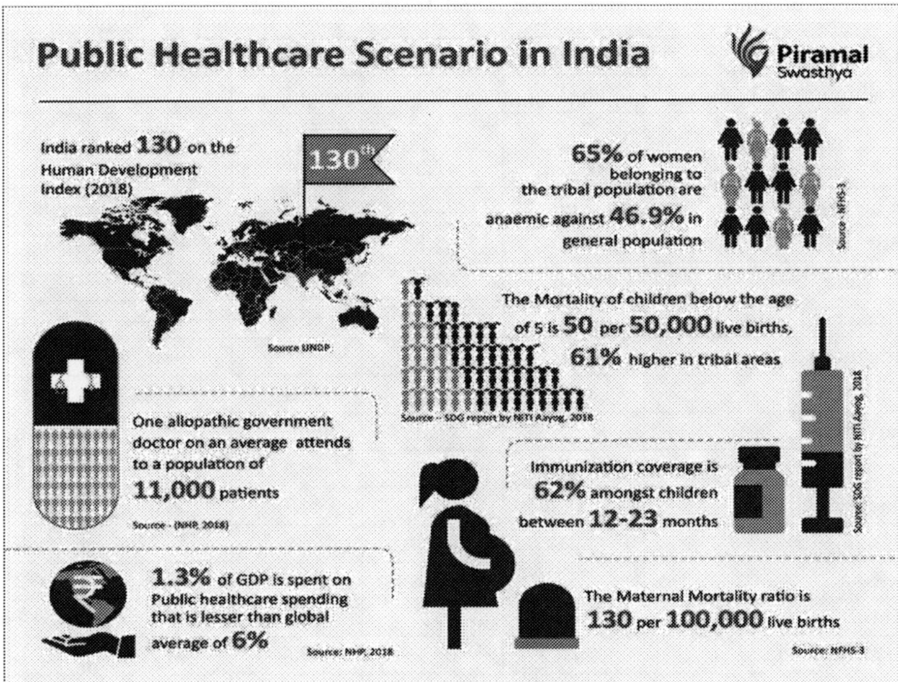

Figure 2.8. Scenario of Public Healthcare in India

Source: The Indian Express, 7 April 2019

Education Structure. Education is considered the most powerful, significant tool to bring about maximum effective change in the world. It is viewed as a passport for a better future; thus, it is identified as a stand-alone goal of the heart of the 2030 Agenda for Sustainable Development. India has been working hard towards achieving this goal. In the last one decade, it has increased its budgeted expenditure on education from INR 3.6 lakh close to INR 4.6 lakh. Despite all efforts, India is not able to achieve success at the expected rates. Although India has raised its current literacy rate of 74.04 per cent (2021) from 12 per cent at the time of Independence in 1947, it still lags behind the world average literacy rate of 84 per cent. Compared with other nations, the Republic of India has the largest illiterate population. The rural population of India represents 65 per cent of the total population, around 88 crore (880 million). As of 2021, the literacy rate in rural India was around 73.5 per cent. This includes 81 per cent male and 65 per cent female literacy in the rural sections of India.

State	*2011*	*2001*	*1991*	*1961*	*1971*
Andhra Pradesh	67.7	60.5	44.1	35.7	24.6
Assam	73.2	63.3	*519*	-	33.9
Bihar	63.8	47.0	375	323	23.2
Chhattisgarh	71.0	64.7	42.9	32.6	24.1
Gujarat	79.3	69.1	61.3	44.9	37.0
Haryana	76.6	67.9	55.9	37.1	25.7
Hlmachal Pradesh	S3.S	76.5	63.9	-	-
Jamrnu and Kashmir	68.7	55.5	-	30.6	21.7
Jharkhand	67.6	53.6	41.4	35.0	23.9
Karnataka	75.6	66.6	56.0	46.2	36.6
Kerala	93.9	90.9	89.8	78.9	69.8
Madhya Pradesh	70.6	63.7	44.7	38.6	27.3
Maharashtra	82.9	76.9	64.9	57.2	45.8
Odisha	73.5	63.1	49.1	33.6	26.2
Punjab	76.7	69.7	58.5	43.4	34.1
Rajasthan	67.1	60.4	38.6	30.1	22.6
Tamil Nadu	80.3	735	6Z7	54.4	45.4
Uttar Pradesh	69.7	56.3	40.7	3Z7	24.0
Uttarakhand	79.6	71.6	57.8	46.1	33.3
West Bengal	77.1	68.6	57.7	48.7	38.9
India	74.0	64,8	52.2	43.6	34.5

The blanks indicate that data is not available for those census years for the states concerned.

Source: Census of India 1971, 1381, 1991, 2001 and 2011.

Table 2.3. Literacy Rate across Indian States

According to ASER 2021, the enrolment in private schools has gradually shifted to government schools over the past few years. Private school enrolment for children aged 6 to 14 has dropped from 32.5 per cent in 2018 to 24.4 per cent in 2021. Both government school enrolments and the percentages of children who are not already enrolled have increased in tandem. Among older children in the age group 15-16, an increase in government school enrolment of 10 percentage points over 2018 levels is driven by significant declines in the proportion of out of school children in this age group, as well as by decreasing private school enrolments.[25]

Age group and sex	ASER 2018					ASER 2020					ASER 2021				
	Govt	Pvt	Other	Not enrolled	Total	Govt	Pvt	Other	Not enrolled	Total	Govt	Pvt	Other	Not enrolled	Total
Age 6-14: All	64.3	32.5	0.7	2.5	100	65.8	28.8	0.8	4.6	100	70.3	24.4	0.7	4.6	100
Age 7-16: All	63.1	32.3	0.7	3.9	100	65.5	28.6	0.7	5.2	100	69.9	24.7	0.7	4.7	100
Age 7-10: All	64.4	33.5	0.7	1.4	100	64.3	30.5	0.8	4.4	100	70.3	24.8	0.6	4.4	100
Age 7-10: Boys	60.6	37.4	0.7	1.4	100	60.9	33.6	0.8	4.7	100	67.9	26.9	0.5	4.7	100
Age 7-10: Girls	68.4	29.5	0.7	1.4	100	68.1	27.0	0.8	4.1	100	72.8	22.3	0.7	4.1	100
Age 11-14: All	64.1	32.0	0.8	3.2	100	68.0	27.4	0.7	3.9	100	70.5	24.5	0.8	4.1	100
Age 11-14: Boys	60.5	35.9	0.7	2.9	100	64.5	30.9	0.7	3.9	100	67.5	27.3	0.9	4.3	100
Age 11-14: Girls	67.6	28.0	0.8	3.6	100	71.9	23.5	0.7	3.9	100	73.9	21.5	0.7	3.9	100
Age 15-16: All	57.4	29.9	0.6	12.1	100	62.1	27.3	0.6	9.9	100	67.4	25.2	0.9	6.6	100
Age 15-16: Boys	55.9	32.2	0.5	11.5	100	60.8	29.7	0.8	8.8	100	66.7	26.3	0.9	6.1	100
Age 15-16: Girls	58.9	27.8	0.7	12.6	100	63.6	24.8	0.5	11.1	100	68.1	24.0	0.8	7.1	100

* 'Other' includes children going to Madarsa and EGS.
'Not rerolled' includes children who never enrolled or are not currently enrolled.

Figure 2.9. Children Enrolled in School: By Age Group, Sex and School Type (2018, 2020 and 2021*)

Human Poverty. The number of poor people in India, according to the country's Eleventh National Development Plan, is more than 300 million. The country has been successful in reducing the proportion of the poor from about 55 per cent in 1973 to about 27 per cent in 2004. However, almost one-third of the country's population of more than 1.1 billion continues to live below the poverty line and a large proportion of the poor live in rural areas. Poverty remains a chronic condition for almost 30 per cent of India's rural population.[26] The bulk of the poor in rural areas belong to the following categories:

- Agricultural labour households, without any land, farming about 60 per cent of all agricultural labour households.

- Agricultural labour households, with very small holdings, constituting about 40 per cent of all agricultural labour households.
- Non-agricultural rural labour households without land holdings, including villages slowly losing their traditional employment and
- Small cultivators cultivating holdings of less than 5 acres.

S. No.	State	Rural		Urban		Total	
		%age of Persons	No. of Persons (lakhs)	%age of Persons	No. of Persons (lakhs)	%age of Persons	No. of Persons (lakhs)
1.	Chhattisgarh	44.61	88.90	24.75	15.22	39.93	104.11
2.	Rajasthan	16.05	84.19	10.69	18.73	14.71	102.92
3.	Manipur	38.80	7.45	32.59	2.78	36.89	10.22
4.	Uttar Pradesh	30.40	479.35	26.O6	118.84	29.43	598.19
5.	Bihar	34.06	320.40	31.23	37.75	33.74	358.15
6.	Andaman & Nicobar Islands	1.57	0.04	0.00	0.00	1.00	0.04
7.	India	25.70	2166.58	13.70	531.25	21 .92	2697.83

Figure 2.10. Number and Percentage of Population below Poverty Line in States—2012-2013

The incidence of rural poverty has declined somewhat over the past three decades because of rural to urban migration. On the map of poverty in India, the poorest areas are in parts of Rajasthan, Madhya Pradesh, Uttar Pradesh, Bihar, Jharkhand, Odisha, Chhattisgarh, and West Bengal. Large numbers of India's poorest people live in the country's semi-arid tropical region. There is also a high incidence of poverty in flood-prone areas such as those extending from eastern Uttar Pradesh to the Assam plains, and especially in northern Bihar.

A major cause of poverty among India's rural people, both individuals and communities, is lack of access to productive assets and financial resources.[27] High levels of illiteracy, inadequate health care and extremely limited access to social services are common among the rural poor. Micro enterprise development, which could generate income and enable the poor to improve their living conditions, has only recently become a focus of the government.

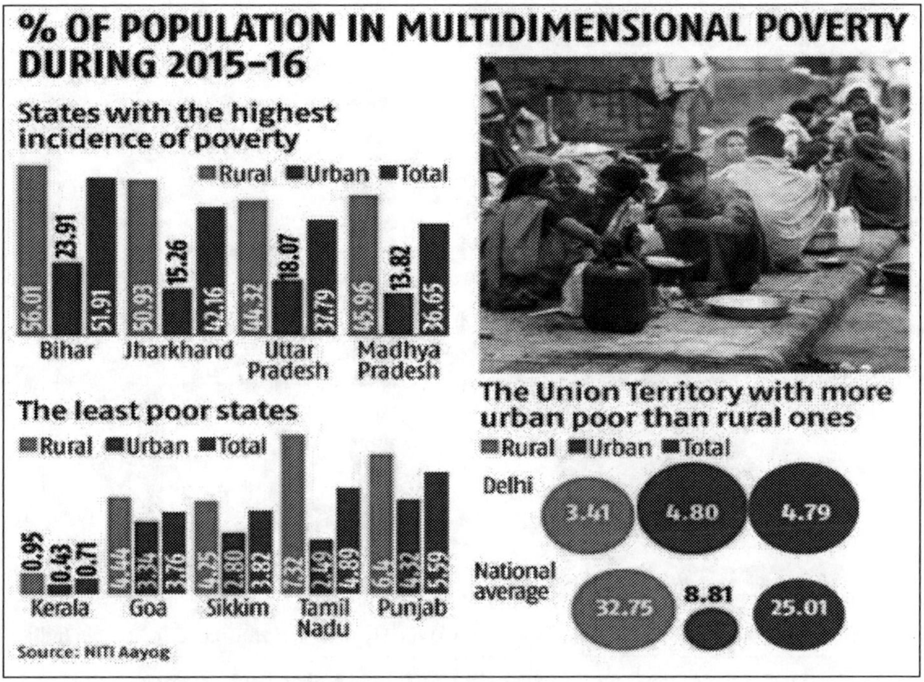

Figure 2.11. Percentage of Population in Multi-dimensional Poverty during 2015-16

Drinking Water. Rural India has more than 700 million people residing in about 1.42 million habitations spread over 15 diverse ecological regions. Meeting the drinking water needs of such a large population can be a daunting task. Water is the basic necessity for the survival of human beings. According to the 76th round of the National Sample Survey, approximately 42 per cent rural households travel every day to fetch drinking water. The distance they cover vary from less than 0.2 km (30.4 per cent households) to over 1.5 km (0.5 per cent households) one way. This means rural India has households whose members travel more than 3 km (round trip from the primary water source) each day to get water. Despite an estimated total of Rs. 1,105 billion spent on providing safe drinking water since the First Five Year Plan was launched in 1951, lack of safe and secure drinking water continues to be a major hurdle and a national economic burden.

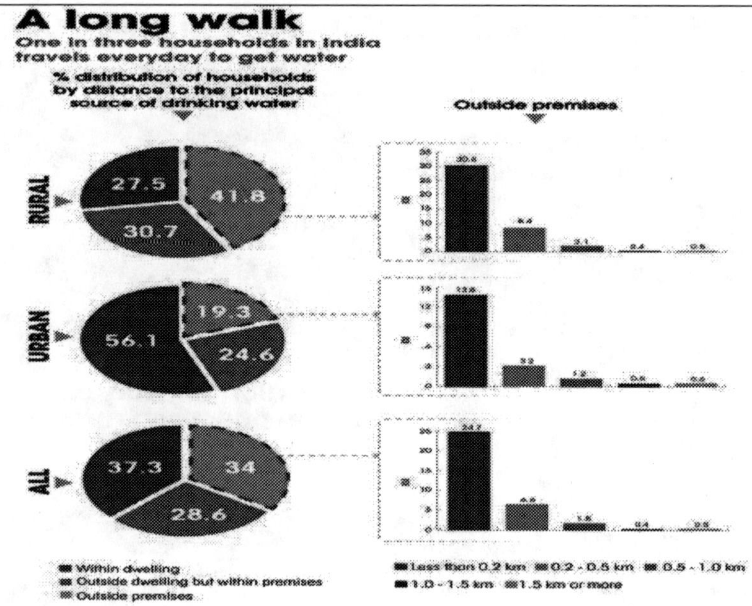

Source: NSSO Report No. 584: Drinking Water, Sanitation, Hygiene and Housing Condition in India.

Figure 2.12. Percentage Distribution of Households by Distance to the Source of Drinking Water

Opportunities and Avenues in Rural India

The impact of globalisation, the proliferation of the media, and the interest of numerous firms and NGOs in rural development throughout the 1990s led to villagers demanding and asking for openness and accountability for their weak economic growth. They discovered in the hard way that the secret lies in their personal engagement, drive, and demand for responsibility and transparency in the conduct of all interaction agents. Rural residents understood that improving their quality of life and achieving economic success would require their own initiative and participation. This insight and shift of perspective is a key factor in the expansion of the rural economy. The rural economy is also fuelled by the expectations, goals, and motivation of the rural folk. To make the rural economy grow, the focus is on economic prosperity, environmental sustainability, and social equity. It is a grand vision, but we can implement it, and achieve it through the public-private-NGO-people model in rural revival and revitalisation to give it a new life and energy. The objective should be to raise the overall scale of resources flowing into rural India, develop ways to increase the scale of locally produced resources from within rural regions, and be much more strategic about the type of investments in rural areas. The challenge today, however, lies as much in sustaining this momentum as ensuring an inclusive pattern of growth through initiatives to integrate the rural economy with the national economy.[28]

Governance in Rural India

The term "governance" today refers to more than just how government institutions run. It is viewed in terms of collaboration and joint ventures between the public, private, and non-profit sectors. The United Nations definition of governance includes specifically the effective cooperation between the government and non-government actors to bring about solutions that are mutually beneficial.[29] With each partner contributing in accordance with their individual resources, strengths, and areas of expertise, this inclusive process is built on common interests. Thus, governance is seen to go beyond the official government structure, to include diverse ways through which civil society can demand, actualise and make more effective the required delivery of services by those in the government. It is also desired that governance be compatible to the principles of equality, justice and human rights.

By including political components into the World Bank's concept of good governance, this idea of good or effective governance has been expanded and tailored to meet the needs of developing nations in terms of their own economic development. Realising the importance of this, most of the countries are now looking towards a transformation from the earlier propagated concept of Inclusive Growth towards new norms of Rapid Growth. This concept includes several interrelated components: rapid growth that reduces poverty and creates employment opportunities, access to essential services in health and education, especially for the poor, equality of opportunity, empowerment through education and skill development opportunities, improving people's participation by way of effective decentralisation through local self-governments and involving civil society and voluntary organisations to accelerate socio-economic developments, reforming civil service to improve accountability and efficiency, administrative procedural reforms for a hassle-free public-government interface, reforming the judicial system for speedy delivery of justice, involving society in the self-help and self-governance models, empowering the marginalised and the excluded to equip them to act as pressure groups to resist bad governance and exploitation by vested interests and using info technology for a transparent and effective administration.

Historical Perspective

Since the beginning of time, villages and rural development have been a part of India. In the past, these areas were self-sufficient, self-sustaining microcosms that resembled little republics, and their rulers made use of their inventiveness to make them more effective. Local self-governments today, however, are structured and run in a British-style manner.

- Keeping Gandhiji's Sarvodaya (upliftment and progress of all) principle in mind, the GoI on 2 October 1952 (Gandhi Jayanti) launched a programme through which all-round development of the population (rural) was sought. It was termed as the 'Community Development Programme' as a part of the first Five Year Plan along with a booster programme called the National Extension Services at the block level headed by the block development officer. However, its implementation disclosed a distinct lack of citizen interest. Therefore, the Balwant Rai Mehta committee to study and diagnose the same was set up and it brought forward the reason for this disinterest which was a dearth of avenues of popular participation in local level development programmes for the people.
- The first local governing body, the municipal corporation, was established in Madras in 1687, marking the birth of local government. The British were not political; their concerns were financial and related to revenue collection. They understood the importance of working with local governments to establish top-to-bottom control at the local level. This led to severe exploitation of the rural areas by the British for their vested interests and a big blow to the economy. Following recurrent famines in the later part of the 19th century and the recommendations of the Famine Commission, Lord Mayo's resolution regarding local government was passed where the majority of officials were to be nominated by the British government.

- The Gandhian view prevailed, and panchayats became the foundation of the local self-government. This principle is enshrined in Article 40 of the Indian Constitution under the Directive Principles of State Policy, which lays down that the State shall take steps to organise village panchayats and endow them with such powers and authority as may be necessary to enable them to function as units of self-government. A large number of rural development programmes was started by nationalists and social reformers of which some gradually diminished due to various technical/administrative reasons and some merged with the government-sponsored schemes later.[30]
- The political tenor of local government in India was set by Lord Ripon's resolution of 1882, sometimes known as "Local Self-Government." Local elections were to choose the members. Non-officials of the British government would elect two-thirds of the members and serve as the chair. The British bureaucracy viewed this with disdain and distrust, and put up a strong fight. This idea was scarcely carried out and later dropped in the late 19th century. In the 1906 session of the Congress, this concept was brought up again for debate and some initiatives regarding the same were taken by the ruling government. With the initiative of Lord Curzon, the Provincial Department of Agriculture with Agricultural College and Provincial Research Institute were established. In 1906, the Indian Agricultural Service was constituted. This was further carried on to the Government of India Act of 1919 (Provision of Object in Transferred List) and followed by the Government Act 1935 as well as some changes to suit the current scenario. During the Independence struggle, and in fact throughout it, national leaders advocated village communities.

The Balwant Rai Mehta Committee. It suggested the following corrective measures in fine perspective in 1957:

- A three-tier Panchayati Raj structure to be established, wherein the uppermost tier would be the zila parishad (district), while the lowermost tier would be the gram panchayat (village level); the intermediate tier was to be the panchayat samiti (block/taluk level).
- Direct elections to the level of gram panchayats while higher-level appointments were to be made through nominations and other indirect means.

- The district collector was to be the chairperson of the Zila Parishad and had an advisory and coordinating role.
- The district or Zila Parishad was seen as a unit for achieving democratic decentralisation and it was recommended as the unit for planning and organising as well as supervising district administrative functions.[31]
- The Panchayat Samiti was to be entrusted with executive powers.
- The Panchayat Samiti would have the headman or sarpanch of the gram panchayat as its members, while the Zila Parishad would consist of ex-officio members and headmen of the panchayat samiti.

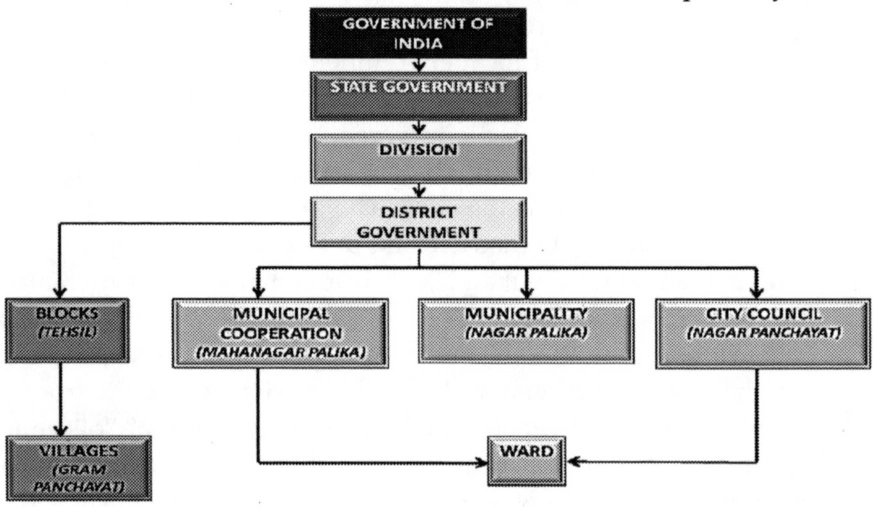

Figure 2.13. Panchayati Raj Institutions in India

Establishment of a three-tier Panchayati Raj System. It is intended to prepare the economic development and social justice plans, implement schemes for economic development and social justice in relation to the twenty-nine subjects listed in the Eleventh Schedule of the Constitution, and levy and collect the proper taxes, duties, tolls, and fees. Panchayats are given the necessary authority to carry out these tasks.

India has two decades of experience of managing village panchayats, panchayat unions (blocks) and zila panchayats (district). Rural development and Panchayati Raj go hand in hand. They were handled by two different ministries, which lacked synergy in implementation. The ministries are those of Rural Development and Panchayati Raj.

Despite having constitutional standing, the way that panchayati raj institutions function has not significantly improved. They are still ruled by bureaucracy. Due to unclear boundaries between their roles, responsibilities, and authority as well as a lack of funding, these institutions were unable to effectively deliver products and services to the villages. Resources must be transferred from outdated, ineffective activities to fresh, potential ones in order for reforms to be successful. Two important questions are raised by this:

- Are the existing concepts, assumptions and values of the theory and practice of development administration, which emerged in the post-colonial phase, still relevant in the 21st century?
- Should we not take into consideration various indigenously available resources within society for the holistic transformation of rural areas?

Present State of Panchayati Raj Institutions (PRIs): Impediments to Growth

The panchayati raj and the municipal system appear to have failed to increase participation and empower people, despite offering a framework for decentralised development even when some panchayat leaders in rural areas have performed honourably. Despite money provided by the government, PRIs have not benefited the common public much. The authority that block level officials have over the infrequently-met village panchayats and gram sabhas not only strengthens corruption and weakens accountability, but has also generated scepticism about the ability of the villagers to improve performance. Today, PRIs are not yet the third tier of the government, but an extension of the second. They are not functioning as institutions of self-governance, but only as agencies for executing a few programs of the state government/GoI.

PRIs at the intermediate and district level and their processes appear opaque and distant to the common person in rural areas. Many significant decisions regarding the identification of beneficiaries under various programmes, the processing of finances, accounting, and paperwork are made behind closed doors and without the knowledge of the general public. Details of several significant laws and plans are still secret and unclear. Only a small number of people in each community are aware of the complexity of the role and authority of government representatives in PRI-related processes. Elected members of the PRIs and the block and district levels behave more or less as contractors, with no institution of the gram sabhas at that level to put moral pressure on them.[32] Zila Parishads and Panchayat Samiti members look upon devolved funds as equivalent to MP or MLA quota funds and the adhyaksha and the block president have been coerced to distribute these funds equally between all members. They independently select contractors and types of schemes. It stands to reason that schemes that offer the highest commission and the lowest chance of verification (like earth work, which is undoubtedly carried out by machines, but has been proven to be done by fake labourers, are favoured.

Most of the time, panchayats are busy implementing construction-related programmes that support contractor-wage labour relationships. Poor people cannot participate in them as equals. However, they encourage the poor's reliance on the sarpanch and the block employees. In this case, panchayat operations are reduced to collaboration between the block engineer and sarpanch. Programs for forestry, pastures, watershed, education, and health that call for collaboration and consensus-building do not involve panchayats.

A detailed analysis of the PRIs indicates nine major defects, which are impediments to growth. These are as under:

- **Administrative Problems**. Panchayati Raj bodies experience several administrative problems. They include the local government's propensity to become politicised, the lack of coordination between popular and bureaucratic forces, the lack of adequate incentives and opportunities for administrative staff to advance, and the lackadaisical attitude of public employees toward development initiatives, among other things.
- **Disillusionment on Structural–Functional Aspects.** The performance of PRIs has been vitiated by political cum-caste-factionalism, rendering developmental projects into chimeras. Panchayati Raj has been hampered by corruption, incompetence, little regard for protocol, political meddling in day-to-day administration, parochial loyalties, motivated actions, power concentration instead of genuine service mindset. Furthermore, it is obvious that the state government's authority to supplant local bodies is contrary to the spirit of democratic decentralisation.

- **Inadequate Finance.** The inadequacy of funds has also stood in the way of successful working of panchayati raj. Panchayati Raj bodies have limited powers in respect of imposing cesses and taxes. The state government only gives them a very small amount of money. Additionally, they typically hesitate to raise the required finances out of concern for their public image.
- **Incompatible Relations between the Three Tiers**. The three tiers do not operate as functional authorities. The tendency on the part of the higher structure to treat the lower structure as its subordinate is markedly visible. From zila parishad to panchayati samiti, and from them to village panchayats, the hierarchical dominance trickles down gradually. Additionally, their mutual interaction does not reflect the true spirit of democratic decentralisation.
- **Lack of Conceptual Clarity**. There is a lack of clarity regarding the concept of Panchayati Raj itself and the objectives for which it stands. Some would treat it as just an administrative agency while some others look upon it as an extension of democracy at the grass root level, and a few others consider it a charter of rural local government. What is even more intriguing is the fact that all these conceptual images could co-exist simultaneously tending to militate against each other every now and then.
- **Lack of Cordial Relations Between Officials and People**. Panchayati Raj was established with the intention of ensuring the people's active participation. However, since government employees hold the important administrative and technical roles, this rarely occurs in practice. Generally, there is a lack of proper cooperation and coordination between the people and officials like block development officers, district officers, etc. Again, the officers fail to discharge development duties more efficiently and sincerely.
- **Politics is an Inevitable Part of a Democratic Framework**. The manipulative nature of rural politics is manifest in the techniques used at elections. Fact-finding research teams observe that the caste system in rural India has made a mockery of the concept of rural development. Even panchayat elections are fought on caste grounds and the traditional dominant castes have manoeuvred in such a way that they still occupy positions of power in the changed set-up. Once the dominant castes have gained control of key positions where choices are made, they can easily sway the plans to work in

their favour. As a result, the caste divide widens daily, further alienating the low castes from taking part in rural development programmes. The political elite in the rural areas develops a stake in seeing that the caste system endures. As a result, the panchayats which were to bring about social change have themselves become victims of caste divisions. The institution which was created to bring change in the socio-economic structure, due to the mere logic of the situation, legitimizes the authority of socially and economically well-off persons.

- **Undemocratic Composition of Various Panchayati Raj Institutions**. Various PRIs are constituted setting aside democratic norms and principles. The indirect election of most of the members of the panchayati samiti only increases the possibility of corruption and bribery.[33] Even the zila parishads consist of mainly ex-officio members. They are, for the most part, government officials. This negates sound democratic principles.
- **Unscientific Distribution of Functions**. The Panchayati Raj scheme is defective in so far as the distribution of functions between the structures at different levels has not been made along scientific lines. The autonomy of local government institutions has been considerably reduced by the integration of development and local self-governance tasks. Once more, it has effectively turned them into governmental organisations. Even the roles entrusted to the panchayat samiti and the panchayat overlap. Resulting in muddling, redundant work, and responsibility shifting.

The Government of India transferred almost four trillion rupees in 2008-09 to the states. If even half of it was to be sent to the sixty million poor families (at 28 per cent as the cut-off line for poverty, 300 million poor would be equivalent to roughly 60 million households) directly by money order, they would have received more than 90 rupees a day! It proves that public expenditure needs to be effectively translated into public goods and services that reach the poor for it to have an impact on poverty and social outcomes. Unfortunately, different kinds of distortions can come in the way of resource allocations reaching the intended beneficiaries.[34]

Although there has been a growing realisation among some chief ministers on the need to improve governance, only a few have been able to translate this into concrete action. This would necessarily involve keeping the MLAs and ministers under check, which is difficult when the state is under a coalition regime, or the ruling party is constrained by a thin margin in the Assembly or is divided into factions. In many states, chief ministers seem to be averse to professionalising administration. When neither politics nor state administration has the capacity for self-correction, only external pressure can coerce states to take hard decisions that will hit at their money-making tactics. In the Indian situation (where foreign donors provide very little aid to the states as compared with what is provided by the Centre) this can come only from the Centre, backed by a strong civil society and media action.

Suggested Reforms

- **CBOs and PRIs**. It is necessary to improve the institutional ties that connect political decentralisation – represented by Panchayati Raj (PRIs) – and administrative decentralisation – represented by user committees supported by central ministries. Links between these two institutions will further strengthen the voice of society's less powerful groups.
- **Connecting the Three Tiers**. There ought to be a system of representation of gram panchayat presidents in the taluka panchayat with direct election of the taluka panchayat president. A similar system ought to be in place for the zila panchayats too.
- **District and Block Level Administration**. Finally, good district and block-level administration is also necessary for functional panchayats/user groups. Therefore, attempts to improve local bureaucratic performance and accountability must coexist with initiatives to strengthen local PRI capacities; otherwise, elected PRI leaders would continue to view the state as an "open treasury."
- **Do we Really Require Three Tiers**? In most states, one of these two tiers is weak; the district units are weak in Tamil Nadu and Rajasthan, whereas the block units are weak in Maharashtra and Gujarat. Some people have suggested that the state should be given the option of doing away with one of the levels in case they so desire. Its implications for efficiency, equity and participation should be studied.
- **Linking MLAs with Block Panchayats**. The exercise of executive power is a hazy area that MPs, MLAs, and PRIs all enter, using either legal or illegal methods. Back-seat driving invites corruption

and encourages making careless decisions. Therefore, why not legitimize the power of MLAs and make them block (taluk panchayat) president by making their constituency co-terminus with the panchayat samiti/taluk panchayat? Giving MLAs a role in the panchayat system will make them fervent advocates for the delegation of tasks and resources to panchayats. Holding that the indirectly elected taluk president or adhyaksha can be trusted with millions of rupees and is trustworthy and committed to the welfare of the public, whereas the directly elected MLA is cunning, corrupt, and irresponsible, is neither good theory nor empirically supported.

- **Local Collection of Taxes**. To lessen their reliance on the state and federal governments, the panchayats should have the authority to independently levy and collect taxes rather than receiving a share of state and federal grants. As they prefer the softer option of receiving funding from the GoI, PRIs nowadays are reluctant to tax and collect. This needs to be discouraged, and local organisations should be encouraged to raise local funds for development in exchange for matching subsidies from the federal government or individual states. A PRI is more likely to use limited resources to support human development and alleviate poverty if it is reliant on the mass of its population for financial support. PRIs become careless and corrupt when they receive external funding without making an effort to raise internal finances. There is an urgent need to transfer the task/function of levying taxes to local bodies. Panchayats should not only collect taxes on land, irrigation, drinking water, power and houses, but also be given the authority to levy taxes on politically unpopular subjects such as agricultural income tax on large holdings.
- **Rank Panchayats.** Through a carefully designed methodology, it is quite possible to measure the performance of panchayats, and to what extent they are inclusive and participative.
- **Untied Grants.** In addition, panchayats would need a share of state and central revenues. States need to increase the share of transfers to PRIs from state governments as united grants. The formula of transfer should no doubt give weightage to population and poverty, but also to efficiency, so that there is an incentive to them for increasing the source of revenues of PRIs through own and assigned taxes and increasing their capacity to collect. State grants should

be given to them only when the PRIs are able to collect a minimum percentage of the taxes assigned to them.

Respecting Civil Society's Autonomy

Despite the enormous burden posed by malgovernance, civil society action has been weak. This could be a reflection of the general state of civil society in the country and its priorities, but largely it is because the government has unwittingly promoted bogus or pliable organisations and have either ignored or have hostile relations with those NGOs that wish to speak for the poor and empower them. In the past 20 years, several organisations have emerged with the intention of enhancing their own status and making quick money. It is important to understand that changes in governance will not happen unless opposing forces in society get the self-assurance and independence they need to fight against government inefficiency and corruption. Therefore, in addition to promoting genuine organisations, the Home Ministry should relax FCRA provisions so that NGOs have access to independent funding.

A vibrant civil society movement towards participatory governance would itself create a demand for better services from the people, thus putting pressure on politics to move away from non-issues or sectarian gains to take more interest in the real livelihood issues of the people. Therefore, governments must involve professional organisations in monitoring programmes and dissemination of information to stakeholders, to increase their sense of ownership and strengthen participatory democracy. Civil society should also take up sustained work among the poor and marginalised people, especially in the rural areas, for increasing their awareness and putting pressure on panchayats/municipalities and making them accountable.

The Role of Government of India. In the Indian situation (where foreign donors provide very little aid to the states as compared with what is provided by the Centre) self–correction in administration can come from the Centre, backed by strong civil society action. The GoI must, at the very least, improve incentive mechanisms by linking fund transfers with performance, improve monitoring mechanisms so that authentic information is available to planners about the quality implementation for all important schemes and amend the All India Services Rules to control the flourishing transfer industry in the states.

The concept of good governance needs to be translated into a quantifiable annual index on the basis of certain agreed indicators such as the infant mortality rate, extent of immunisation, literacy rate for women, child sex ratio, feeding programmes for children, availability of safe drinking water supply, electrification of rural households, rural unemployment, percentage of villages not connected by all-weather roads, number of class I government officials prosecuted and convicted for corruption and so on. Some universally accepted criteria for good budgetary practices may also be included in the index. Once these figures are publicised, states may get into a competitive mode towards improving their score. Central transfers should be linked to such an index.

Rural Reconstruction

Rural reconstruction implies renovation of the villages for the total well-being of the rural population. It is oriented to their social, economic and political development. The principal objective of rural reconstruction includes eradication of poverty by regeneration of cottage industries, establishment of cooperative societies and improvement of transport, spread of education, progress of health and abolition of social malpractices like casteism, untouchability, etc. The concept of rural reconstruction has been advocated by three schools of thought are known as the Philanthropic group, the Reformist group and the Revolutionary group as under:

- The Philanthropists offer a pragmatic approach. They plead for improving the condition of the rural population within the purview of the existing rural institutions and structure of rural society. They attach supreme importance to purely humanitarian endeavours like establishment of schools and hospitals, creation of charity funds to cater to the needs of the rural poor and moral appeals to landlords/ moneylenders to relax their pressure on peasants and labourers.
- The Reformists assume that it is the malfunctioning of the existing social institutions that causes economic misery and socio-cultural backwardness of the rural population. They, therefore, stress the need for reformation of social institutions for the healthy functioning of the social system in order to bring about holistic development of the rural community.
- The Revolutionary group supports the programme of revolutionary transformation of the rural matrix. People belonging to this group

are of the opinion that the evils of the rural community are not an outcome[35] of the malfunctioning of the rural social institutions but are concomitant of the social system. These evils are the inevitable product of the normal functioning of the contemporary social order. Therefore, they recommend radical transformation of rural social institutions to bring about a revolutionary change in the social system.

Aspects of Rural Reconstruction. Broadly speaking, the rural reconstruction programme entails three aspects. They are material, intellectual and moral. So far as the material aspect is concerned, the rural reconstruction programme is oriented to improve the health and raise the standard of living of the rural community. The former is achieved by encouraging better sanitation and provision of medical aid. To realise the latter, better methods of cultivation, finance and marketing are needed. As regards the intellectual aspect, educational facilities are provided to boys, girls and adults. Information and instruction are also made available to them through the radio, newspapers, television, lectures, demonstrations, etc. The moral aspect, however, is the most fundamental. It seeks to awaken the villager from the long stupor of ages, so that he may realise his due in life as well as shake off his lethargy and work in cooperation with government agencies to ameliorate his lot. It aims at creating in him the desire for self-improvement and self-discipline by individual and collective action so that he may be freed of his inhibitions standing in the way of his self-realisation. It seeks to release his pent-up energies for removing defeatism, superstition, and baseless fears created by centuries of depression.

Importance of Rural Reconstruction. The importance of rural reconstruction cannot be understated. Rural reconstruction puts an end to exploitation, disease, illiteracy, gambling, drinking, corruption, or class struggle. It seeks to establish a socialistic system in the country and thereby bring about the social and economic development of the rural population. By establishing agricultural and cottage industries, rural reconstruction solves the food problem of the country and saves millions of rupees in foreign exchange which goes towards the import of food grains. It also increases national income. Indian culture will be regenerated and will forge ahead through reconstruction. Rural reconstruction, in this way, will pave the way for the establishment of a true democracy in India since most of the population lives in villages.

Success of Rural Reconstruction Programmes. A few of the many recommendations which will ensure success of these programmes are as under:

- A balance should be restored between human and material resources through the control of population and maximum development of resources.
- Agricultural productivity should be increased through adoption of improved techniques of production and physical changes by means of soil conservation, irrigation, quality of seeds, etc.
- Efforts should be made to accelerate the process of urbanisation and rural industrialisation to eliminate unemployment and relieve the pressure on land.
- Last, but not the least, the programme of rural reconstruction should have a high survival value.
- Local people should shoulder more and more responsibility towards the effective implementation of rural reconstruction programmes.
- Success in the simpler programmes should pave the way for more difficult and complicated programmes of bigger dimensions.
- The existing institutions of the rural community should be transformed in view of the needs of the rural population.
- The level of education of the rural population should be raised and their level of interest and skill should be developed to enable them to play an effective role towards the success of the rural reconstruction programme.
- There should be a cumulative growth with an ever-rising tempo in each successful field. An upward trend should be maintained till a particular programme reaches saturation point by achieving the end set out for it.
- There should be adequate provision of greater amenities, services and physical resources in order to provide optimum conditions for the full development of the sectors of agriculture, industry and social services.
- There should be proper coordination among the various aspects of the programme. There should be simultaneous progress on several fronts in an organically correlated manner.

Conclusion

As opposed to the other way around, development results from effective institutions. Therefore, the emphasis must be changed from increasing the amount of cash for development to increasing development outcomes and the efficiency of public service delivery. India confronts huge problems and must make some difficult political choices despite making progress on the front of prosperity. Concerted policy actions by the Government ensuring audit and corresponding accountability with regular monitoring of progression is needed to lift the 250 million poor out of poverty, who are increasingly concentrated in the poorer states. This requires not much additional resources, but better participation of stakeholders and sound delivery mechanisms. It mandates improving the environment considerably with procedures enunciated and enforcing a detailed feedback system from the populace in which the three agencies of delivery – civil services, panchayats and local bodies – function. The responsiveness of government functionaries at all levels with alacrity and sense of commitment towards the nation alleviates existing conditions to a very great extent.

NOTES

1. Debroy Bibek, Ashley J. Tellis and Reece Trevor. *'Getting India Back on Track: An Action Agenda for Reform'*, Random House, India, 2014.
2. Debroy Bibek, Ashley J. Tellis and Reece Trevor. *'Getting India Back on Track: An Action Agenda for Reform'*, Random House, India, 2014, pp. 7-22.
3. Debroy Bibek, Ashley J. Tellis and Reece Trevor. *Getting India Back on Track: An Action Agenda for Reform*, Random House India, Feb 2014, pp. 25-40.
4. Arvind Panagariya. *"India: The Emerging Giant"*, Oxford University Press, 2011, pp.10-32.
5. Ibid., pp. 40-51.
6. V. Kumaraswamy. *Making Growth Happen in India: A Road Map for Policy Success*, Sage Publications India, New Delhi, 2014, pp. 15-43.
7. Gurcharan Das. *India Unbound*, New Delhi: Viking Pub, 2000, pp. 13-27.
8. Shriram Maheshwari. *Rural Development in India: A Public Policy Approach*, New Delhi: Sage Publications, 1995, pp. 23-29.
9. Debroy Bibek, Telis, Ashley, J. and Trevor Reece. *Getting India Back on Track: An Action Agenda for Reform*, Random House India, Feb 2014, pp. 65-73.
10. Anjan Chakravarty. "The Evolving Scope of Rural India" *Advances in Economics and Business* 3(7): 261-271, 2015.
11. Abdul Kalam, A. P. J., Dr. & Singh, Srijan Pa. *Target Three Billion, PURA: Innovative Solutions towards Sustainable Development*, Penguin UK, Nov 2011, pp. 14-33.
12. J. Dreze and A. Sen, *"India: Development and Participation"*, Oxford University Press, New Delhi, India, 2002, pp. 13-18.

13. R. Islam. "Rural Industrialization and Employment in Asia", *ILO Asian Employment Programme,* New Delhi, pp. 3-5.
14. R. Chand and J. Singh. "Workforce Changes and Employment: Some Findings from PLFS Data Series". NITI Aayog, Government of India, New Delhi, p. 11.
15. U. Patnaik. *The Long Transition: Essays on Political Economy,* Tulika Books, New Delhi, 1999, pp. 22-30.
16. "Sixth Economic Census All-India Report (2016)", Govt. of India, Ministry of Statistics and Programme Implementation.
17. S. Mahendra Dev. *Inclusive Growth in India: Agriculture, Poverty and Human Development,* Oxford University Press, 2008, pp. 3-4.
18. *India's Electricity Reforms: A Power Shortage May Thwart India's Rush to Modernity, Economist* (2005), September 22, pp. 83-84.
19. "Planning Commission (2000) Report of the Task Force on Employment Opportunities". *Government of India*: New Delhi, pp. 23-29.
20. *"Planning Commission (2000) Report of the Task Force on Employment Opportunities". Government of India:* New Delhi, pp. 45-48.
21. A. Saith. *"The Rural Non-Farm Economy: Processes and Policies,"* International Labour Force, Geneva (mimeo), (1992), pp. 12-16.
22. G..K. Chadha. *Rural Nonfarm Sector in the Indian Economy: Growth, Challenges and Future Direction.* (mimeo), (2003), International Food Policy Research Institute, Washington D.C.
23. M. Saxena. India (1) in Non-farm Employment Opportunities in Rural Areas in Asia, (2000,) Tokyo, p. 90.
24. Aijaz, S. in his articles on *"Uneducated India: Learning at the rural juncture"*, 20 Feb 2015.
25. ASER 2021 – Rural.
26. Puja Mondal. "Brief Essay on Rural Poverty", Article Library.com, Feb 2014.
27. K.N. Prasad. "India's Rural Problem", *Concept Publishing Company,* California, pp. 45-49
28. *Uma Narula. Dynamics of Indian Rural Economy,* Atlantic; Edition (1 December 2010), pp. 25-38.
29. *United Nations Development Programme, Human Development Report, United Nations,* New York 2004, p. 103.
30. *The Indian Journal of Public Administration, Jul-Sep 2008,* S.L. Goel, pp. 428-429.
31. B. Bhattacharya. *Urban Development in India since Pre-Historic Times*, Shree Publication House, New Delhi, 2009, pp. 23-35.
32. P.K, Gera, Y. K. Dewan and Sandeep Singh. *Comprehensive National Power: A Model for India,* Vij Books India Private Limited, February 2013, pp. 150-154.
33. Puja Mondal. "Panchayati Raj System in India," Article Library, May 2014.
34. PK Singh, Gera YK, and Sandeep Dewan. *Comprehensive National Power: A Model for India,* New Delhi, IND: Vij Books India Private Limited, 2013, pp. 160-163.
35. Puja Mondal. Rural Reconstruction in India, Article Library, May 2014.

3

SUCCESS STORIES OF RURAL DEVELOPMENT IN INDIA

"New markets could be created by rural potentials, which could lead to rise in the employment".

—APJ Abdul Kalam

Introduction

A topic of long running interest to social scientists has been the processes that surround the transformation of economies along the development path. As is well documented, the process of development tends to generate large-scale structural transformation of economies as they shift from being primarily agrarian towards more industrial and service-oriented activities. A related aspect of this transformation is how the workforce in such developing economies adjusts to the changing macroeconomic structure in terms of their labour market choices such as investment in skills, choice of occupations, location and industry of employment.[1] Indeed, some of the more widely cited contributions to development economics have tended to focus precisely on these aspects.

India has been on precisely this path of structural change for the past three decades. As a result of a series of changes that were initiated in the middle of the 1980s, the nation now consistently experiences yearly growth rates that are higher than 8 per cent. This is in sharp contrast to the first 40 years since 1947 (when India became an independent country) during which period the average annual output growth hovered around the 3 per cent mark, a rate that barely kept pace with population growth during that period.[2] The output composition of the nation has undergone a substantial change throughout this phase, with the agricultural sector gradually losing its share in both output and employment. Although the country is on the path of rapid growth, the gap, however, between the urban and rural areas is fast widening. The focused and concentrated efforts by some of the states have tried to bridge this gap to ensure a holistic growth of the region. Some of the states which have been able to develop a growth model are Gujarat and Tamil Nadu. However, much is left to be desired by the rest of the states. This chapter aims to analyse the various growth models implemented in the country, identify the strong points of each of these and try and bring out their shortcomings and inadequacies.

Concept of an Ideal Village (*Adarsh Gaanv*)

In India, 68.9 per cent of our population lives in rural areas (Census 2011). Though the number has fallen in the last five years, it is still estimated that more than half of our population will be rural even in 2050. Despite there being several initiatives by governments at all levels – Central, state and local – in the past as well as the present, the level of improvement has not kept pace with the rising aspirations of Indians. On most development parameters, there is still a significant gap between rural and urban India. One reason for the failure of rural development schemes has been the lack of a holistic focus on the village as a unit. Separate flagship schemes targeting different sectors such as health (NRHM), education (SSA) and livelihood (NREGA, NRLM) have been launched in the past, but met with limited success.[3] It is therefore imperative to lay down a vision for an Ideal Village (*Adarsh Gaanv*) which is not only self-sustaining but also contributes positively towards the overall growth of the nation towards our aspirations to become a global superpower. Before analyzing the rural success story in a few of our states, it is necessary to lay down the objectives for an 'Ideal Village'. These could be indexed as under:

- A typical phenomenon in Indian villages is the distress migration from rural to urban regions, which is spurred by a lack of opportunities and amenities that ensure a good standard of living.
- Access to urban markets should be made simpler, quicker, and less expensive for agricultural products or other commoditised goods produced in such settlements.
- Contribute towards social empowerment by engaging all sections of the community in towards village development.

- Create a "hub" in the village to draw resources for the growth of neighbouring settlements.
- Create and sustain a culture of cooperative living for inclusive and rapid development.

A 21st Century model village in India needs to incorporate certain key themes which would be essential for its success. Figure 3.1 highlights these broad thematic focus areas and mentions the important elements under each such theme.

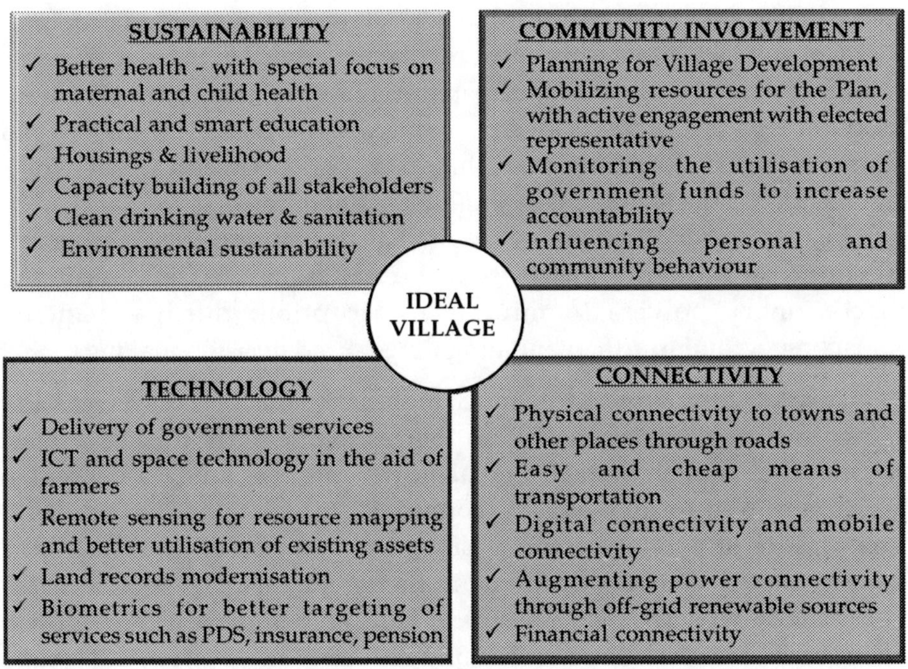

Figure 3.1. Key Elements of a Modern Village

One of these regions might be affected by an intervention that also affects other areas. The quality and delivery of other services like health and education might be improved through the use of technology, which would support sustainable development. Similar to this, using renewable energy not only helps to meet energy needs but also promotes environmental sustainability. Village tree plantation drives could encourage community participation, benefit the environment, prevent soil erosion and benefit agriculture, conserve water, and finally contribute to the aesthetics of the village. A number of these initiatives have already been taken in different parts of the country, but most of them have been attempted in isolation. The urgent need is to bring about a convergence of all such initiatives, for which two things would be essential: grassroots level planning and mobilisation of resources.[4] The 'Mera desh badal raha hai, aage badh raha hai' initiative of PM Modi is a right step in this direction, thereby promoting convergence of a multitude of projects at varying levels.

SUCCESS STORY OF GUJARAT

According to a 2011 survey by the Hong Kong-based Political and Economic Risk Consultancy, India is the most regulated country in the world and its rules 'were complex and non-transparent, while standards and certifications procedures were onerous'.[5] Governance impedes individual aspirations and restrains the country from maturing as a world power. In order for a significant change to take place and higher standards of governance to be possible, a number of actions are required: first, ensuring greater economic freedom by reducing an onerous bureaucracy; second, reducing discretionary powers to minimise corruption; third, enhancing transparency; and fourth, mandating time-bound decision making.

Gujarat, with a growth rate much higher than that of India, is seen as a classic success story of neoliberal policies, particularly during the last decade. The state achieved an annual growth rate of around 6-7 per cent in agriculture, a sector in which the country is struggling hard to achieve a growth rate of even 4 per cent. Bibek Debroy was impressed by the performance of Gujarat's economy in the recent past. His book, *Gujarat: Governance for Growth and Development* (2012) highlights the high growth achieved by the state along with 'rapid reduction in poverty', praises the improved governance and infrastructure in the state, and discusses the improvements in health, literacy, and education in the state.[6]

Less government, more governance has long been Prime Minister Narendra Modi's catchphrase. But is it real? Deficit funding is not the best approach to boost the economy; instead, taxes and regulations should be reduced, along with the size and scope of the government. The government can also assist by funding the infrastructure and benefits that make it easier and more efficient for people to work, such as roads, irrigation, education, and healthcare. By stimulating growth, it can sustain investment-focused budget deficits, as Gujarat has tried to do.[7]

Taking the five shakti pillars, he grouped them under a collective name, 'Panchamrut', in the form of Jal Shakti (Water Power), Gyan Shakti (Knowledge Power), Urja Shakti (Energy Power), Raksha Shakti (Security Power), and Jan Shakti (People's Power). Panchamrut, stands in contrast to "shakti," which is universal in its notion. Panchamrut is a practical concept where it comes from everyday rituals, daily puja or home offerings and contains ingredients like milk, dahi (yoghurt), ghee (clarified butter), honey, and sugar. The communities initially saw a virtually unbroken full voltage power supply together with a tightly adhered to schedule. Farmers were also happy that they were spared the very high repair and maintenance cost that poor power supply imposed on them.[8]

Electricity-Jyoti Gram Yojana

When Modi assumed office in 2001, Gujarat had a shortage of around 2,000 MW. He initiated a scheme named the Jyotigram Yojana, which is an initiative of the Government of Gujarat to ensure availability of 24-hour three-phase quality power supply to rural areas of the state and to supply power to farmers residing in scattered farm houses through feeders having specially designed transformers.[9] The scheme was dedicated to the nation by President A. P. J. Abdul Kalam in 2006. Gujarat has altered lives in rural Gujarat by delivering uninterruptible power supply to all families under this initiative. The programme, which encompasses 18,000 communities, was the first to implement real-time co-management of groundwater irrigation and energy. It has unshackled domestic and non-farm rural electricity supply from the clutches of an invidious political economy of farm power subsidies and has transformed what was a highly degenerate power-pricing-cum-supply regime into a rational one.[10] Gujarat has transformed from a power deficit state to a power surplus state. Several states do not even have 5,000 megawatts of power. Gujarat generated 10,000 megawatts of power in only one district of this state. The Panchamrut revolution of Gujarat began with Jyotigram.

Drinking Water

Gujarat's 'State-Wide Drinking Water Grid' construction started in 2002. Like the Jyotigram power infrastructure, the nearly 2,000 km of water mains, 115,000 km of auxiliary pipelines, 11,000 water towers, and an equal number of sumps and reservoirs were quickly constructed. 10,000 villages received daily access to 2,250 million litres of potable water thanks to more than 150 water treatment, filtration, and, more recently, coastal desalination plants. Agricultural supplies were supplemented when drinking water availability improved. A programme was begun to construct 113,000 check dams (small dams across water channels that irrigate a maximum of 10 hectares, built through the Sardar Patel Participatory Water Conservation Scheme), stockpiling 56,000 sandbag stores – 'bori bunds' – for use in the event of floods to trap water, digging quarter of a million new farm ponds and erecting 60,000 other structures.[11]

Agriculture Initiatives

The second step of "micro water harvesting" infrastructure development involved training farmers how to micro-irrigate, which uses much less water to produce the same results. The newly-established Gujarat Green Revolution Company promoted drip irrigation. Urja Shakti grew Jal Shakti, and both in turn helped to transform Jan Shakti –the abilities and potential of people. The education of farmers would further embed and improve agricultural production and the quality of rural life. Thus, in 2005, the 'Krishi Mahotsa scheme was inaugurated – a travelling road show and mobile education centre that visits every single village in Gujarat annually. It consists of a set-up of booths and exhibitions staffed by government employees from agricultural universities and businesses, both home and abroad, who advise farmers and demonstrate innovative techniques for enhancing land productivity and crop production. Farmers were issued with soil cards to test the state of the soil and were educated about how best to nourish and improve it. It may sound very simplistic and frugal, but soil nurtures the plants and crops qualitatively and enhances productivity levels multi-fold, thereby leveraging the volume of production and ushering greater prosperity in agriculture, providing a higher GDP of the country. Agriculture contributes over 20 per cent to GDP after the manufacturing sector towards development.

Better strains, such as castor for oil and bajra (pearl millet, which is heavy in iron), were promoted to be planted by seed firms. The acceptance of Bt cotton, which is resistant to several common plant diseases, has caused the production of that crop in particular to soar, rising from 3.05 million bales (each weighing 170 kg) in 2002–03 to 11.2 million bales in 2007–08 – and it has not stopped since. Similarly, The Garib Kalyan Mela is an ambitious programme for social transformation that has combined benefits from many programmes and dispensed with intermediaries to ensure that benefits reach the most vulnerable. The Gujarat government[12] has so far conducted 1,000 Garib Kalyan Melas and distributed Rs. 11,000 crore assistance to around seventy-five lakh beneficiaries.

Governance and Administrative Issues

The drift towards a centralised bureaucracy was reversed by Modi offering a bounty, under his 'Samras Yojana Programme', of one lakh rupees to any village that could unanimously elect a representative. As per Modi, each citizen of Gujarat is an initiator, creator and implementer. This has resulted in micro-level involvement of the local population towards the growth of their respective areas and villages. Roads continued to be built; over 98 per cent of rural habitations at village level have been connected.

Meanwhile, the amount of red tape for businesses looking to open offices in the state was reduced, and news quickly travelled around the world that the western region of India had a helpful government that did not require bribes. With the help of "Vibrant Gujarat," investment started to pour into Gujarat. Clone capitalism was criticized for it, with claims that land was being sold to manufacturers cheap. However, a lot of the criticism was subdued by the riches and employment these new manufacturing facilities brought to the neighbourhood. A few examples of the investments done by private players, both global and Indian, are as under:

- Its workers were now employing 10,000 diamond polishing machines and 500,000 high-tech looms. A state-of-the-art, all-weather seaport was being constructed by Shell, and it would be well served by new roads and flyovers lacing together the busy city.[13]

Like its drainage system, Surat's water distribution has been automated. Surat even operates a sewage treatment plant which transforms waste into energy, as well as one of the best water treatment plants in India.[14]

'E-gram Vishwagram' in which all the 13,700 panchayat villages in the State were linked with an internet pathway and impressive financial management in which his government wiped out Gujarat's 16-year-old fiscal deficit in 2006. Establishing Seva Sadans (core service centres) in each district and Jan Seva Kendras at tehsil headquarters to provide hundreds of day-today services online to the people for which they had to wait for days together earlier are praiseworthy.

As per Modi, "If Gujarat follows a five-step formula – 'farm; farm to fibre; fibre to fabric; fabric to fashion; fashion to foreign, then only will the farmer will be a beneficiary. So we must have a value-addition chain right up to exports." This showed how a city that was a slum with a hopelessly insufficient infrastructure, an ineffective municipal government, and even visits from mediaeval mass murderers only two decades earlier could be changed by reformist municipal commissioners who have support from the state government but also independence. Just as Jan Shakti fostered the skills and resources of Gujarat's farmers, Gyan Shakti, or knowledge power, was directly responsible for the advancement of education. A 'Narmada Bond' of Rs. 1,000 was introduced for girls to save for their school expenses starting in 2002. It was assumed that for society to advance organically and sustainably over time, FDI in industry would not be sufficient to ensure Gujarat experienced an even distribution of prosperity. Gujarat's growth is based on manufacturing, not services.[15] The fifth and last pillar of Modi's Panchamrut is Raksha Shakti-security.

Gujarat Growth Model: A Critical Analysis

The "Gujarat model of development" and the notion that the State of Gujarat and its residents have prospered because of effective and decisive government, particularly in the field of economic policies, have been heavily promoted in the media for at least the past two years in India. This public opinion most likely contributed significantly to the Bharatiya Janata Party's (BJP) victory in the general election. However, how valid is this perception? Are people in Gujarat materially so much better off than their counterparts in other comparable States? What are the elements of Gujarat's economic success, and what are the economic policies that have been employed in the State? These questions become even more pressing now that Narendra Modi is India's Prime Minister and can be expected to put in place similar policies at the national level. Unfortunately, much of the recent literature on the State, even by reputed economic analysts, has been uncritical and verging on the hagiographic, and so has not provided a sober assessment of actual trends.[16]

The rapid growth of Gujarat, as compared to other states, is largely due to its significantly higher comparative advantage in agriculture and manufacturing. Easy availability of land and infrastructure facilities has also aided the growth of the state. Gujarat has been one of the best performers in the electricity sector. What is remarkable is that Gujarat has been able to maintain and enhance its comparative advantage despite a high level of per capita income, when all other highly industrialised (and high income) states have, as expected, steadily lost their comparative advantage with per capita growth. Low labour costs in the state (on account of repressed wages and poor quality of employment), higher rate of savings (given high income inequality), high tax concessions and other incentives to corporate investments, vast migrations to Gujarat, and the increasing use of capital-intensive machinery in Gujarat – all these factors may have allowed the State to hold on to its advantage. The Narmada project and particularly ample rainfall over the period under consideration may have enhanced it as well.

Gujarat has, unlike many other states, followed the classical model of transition from agricultural development to industry-led development before transforming into an economy dominated by the services sector. In the last decade, the State has seen an exceptionally large inflow of industrial investments backed by huge investments in infrastructure both by the private sector and under the PPP model. Some of the favourable factors for industrial growth in Gujarat have been power supply, good quality roads, small and large all-weather ports and shore jetties, large-format industrial estates and industrial parks, and over 50 special economic zones (SEZs). However, environment degradation caused by industries in the State is a cause for concern as also the nature of industrialisation in the State has not created substantial direct employment in the organised sector and in fact has increased casualisation of workers.[17]

The last decade has seen an unprecedented growth in Gujarat's agriculture sector. This is noteworthy not only because of the phenomenally high rates of growth experienced during most of 2000, but also because the high growth seems to have been steered through a series of policy measures coupled with favourable monsoons. It shows that even in a state, which is considered a classic success story of neoliberal policies, inclusive growth is not forthcoming easily.[18] The problem lies in both the policy framework of the neoliberal policies as well as its translation in Gujarat. At the conceptual level, it is not feasible to have growth first, followed by development under the neoliberal policy framework. It is necessary, therefore, to integrate distribution or development within the growth process itself by creating productive employment with decent work conditions.

Limitations in Gujarat Model. The following are some of the limitations which appear at the face value of research:

- Assessing the impacts of agricultural growth (crop farming, animal husbandry, fisheries, forestry, and so on) and industrial growth on environmental resources, the sustainability of growth in Gujarat is questionable.[19] Since natural resources are not integrated with the growth process or with major decisions about projects, several problems are created.
- 'Crony capitalism' in the State denies a level playing field to lakhs of small enterprises and small units, which struggle hard and frequently fail to get adequate credit for their survival and growth.
- Despite its high economic status, the State lags behind in several other parameters like drinking water, toilets and library facilities. While privatisation of education has increased, the quality of education has not improved. The commoditisation of education has been facilitated by the global understanding that has emerged about knowledge.
- Environmental Concerns. Some of the major environmental concerns caused by the industrial expansion in the State are industrial pollution and waste disposal into the water bodies and coastal wetlands, massive conversion of prime farmlands, including protected areas for creation of SIRs and setting up industry and pollution of coastal and marine ecosystems and their impacts on marine biodiversity, mangrove ecosystems, coral reefs, and so on.
- Finally, the huge expenditure on incentives and subsidies has left less public funds for social sectors, with Gujarat having a much lower per capita expenditure on social sectors as compared to other states (both slow growing as well as fast growing). In fact, in this

regard, Gujarat is almost at the bottom among the 20 major states in India.

- Growth of ST Talukas and Tribal Areas. The STs in Gujarat constitutes 17.7 per cent of the total population. Their area covers approximately 15 per cent of the total geographical area of the State. These talukas have remained backward in socio-economic infrastructure, health and education, economic growth, and poverty reduction. Despite high annual rainfall (800-2,000 mm), half the tribal talukas are Drought Prone Area Programme (DPAP) or Desert Development Programme (DDP) talukas, which suffer from uncertain crop production. The depletion and degradation of natural resources in the tribal region is thus primarily because natural resources are mainly used as resources to be consumed/ destroyed for economic growth, and not as natural capital to be used and strengthened as a major factor of production and a major source of livelihood in the region.[20] Also, the tribal areas have poor socio-economic infrastructure for education, health, water and sanitation, electricity, roads and transportation, and so on.
- The State also has given huge favours to corporate sector units in terms of land, water, and other infrastructure, with the result that these markets are highly distorted, posing serious problems for the life and livelihoods of people on the one hand and misallocation of these resources in the State, on the other.
- Urban Development Paradigm. It is pertinent to note that 55 per cent of the urban population in Gujarat (2011) lives in four metropolitan cities, namely, Ahmedabad, Surat, Vadodara, and Rajkot. Tamil Nadu has a relatively less skewed urban settlement structure. Though urban Gujarat has been projected as a success story, there is a growing schism between high growth and poor employment for a very large section of population, as well as between high investments in urban infrastructure and inadequate attention to housing for the urban poor.[21]

Analysis of the Gujarat Model

There was reluctance to accept the Gujarat growth story, dismissing it as hype. Since growth is reflected in data, that growth is finally no longer contested. How can objective facts be hype? Gujarat has registered double-digit growth since the 10th Plan (2002-07). Among large states, so have

Bihar, Maharashtra and Tamil Nadu. Relatively more advanced states find it difficult to find sources for growth, a point to remember for Bihar. Had historical trends alone provided momentum, Karnataka should have grown fast.

Volatility of growth has declined in Gujarat, a reflection of agricultural performance. Triggered by roads, electricity (the Jyotigram Yojana) and water (inter-basin transfer of water), there has been agricultural diversification and commercialisation in many historically deprived districts. Dairy, animal husbandry, horticulture are examples. Second, the growth story is still misunderstood. In popular perception, Gujarat's economic growth is about large-scale industry. However, there has been an increase in the number of factories and MSME (micro, small and medium enterprises) clusters. The share of manufacturing in GSDP has declined. It is the non-manufacturing industry and services that have increased. Therefore, Gujarat's growth is also about agriculture, MSMEs, non-manufacturing industry and services.

Development. As regards development, the argument which has always been quoted is that growth is not synonymous with development. Gujarat does not do well in social sectors. Poverty ratios show a sharp decline in rural poverty between 2004-05 and 2009-10. While urban poverty has not declined that much, if rural poverty has declined sharply, growth must have been inclusive. There is no evidence that inequality has increased.

- **Health.** In health, the percentage of institutional deliveries has risen from 55.87 per cent in 2003-04 to 93.5 per cent in 2011-12. Immunisation coverage has increased. Extremist violence has been contained despite geographical proximity with violence-prone states. Despite the emphasis on industrialisation, refineries and port-led development, there have been no major environmental disasters along the coast or elsewhere.
- **Social Growth**. In social sectors, the timeline of data is important since explicit focus on social sectors started in the 11th Plan (2007-12). Gujarat has not done well in the social sectors but have there been temporal improvements over time and have remedial measures been taken? As one example, there has been a sharp decline in the number of out-of-school children between 2006 and 2011.

The growth story is reluctantly accepted; the development story rarely and governance story never. However there is a governance story. It is partly based on fiscal consolidation and using fiscal space to plug gaps in the central sector and centrally-sponsored schemes with state-level ones.[22] The story is not that much about increasing public expenditure. It is more about creating an environment for private expenditure. In both education and health, there are instances of moving away from traditional government monopolies in delivery. The story is also about increasing efficiency of public expenditure. There is an important e-governance component too; discretion having been removed for assorted certificates. There is also decentralisation down to talukas, facilitated by Gujarat's long tradition of Panchayati Raj Institutions (PRIs) and participatory planning. Since 2003, Chintan Shabbir's are also illustrative, ensuring the government does not work in silos and departments and enabled cross-fertilisation of ideas which resulted in better formulation of schemes and better implementation. Transfers, postings and implementation have become more insulated from political interference. The governance story is a standard development template that every state ought to adopt and implement.

It is always difficult to disentangle various factors that go into ensuring the growth, development and governance story. First, there is a legacy factor, and Gujarat governments prior to 2002 have left a positive impact. Second, Gujarat has had a healthy tradition of private entrepreneurship and an equally healthy scepticism of government. Third, in sectors like water and roads, Gujarat has also benefited from favourable exogenous circumstances, including locational and geographical advantages, as it has from negative push factors in other states, automobiles and auto ancillaries being an instance. Last, but not the least, there is no getting away from Chief Minister Narendra Modi's leadership role. More specifically, social sector push, empowerment of bureaucracy and insulation from political interference, clamping down on corruption, decentralisation, emphasis on private sector and message of pride in Gujarat's growth and development bear his personal stamp. That part is thus person-specific and not systemic, a phenomenon also true of some other fast-growing states.

To sum up, it will not be incorrect to say that the Gujarat development model is a clear example of neo-liberalism and is often presented as a major success of neoliberal economic policies in ensuring economic growth and improving social welfare. Gujarat's growth under Modi's leadership is widely seen as a miracle produced by a strong form of state-led market fundamentalism. The main ingredients are economic freedom and innovation, while the function of the state is to facilitate and support private initiative by removing obstacles and providing adequate incentives.

TAMIL NADU: GROWTH ORIENTED DEVELOPMENT

Development, in the perspective of a state, is about growth that generates employment; employment provides income; income enhances consumption and thereby, improves people's standard of living. Thus, the higher the growth rate, the higher is the employment. This is the mantra that the youth, the neo-informed vote bank, understands as development. In turn, their parents, who are a large vote bank, think similarly. In order to benefit from growth, however, there should be quality educational institutions that can produce professionally qualified youth. This is the first growth cycle. A capable person from any socio-economic strata can dream of becoming a part of this growth cycle and benefit without discrimination. Growth requires investment. Investors come to invest in a state that has a positive political environment, encourages policies, good infrastructure facilities, technical personnel and peace. When a state plays this role effectively, growth will result. This is the second growth cycle. The third growth cycle is about the growth of the sector that services the above two growth cycle as well as the primary sectors.

The growth of a state, that is, how the growth cycles actually operate, depends on the vision and mission of the political head of the state. The growth rate of a state, seen as a function of the performance of the state leadership, has, thus, become the crux of political debate as much as of economic. Development has been traditionally viewed as a process of economic and social transformation, and as a process of adding improvements. It is also about the rate of growth and loosely about 'progress'. While the above concepts of development might seem complete, they are still inadequate. Development is qualified: 'sustainable and green'. This is because of the alarming level of legal and illegal extraction of natural resources to meet human needs, and of natural resources getting depleted and the environment getting polluted.[23]

Given the non-sustainability of the current economic growth that is taking place, a new and sustainable approach to development is urgently needed. Sustainability of economic growth cannot be compromised. Now, the word 'sustainability' is also qualified: environmental, economic and social sustainability. Development, in the perspective of people, is about well-being, welfare and good governance. Growth improves well-being as well. So is good infrastructure. Thus, development is multi-dimensional. The Tamil Nadu model of development is a balanced combination of growth, well-being, welfare and exemplary governance. The earlier chief minister of Tamil Nâdu, Mrs. Jayalalitha (commonly referred to as Amma), had emphasised many times that she wanted to put Tamil Nadu First among the Indian states in development, and also that "Ellarum Ellavum Pera Vendum, Illamai Illai Entr Nilai Vendum" (All should get everything and there should not be a condition of have-not).

Any 'model' is about causes, processes and effects (outputs, outcomes and impact) in a functional relationship. The 'Amma Model of Development'[24] has contributed enormously to the growth, well-being, welfare and exemplary governance of Tamil Nadu and its people. The hon'ble chief minister has formulated a 'Tamil Nadu Vision 2023' document for the State, with clear goals to be achieved by 2023, coinciding with the next two five-year plan periods. The 'Vision 2023' aims at making Tamil Nadu the state with the best infrastructure services in all vital sectors as well as the highest Human Development Index (HDI) ranking in India. The outcome of the entire planning process will be the eradication of poverty, creation of more and better job opportunities and overall growth of rural areas.[25]

Sectors Contributing to Tamil Nadu's Growth

Industrial Growth. The 'Tamil Nadu Vision-2023' document states that the contribution of the manufacturing sector is currently at about 17 per cent of the Gross State Domestic Product (GSDP). The target to be achieved by 2023 has been increased to 22 per cent. Thus Tamil Nadu has been consistently at the frontline of industrial development contributing in substantial measure to India's economic growth. The Vision-2023 document has set the following objectives with respect to industrial growth in the state. It seeks to:

- Ensure peace, security and prosperity for all citizens and businesses, enabling free movement and exchange of ideas, people and trade with other Indian states and the rest of the world.[26]

- Make Tamil Nadu one of the top three preferred investment destinations in Asia and most preferred in India with a reputation for efficiency and competitiveness.
- Make Tamil Nadu known as the innovation hub and knowledge capital of India, on the strength of world class institutions in various fields and the best human talent.
- Provide the best infrastructure services in India in terms of universal access to housing, water and sanitation, energy, transportation, irrigation, connectivity, health care and education.

Contributing Factors. In Tamil Nadu, there are a number of contributing factors which make the targets listed in the vision document a possibility. They are as under:

- ***Availability of good quality manpower at a low cost compared to other metros and cities***. A large pool of labour comprising well-qualified, skilled, disciplined, productivity-oriented and English-speaking workforce.
- ***Contribution of the micro, small and medium-size industries***. In Tamil Nadu, MSMEs produce more than 8,000 varieties of products that include engineering products, electrical, electronics, chemicals, plastics, steel, cement, paper, matches, textiles, hosiery and readymade garments.[27]
- ***Joint Ventures and provision of Special Economic Zones (SEZs).***
- ***Many prestigious educational institutions*** providing high standards of education.
- ***'Single Window Clearance' for promotion of industries*** and starting of a business.

Agricultural Production

During 2011-2012, Tamil Nadu created a history in the annals of agriculture of the State with the highest food grain production of 101.52 lakh MT. This is an all-time high in the last ten years. The State has also achieved the highest production in rice, millets and pulses. This record-breaking production has been possible due to the following proactive measures implemented by the government. It had also implemented a multitude of crop-oriented schemes for the welfare of the farming community which is a whole village concept. Nearly 1,880 SRI villages were organised throughout the State. Precision farming and micro irrigation, that is, promotion of high-end technologies, quality and input efficiency increased production of millets through increased yield. Hence, sanction of a sum of Rs. 10.48 crore was made towards micro irrigation exclusively for pulses.

In order to further step up the momentum towards the Second Green Revolution, the government framed certain strategies, namely, increased water use efficiency, soil nutri-care and rebuilding of agricultural infrastructure, appropriate land use system and dry land farming, organic and integrated farming, group farming/cluster approach, disaster risk reduction, crop diversification and IT based extension deliverance:

Energy Security

The present power demand of Tamil Nadu is approximately 12,000 MW. On an average, the availability of power from the existing conventional and non-conventional energy sources is about 8,000 MW. Currently this deficit is managed through power purchase and restriction and control measures. However, the State has already chalked out a sound plan to tide over this problem by investing in the field of renewable sources of energy.[28] Tamil Nadu accounts for 39 per cent of the wind power generation in India with an installed capacity of 7,178 MW wind power. Thermal plants are coming up in a big way across the State. It is planned that in the next five years, as much as 14,460 MW electricity will be generated through thermal and hydro generation systems alone. The present progress will increase over the years.

First Solar-Power Park. The first solar energy park has been established in Paramakudi (Ramnathapuram District) to generate 100 MW power at a cost of Rs. 920 crore, with Rs.500 crore in partnership with M/s Rassi Green Earth Energy Private Limited. This park is the first of its kind in the whole of India, set up exclusively for solar power generation in the public-private partnership mode.[29] The Parmakudi Solar Power Plant has been set up with necessary infrastructure like roads, drainage, water facilities, enriched landscape and power transmission lines so that power projects can be located there effectively. This is to attract more investors in solar power projects.

Concept of Well-Being. Well-being means a state or condition of being content, healthy, happy, prosperous, comfortable or successful. It is a state of well-being, where all human needs are met. It is about the quality of life and the absence of negative conditions and presence of positive attributes.[30]

Amma Unavagam (Budget Canteen). The policy of subsidised 'Budget Canteens' has been announced in all the 200 wards of the Chennai Corporation in an effort to provide them healthy and hygienic food at low prices. This scheme is implemented by the municipal corporations. Officials of the Corporation's revenue and health department oversee the canteens. A separate department is proposed to be created for managing them. The required infrastructure including buildings, kitchens, and cooking and serving utensils is provided by the corporation. The women's self-help group members do the cooking and run the canteens. They are trained at the State Institute of Hotel Management and Catering Technology.

Education System. The State had allocated an unprecedented amount of Rs. 14,553 crore for school education in 2013-14. To improve the infrastructure in schools, works costing Rs. 1,660 crore have been taken up. To make Tamil Nadu an illiteracy-free State, the government has been extending several concessions to students. Schools are being started in rural areas near their places of residence. Elementary schools have been upgraded to middle schools, middle schools to high schools and high schools to higher secondary schools. In the last two years 1,075 schools have been upgraded which has pushed up student enrolment in the State. Free education is being provided from class 1 to class 12.[31] To promote collegiate education in areas where there are not many colleges 11 arts and science university-affiliated colleges and one engineering college was started in 2011-12. During the last four years, 12 government arts and science colleges, two university affiliated colleges, three government engineering colleges, 11 polytechnic colleges, National Law School, Indian Institute of Information Technology, a fisheries university, two veterinary colleges, six livestock research centres and two institutes of fisheries technology have been set up. There will be tremendous progress from the retrospective statistical details given, till the current year in education infrastructure with modernity and contemporariness.

Skill Development. There are 38,601 industrial units in the State. On the one hand, there is an acute shortage of skilled manpower and, on the other, 68 lakh youth are registered with employment exchanges. The CII has estimated that the skilled manpower requirement of Tamil Nadu will be about 130 to 150 lakh. National Association of Software and Service Companies (NASSCOM) has estimated that only 20 per cent of the 340,000 graduates coming out of colleges every year are employable; the rest are unemployable as they lack skills. Under the Tamil Nadu skill development mission, the state government forges partnerships with industry to identify skill gaps and design course materials leading to 'Modular Employable Skills Certification'. To instil a sense of pride in the skilled workers, a Skill Smart Card is issued to all government ITI pass–outs.[32]

Rural Infrastructure Development. The assets created under Mahatma Gandhi National Rural Employment Guarantee Scheme (MGNREGS) are stabilised under the Rural Infrastructure Scheme and the basic infrastructure facilities especially the road network is maintained. The Government continues with the implementation of rural infrastructure schemes. The priority works are given below:

- Construction of culverts and retaining walls in new roads under MGNREGS.
- Construction of retaining walls in water bodies desilted under MGNREGS.
- Existing earthen and gravel roads are upgraded into WBM roads.
- Existing WBM roads are converted into BT roads.
- Sluices and surplus weirs are repaired.

Self-Sufficiency Schemes. To ensure an open and accountable process through which individuals and groups can exchange views and promote useful community assets through community participation in collaborative decision making, mediation, community building and consensus building, the Government has reintroduced the Self-Sufficiency Scheme in 2011-12. This is a measure to promote public participation in government schemes. Selection of works will be as under:

- A work may originate based on petitions from individuals, groups, institutions, public or private companies or from the community.
- After ascertaining the need and the feasibility of the work, proposed, estimates will be prepared.
- Application from the public on the work identified and also the consent letter for contributing not less than one-third of the estimated cost will be received by the district collector.

- **Execution of Works**.
  - Local bodies or the department concerned will execute the works through tenders as per the Tamil Nadu Tenders Act, 1998.
  - If the public or contributors opt to execute the work themselves or through their agency in order to facilitate larger participation of the people in this scheme, willingness should be given by them in writing while applying for the work under the Self-Sufficiency Scheme.
  - The district collector will examine the request and permit the contributors or the agency to execute the works if the public contribution is 50 per cent more than the estimated work.
- Major contributions from public or private companies for specific projects to be implemented across the State will be received by the Commissioner of Rural Development and Panchayati Raj.
- The district collector will arrange the works in the order of priority and accord administrative sanction in case the requirement exceeds the allocation.

Tamil Nadu Village Habitations Improvement (THAI) Scheme

- The government has initiated from 2011-12 onwards a flagship programme called the Tamil Nadu Village Habitations Improvement (THAI) Scheme to provide even distribution of resources and provide minimum basic infrastructure facilities to all the habitations. It is only Tamil Nadu that is focusing on 'Habitation' as a unit for development. With 79,394 habitations in 12,524 village panchayats in Tamil Nadu, there is an average of seven habitations per village panchayat. The number of habitations varies from district to district. In the Nilgiris district, the average number of habitations in a village panchayat is 37, but is only three in Villupuram district. With varied number of habitations per village panchayat, allocating an equal amount to all the village panchayats has led to disparity in development, disproportionate distribution of assets and uneven progress. This issue requires proper intercession by strong leadership to ensure that weaknesses are eradicated.
- The THAI scheme is a boon as it aims at extending the basic facilities in each habitation. The population of 12,524 village panchayats in the 31 districts of Tamil Nadu (except Chennai) varies widely. Some village panchayats have populations even below 500 while some

have populations exceeding 10,000. A village panchayat will require more funds if it has a greater number of habitations. So, the village panchayats have been grouped into four categories based on the number of habitations for the purpose of allocation of funds. Under this formula, a village panchayat having a greater number of habitations and having a larger population shall receive more funds.

- Under the THAI Scheme, works are categorized in three areas:
  - ❖ Minimum basic requirements.
  - ❖ Additional requirements.
  - ❖ Other works.
- The scheme has been programmed to be implemented in five phases as under:

Year	No. of Village Panchayats	No. of Habitations
2011-12	25,335	2,020
2012-13	18,581	2,250
20113-14	2,500	15,115
2014-15	2,740	12,093
2015-16	3,014	8,270
Total	12,524	79,394

Table 3.1. Expanded Social Security Scheme for Farmers and Agriculture Workers

- ❖ The State has unveiled a special 'Expanded Social Security Scheme for Farmers and Agriculture Workers', which includes a monthly pension of Rs. 1,000 for those who have crossed 60 years, educational assistance for their children and marriage and maternity assistance. The Chief Minister's Farmer's Security Scheme covers small and medium farmers in the age group 18 to 65, and who own 2.5 acres of wetland or five acres of dry land. Agriculture workers and lease holders in the same age group are also eligible for the benefits. Unlike the earlier schemes where only the head of the family was given an identity card, the new scheme covers all the family members.
- ❖ On educational assistance, the children of the beneficiaries studying in industrial training institutes (ITIs) get Rs. 1,250 to Rs. 1,950 per year. Undergraduate students are given Rs. 1,750 to Rs. 2,500 and postgraduate students Rs. 2,250 to Rs. 3,750. Students of undergraduate professional courses get Rs. 2,250

to Rs. 4,750 and postgraduate students Rs. 4,250 to Rs. 6,750.

- Marriage assistance is given to those who cannot get similar benefits under the scheme of the Social Welfare Department. Men get Rs. 8,000 and women Rs. 10,000. The beneficiaries of the new scheme are eligible for maternity assistance given by the Health and Family Welfare Department. To simplify procedures, the government issues certificates through special tehsildars (Social Security Scheme).
- Besides a monthly pension of Rs. 1,000 for farmers, relief is given to the family of farmers in the event of death due to natural causes or accidents. Since both the farmer and his wife get separate identity cards, both are eligible for the relief. The scheme is implemented through district collectors and revenue officials. A high-level committee has been constituted to oversee its implementation.

Socio-Economic Development of Naxal-Affected Areas. In the backward districts of Dharmapuri and Krishnagiri, a socio-economic development programme (SEDP) was launched in 2003-04 to curb the rise of Naxalite elements. Works such as construction of new houses, repair of group houses, distribution of tool kits and implements for youth and individual assistance to differently-abled/widow and destitutes are undertaken under this scheme. Nearly 3,762 works were taken up in 2012-13 with a total allocation of Rs. 7.5 crore. The allocation was enhanced to Rs. 20 crore for Dharmapuri and Rs. 1 crore for Krishnagiri District for 2013-14.

Welfare of Citizens. On June 1, 2011, the State Government launched a scheme to provide 20 kg rice free to all ration-card holders in the state through ration shops, and from a government-run outlet at Alwarpet, fulfilling the promise made in Jayalalitha's party election manifesto for the April 2011 polls.[33] The new scheme will benefit more than 1.67 crore ration card holders in the State. Another scheme, to provide 35 kg of rice per month free to 18.62 lakh beneficiaries under the 'Antyodaya Anna Yojana' (AAY) scheme, was also launched. The Tamil Nadu Government is implementing the universal public distribution system (UPDS) and no exclusion is made on income criteria. So far, rice was given at Rs. 1 a kg to those who are entitled to receive it. As per existing norms, rice of 4 kg per adult and 2 kg per child is supplied subject to a minimum of 12 kg and a maximum of 20 kg per month per card except in the Nilgiris where the minimum will be 16 kg and the maximum 24 kg. The Civil Supplies Department has made arrangements for distribution of rice in 33,222 ration shops across the State. Over 381,000 tonnes of standardised rice is distributed.

Student Welfare. The welfare measures announced by the Chief Minister have made universalisation, 100 per cent enrolment and retention, and quality education achievable. The welfare schemes for children announced in the 2011-12 and 2012-13 budgets have all been successfully implemented.[34] The main objectives are to improve enrolment in government schools. The following initiatives have also been taken to motivate children towards education:

- Special cash incentives to reduce dropouts.
- Supply of bicycles to 631,000 students studying in standard XI in government, government-aided and partly-aided schools in 2012-13.
- Supply of four sets of uniforms.
- Supply of free textbooks and notebooks for students studying in standards I to X.
- Supply of laptops to students of class XII.

Exemplary Model of Governance

- **Concept of Good Governance**. The International Monetary Fund (IMF) declared in 1996 that promoting good governance in all its aspects, including by ensuring the rule of law, improving the efficiency and accountability of the public sector, and tackling corruption, as essential elements of a framework within which economies can prosper.[35] The IMF feels that corruption within economies is caused by ineffective governance of the economy, either too much regulation or too little regulation. To receive loans from the IMF, countries must have certain good governance policies, as determined by it, in place. The IMF declared in 1996 that promoting good governance in all its aspects, including ensuring the rule of law, improving the efficiency and accountability of the public sector, and tackling corruption, as essential elements of a framework within which economies can prosper. The IMF feels that corruption within economies is caused by the ineffective governance of the economy, and either too much or too little regulation. To receive loans from the IMF, countries must have certain good governance policies, as determined by the IMF, in place.

- According to the UN, good governance has eight characteristics. Good governance is consensus oriented, participatory, following the rule of law, effective and efficient, accountable, transparent, responsive, equitable and inclusive. The World Bank underlined three aspects of society which it feels affect the nature of a country's governance, that is, type of political regime; process by which authority is exercised in the management of the economic and social resources with a view to development; and lastly the capacity of governments to formulate policies and have them effectively implemented.

E-Governance. Effective delivery of public services has been initiated to eliminate corruption. The AADHAR scheme has been implemented successfully for introducing biometric-based unique identification of all beneficiaries under various welfare schemes. Five departments, namely, Revenue, Registration, Municipal Administration, Civil Supplies and Transport, are introducing e-Governance. The pilot implementation of the e-district project in Krishnagiri district is extended to other districts. Steps have been initiated to computerise the details pertaining to land in the State to expedite steps such as patta transfers.

Getting the Best Out of Civil Service. Equitable development of a state is possible when the civil service in the state is allowed to act in a impartial manner without any discrimination based on region, caste, creed, religion or political affiliation. Political will to usher in a climate of true welfare, respect for human rights and natural justice is possible only in a mature democracy. In Tamil Nadu, a fair amount of autonomy to the civil service to implement both central and state government schemes and externally-funded projects has been accorded.

There are many who love development but hate politics. The science of political economy establishes a strong relationship between politics and economy and, how one impacts the other. The importance of this relationship can be more easily understood by looking at the Indian states that are hugely endowed with mineral wealth but still remain the poorest,.

while states with minimal natural resources like Tamil Nadu are pioneers in this field. This explains the critical importance of the political leadership of a state and its vision and mission. The following is the emerging functional relationship of the Amma Model of Development:

Development = Growth + Well Being + Welfare + Exemplary Governance

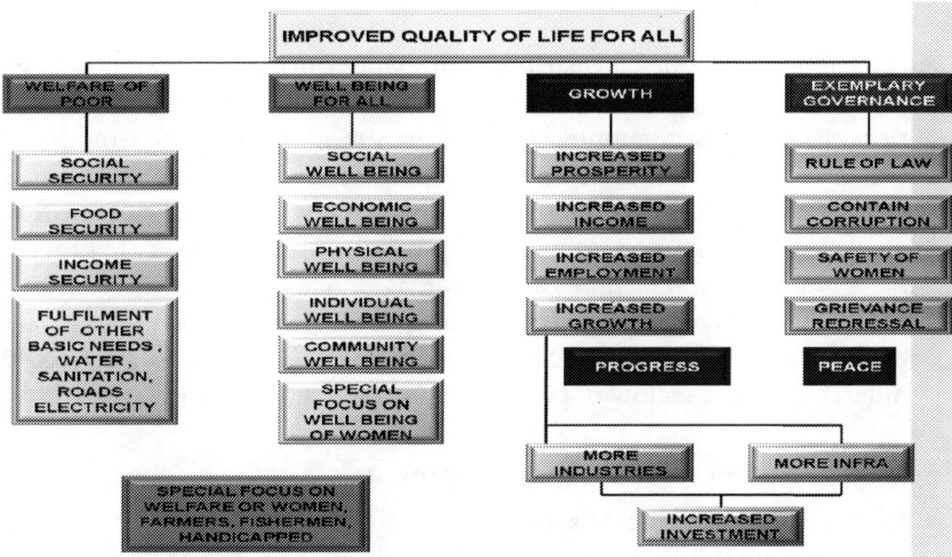

Figure 3.2. The Amma Model of Development

PROVISION OF URBAN AMENITIES IN RURAL AREAS (PURA)

The speed of urbanisation poses an unprecedented policy change, yet India has barely engaged in a national discussion about how to handle this seismic shift in the make-up of the nation. By 2030, there will be 590 million more people living in urban areas in India than there are now (340 million). India's urbanisation is predicted to accelerate, having an effect on practically every state. India's economic structure will alter as it grows. In 1995, India's GDP had split almost evenly between its rural and urban economies. In 2008, its urban GDP accounted for 58 per cent of its overall GDP and if the current trend continues it is expected that urban India will generate 70 per cent of India's GDP by 2030. The challenge for India will be to ramp up investment in line with economic growth.[36]

Urban dwellers in Indian cities are not getting a decent standard of living, and as cities grow, the situation can get even worse. Every major service will see a five to sevenfold increase in demand as the urban population and its earnings rise in cities of all sizes and shapes. Gridlock and urban deterioration will follow if India keeps investing at its current rate in urban infrastructure, which is extremely low by worldwide standards. India must control urbanisation immediately by implementing a new strategy.

Urban India today is distributed in shape with a diverse range of large and small cities, spread widely across the nation. To address the issue of urbanisation, India should continue to aim at a distributed model of urbanisation, because this suits its federal structure and also helps to ensure that migration flows are not directed towards any particular city or cities. To control the migration from rural to urban areas, it is necessary to provide basic amenities and facilities in rural areas similar to those in urban areas. In an effort to close these disparities and give rural India the same amenities as urban India, programmes like PURA make an effort to do so. This would aid in reducing the flow of people from rural to urban areas.

PURA: Model for Rural Development

PURA is a central sector scheme re-launched by the Ministry of Rural Development (MoRD), Government of India, during the remaining period of the XI Plan with support from the Department of Economic Affairs and technical assistance of the Asian Development Bank. MoRD intends to implement the PURA scheme under a public-private partnership (PPP) framework between gram panchayat(s) and private sector partners. The scheme envisages linking rural infrastructure development with economic re-generation activities and is the first attempt at delivering a basket of infrastructure and amenities through PPP in the rural areas. By using private sector efficiency in the administration of assets and service delivery, it aims to offer a different framework for implementation of rural infrastructure development initiatives. This could be the world's first PPP effort for integrated rural infrastructure development and administration.

It would provide holistic and accelerated development of compact areas around a potential growth centre in a gram panchayat (or a group of gram panchayats) through the PPP framework for providing livelihood opportunities and urban amenities to improve the quality of life in rural areas.[37]

Features of PURA

The key characteristics of the scheme are:

- Combining livelihood creation with infrastructure development.
- Enforcement of service standards through a legally binding arrangement.
- Enforcement of standards of service delivery in rural areas almost at par with those obtaining in urban areas.
- Provision of funds for O&M of assets for 10 years' post-construction, along with capital investment for creation of assets.
- Simultaneous delivery of key infrastructure in villages leading to optimal use of resources.
- Transformation of several schemes into a single project to be implemented as per set standards in a defined timeframe with the requirements of each scheme kept intact.

The objectives of PURA are proposed to be achieved under the framework of public private partnership between gram panchayats and private sector partnered with active State Government support. Core funding shall be sourced from the central sector scheme of PURA and complemented by additional support through convergence of different Central Government schemes. The private sector shall also bring on board its share of investment besides operational expertise. The scheme would be implemented and managed by the private sector on considerations of economic viability but designed in a manner whereby it is fully aligned with the overall objective of rural development.[38]

PURA Architecture

The model of a PURA creation begins at the individual village household level, which is the atomic level of PURA implementation. Here, it has to ensure the participation of all households according to their skills and needs, with an opportunity for capacity-building and gaining access to basic amenities. The next in the PURA hierarchy is the village. It is in this area that the acceptability of PURA's various initiatives needs to be developed to make it a process of community participation.

PLANNING	EXECUTION	SUSTENANCE	GROWTH
• Assessment of Core Competencies & Priority Needs • Technological Customisation & Assimilation • Role of PRIs	• Determining & Executing the Investment Model • Helping Implement Through Convergence of Schemes and People's Efforts • Formation of SHGs & Cooperatives	• Generating & Augmenting Local Markets • Promoting Participations Usage of the Amenities Created • Monitoring of & Feedback from the Impact Created by Initiatives	• Creating & Managing Vertically Integrated & Balanced Systems • Promoting Participation by the Maginalised Sections for Better Inclusion • Quality Adherence

Figure 3.3. Provision of Urban Amenities in Rural Areas 'PURA': Four-Fold Cycle

The next higher grouping is the PURA Village Cluster, which is a group of villages sharing basic economic and social assets, such as connecting roads, markets, advanced health-care services, higher educational facilities and electronic connectivity. The size of a PURA cluster can vary from ten to fifty villages. The clusters would be located close to each other, physically as well as culturally and linguistically, and may typically have some common elements in the resources they possess or the skills they have developed. A PURA cluster would be the basic 'element' of the PURA design, each possessing its unique qualities, economic inputs and outputs, and be capable of existing independently. Each cluster would exist independently as a socio-economic entity. Beyond this level, the focus would move to inter-PURA coordination. PURA clusters may collaborate for mutual benefit, dividing fixed costs, exchanging knowledge and sharing markets, and core competencies of products.

India, taken as an entire country, needs 7,000 PURAs covering more than 600,000 villages. The theme of PURA, apart from concentrating on reinforcing agriculture, is to emphasise agro-processing, and develop local crafts, dairy farming, fishing and silk production, so that the non-farm revenue for this sector is enhanced, based on the core competency of the region. Moreover, its economy will be driven by sources of renewable energy, such as the sun, wind, biofuels and the conversion of municipal waste into power.

Types of PURA Clusters. There is Plain PURA, Coastal PURA, Desert PURA, Hill PURA, Island PURA and Delta PURA.

PURA Connectivity

PURA aims at achieving the following forms of connectivity between urban and rural areas:

- **Economic Connectivity**. Economic connectivity would essentially lead to the creation of employment, entrepreneurship, and income augmentation of rural areas through the setting up of agro-based, manufacturing and service industries. Its role in the overall PURA scenario is important since PURA complexes strive to be economically independent.[39]
- **Electronic Connectivity**. Villagers, wherever they are, must have access to good education from the best teachers, the benefit of good medical treatment and the latest information on their occupations such as agriculture, fishery, horticulture and food processing.
- **Knowledge Connectivity**. This can facilitate an increase in productivity; utilisation of spare time to tackle underemployment; and the spread of awareness of health welfare, schools/hospitals, vocational training, knowledge training and use of IRS imagery for land and crop management, water management, forest management, environment, proactive health care, cooperative product marketing, etc.
- **Physical Connectivity**. Villages must relate to each other and with main towns and cities with good, well-networked roads. In the case of deltaic, island or coastal PURAs, the most efficient way could be to use carefully planned waterways or seaways with a proper traffic management system:
  - ❖ Ring Road.
  - ❖ Rail Connectivity.
  - ❖ Public Infrastructure.
  - ❖ Enabled movement of people and goods.
  - ❖ Improved access to schools and health-care centres.
  - ❖ Reduced investments in distribution of power, water and communications networks.

Pilot Phase for PURA

The pilot phase of PURA was implemented from 2004-05 to 2006-07, with the consent of the Planning Commission and a total budget of Rs. 30 crore. Seven clusters were selected in seven states, with a budget of Rs. 4-5 crore per cluster. The identified agencies for the implementation of PURA projects were responsible for providing village-level connectivity relating to basic services, transport, power, electronic knowledge and market and providing drinking water and healthcare facilities.[40] The implementation of the pilot phase did not yield the desired results as it faced the following issues:

- The pilot projects lacked a detailed business plan, which would have identified the potential of each project. In addition, the delivery of the projects was patterned on the conventional mode of scheme delivery. These two factors ensured limited participation by private sector entities.
- The pilot projects were predominantly infrastructure-oriented, with limited attention being given to the implementation of economic activities, which would have improved the standard of living of the local populace.
- The criteria for the selection of the clusters did not factor the growth potential of that area.
- In addition, there was no ownership at the state government level and the entire implementation lacked an appropriate institutional structure with dedicated professional support.
- Finally, there was no convergence with other schemes of rural development or other departments.

The Precision Farming Project in Tamil Nadu. One of the examples of the pilot projects initiated under the PURA scheme was the 'Precision Farming' project in Tamil Nadu. Its details are the following:

- Under this scheme an amount of Rs. 75,000 for the installation of drip irrigation and Rs. 40,000 for crop production expenses was given to farmers. The Government of Tamil Nadu undertook the task of implementing the Precision Farming Project on 400 hectares as a turnkey project, with the main focus on a 40-60 per cent enhanced yield and effective market linkage. Later, the project was scaled up to 40,000 hectares across the state with budget support by the Government of India, under the National Development

Project (NADP). The states of Kerala, Karnataka, Andhra Pradesh, Odisha and Maharashtra have adopted this project on a large scale, and training has been provided to farmers and developmental workers at Dharmapuri in Tamil Nadu.

- The process finally led to the establishment of a farmer-owned producing company called Dharmapuri Precision Farmers' Agro Services Ltd. registered under the Companies Act, the first producing company in Tamil Nadu state, in which 166 farmers of Dharmapuri are shareholders. Later, a second producing company owned by the farmers—Erode Precision Farm Producers' Company Ltd.—was established during 2008-09. The precision farmers have doubled the yield in 45 crops, as compared to the national and state averages.
- The Krishi Vigyan Kendra (KVK) of Agriculture Science Centre is an initiative by the Indian Council of Agricultural Research (ICAR) to promote the transfer of technology in agriculture, animal husbandry, beekeeping, and many other fields to farms. Each KVK adopts five to six villages in a radius of 10-20 km for upgrading farm technology, agriculture extension services, conducting training courses and live demonstrations. At present, there are approximately 667 KVKs in the nation with the number likely to go up in the near future.

- The next tier of the system consists of the Conventional Farmers' Clubs at the village level. There are 148 clubs with a membership of 2,977 farmers.

- The last tier of the system is the self-help groups of farmers. There are 485 SHGs with over 7,275 members. They help disseminate technology at the field level and undertake the vital task of credit mobilisation to give the farmers financial power to adopt the technology.

Challenges during the Pilot Phase

The issues with the current design of PURA have been classified into five categories, details of which are presented in the succeeding paragraphs.

Issues Relating to the Convergence of Various Schemes

- A guideline can be given to future bidders regarding the potential non-MoRD schemes that could be integrated within PURA projects. This guideline could be a useful databank for bidders and reduce their efforts in searching for the relevant scheme for their cluster.
- It will be necessary to arrive at an optimal size and number of the villages to be covered under a PURA project to ensure a holistic approach for all.
- There is a lack of funding for various capital-intensive mandatory activities under MoRD schemes. For instance, there is no provision under the TSC Scheme for the development of a sewage treatment plant. In addition, there are no schemes pertaining to the development and maintenance of village streets and storm water drainage. The lack of funds for these activities limits the coverage of facilities in the PURA cluster.
- There are differences between the specifications given out in the scheme guidelines vis-à-vis specifications for the PURA projects, highlighted in the bid documents. An assessment of the specifications may be undertaken to formalise the same for future PURA projects.
- The current approval process for activities under non-MoRD schemes is twofold. The first step is the independent sanction of the project proposal by the concerned ministry and then its approval by the empowered committee for PURA projects. There needs to be a better co-ordination procedure for granting approvals to projects under non-MoRD schemes, to ensure single-window clearance for the bidders.

Adopting an Integrated and Participatory Approach

- During the evaluation of the DPRs, it was found that considerable efforts were made for consensus-building at the gram panchayat level; however, similar efforts for consensus-building at the district administration level was lacking. This flaw was clearly reflected in the results of the baseline survey wherein the actual ground situation was not reflected. This could have been easily addressed through interaction with various technical departments of the district administration.
- Each PURA project has a limited capacity to address the needs of all the villagers. It was felt in some of the clusters that the bidders had not adopted a consensus-building process and hence had failed to incorporate many of the demands of the villagers. A pro-active consensus-building approach may be given as a guideline to the bidders with each step being documented. Each demand should be documented and if the same is not accommodated by the bidder, then a logical reason for the same should be documented.
- The guideline, mentioned in the above point (a) may be extended to consensus-building at the district administration level.

Strengthening Administrative Process

- A project implementation unit needs to be established within MoRD to undertake a monitoring role for all PURA projects within the country.
- Due to multiple activities involved in a PURA project, the bidder is required to approach various departments within the state government. This process can be time-consuming. Hence, a project-level co-ordination committee may be constituted at the state government level to grant various approvals or take decisions on the implementation challenges associated with PURA projects. An example is the committee constituted by the Government of Kerala to address issues relating to PURA projects.
- It is requested that state governments give access to resources in its control for fulfilling the needs under mandatory activities of the PURA project. For example, in one of the clusters, there exists a reservoir which is owned by the Irrigation Department of the State Government. This reservoir has enough water to meet the drinking water requirements of drought-prone villages under PURA. The

utilisation of water would be limited to 2 per cent of its total capacity. By granting an approval to tap this source, the entire drinking water needs of the PURA cluster can be fulfilled.[41]

Implementation Challenges Associated with PURA Projects

- There is an imperative need for officials of the gram panchayat and the district administration to undertake capacity-building activities. This capacity-building is aimed at providing officials with the necessary skill sets to meet their obligations under the concession agreement and state support agreement. A possibility of handholding by the MoRD in the pilot phase may be undertaken to achieve smooth implementation of the projects.
- An accurate baseline survey is crucial to determine the PURA grant for the project. It may be explored to provide the broad contents of the baseline survey to bidders as a standard document.
- Given the diverse backgrounds of the bidders, it may be considered suitable to provide standard technical solutions (like sample designs of various structures) as a manual to bidders. Such a reference document would enable standardisation of the DPRs and enable a smoother approval process for MoRD.
- In addition to technical solutions, it may be considered to provide a manual of various innovative (but cost-effective) technologies. These could be adopted by the bidders in their projects.

Improvements that can be Adopted in the Procurement Process

- Circulating the present specifications under PURA to each state government may be explored. Customisation may be undertaken based on the inputs of state governments. An example: the Government of Rajasthan has specified the provision of 70 lpcd of drinking water to gram panchayats as against a requirement of 100 lpcd in the case of PURA projects.
- It has been found that there exists significant variance in the efforts undertaken by the bidders during the concept plan stage and the DPR stage. It may be explored to strengthen the concept plan stage so as to ensure that variation in the PURA grant quoted in the DPR stage is not beyond 20 per cent of the PURA grant quoted at the concept plan stage.

PURA: Demand Driven PPP Scheme

Given the experience of the pilot projects, the Planning Commission undertook an appraisal of the projects in 2007. After appraising in 2007, it advised redesigning PURA as a demand-driven PPP scheme with the following key features:

- Commitment of the state government for facilitation support.
- Selection of clusters based on economic growth potential.
- Selection of lead agency/anchor partner with a clear articulation of the roles, rights and responsibilities of the lead agency.
- Creation of a sustainable revenue model to encourage commercial banks and the private sector to participate.
- Financial outlay for a PURA cluster to the tune of Rs. 70-80 crore, with Central Government participation limited to Rs. 20-25 crore.
- Focus on livelihood opportunities.

PURA Project Transaction Structure. There exist two main relationships in the project, namely, (1) Relationship between the gram panchayat, the district rural development authority (DRDA), and project special purpose vehicle (SPV) for the development of PURA projects; and (2) Relationship between the Ministry of Rural Development (MoRD), the state government and the project SPV. These relationships are governed by the concession agreement and the state support agreement respectively and shall be operational for a concession period of 13 years. Of the total concession period, three years are allocated for the development of the project facilities and 10 years for operating and maintaining them. The following transaction structure was conceived to implement the project.

Is this Model of PURA Sustainable?

A decade-old central scheme introduced by the erstwhile UPA government for providing urban amenities in rural areas will soon pave the way for implementation of Gujarat's 'Rurban Model' across India. In the Union Budget 2014-15, unveiled by Finance Minister Arun Jaitley, the government made no allocation for the central scheme PURA (Providing Urban Amenities in Rural Areas) and instead introduced the Rurban Mission, similar to the one running in Gujarat, with an initial allocation of Rs. 100 crore. The new government now wants to replicate the Gujarat model at the national level to provide urban amenities in rural parts of the country.

"Consequently, we will subsume PURA into the Rurban Mission," a senior government official told ET.[42]

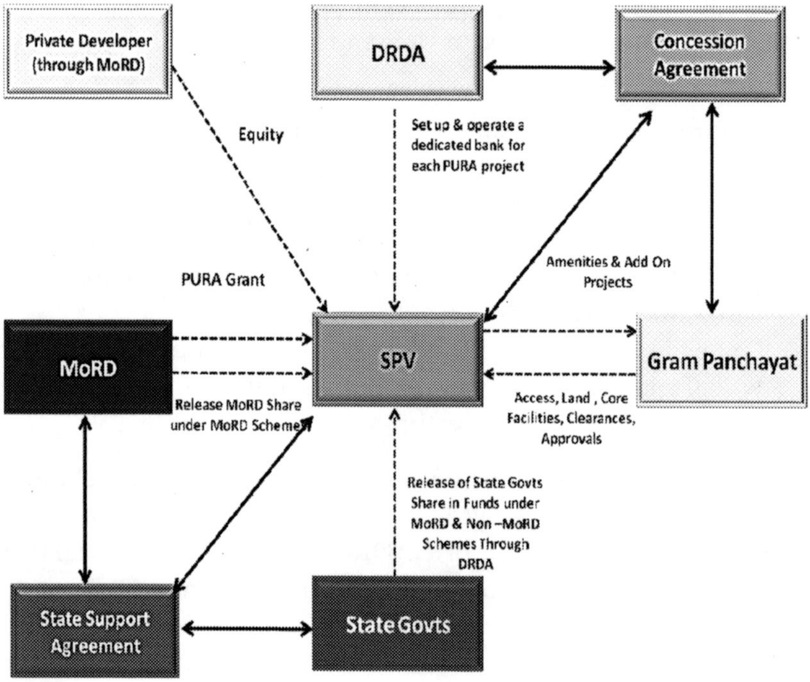

Figure 3.4. Structure to Implement PURA Demand Driven PPP Scheme

Conclusion

According to the official, the rural development ministry will closely follow the Gujarat model while preparing the road map for implementation of the Rurban Mission. "We will look at the cluster of villages holistically and do the resource mapping as well as gap analysis to come up with a framework for the new scheme to be delivered through a convergent resource pool," the official added on condition of anonymity. Citing the success of Gujarat in providing urban amenities to rural parts of the state, the finance minister had said in his budget speech, "Gujarat has demonstrated successfully the Rurban development model of urbanisation of the rural areas. The Shyama Prasad Mukherji Rurban Mission was planned to be launched to deliver integrated project-based infrastructure in rural areas, which would also include development of economic activities and skill development, preferably through the PPP (public-private partnership) mode."

NOTES

1. A. Banerjee and T. Piketty (2001): Are the rich growing richer: Evidence from Indian tax data working papers, MIT and CEPREMAP.
2. K. Munshi and M. Rosenzweig (2009): Why is Mobility in India so Low? Social Insurance, Inequality, and Growth, Working paper, Brown University, Department of Economics.
3. www. Swaniti.in
4. Ramgopal Agarwala. 'Developing Modern Village Clusters', *The Hindu*, 18 Sep 2014.
5. 'Indian bureaucracy rated worst in Asia, says a Political & Economic Risk Consultancy report' *The Economic Times*, 11 January 2012.
6. Bibek Debroy. *Gujarat: Governance for Growth and Development (2012)*, Academic Foundation, 2012 edition.
7. Prof. Mukul G. Asher. For good statistics and links on Gujarat development and budget, etc, 'Gujarat's budget reflects sound development strategy', *East Asia Forum*, 3 April 2012.
8. Andy Marino, *Narendra Modi: A Political Biography*, Harpers Collins Publishers, India March 2011.
9. http://guj-epd.gov.in/epd_jyotiyojna.htm. Energy & Petrochemicals Department.
10. Tushaar Shah and Shilp Verma. 'Real-time Co-management of Electricity and Groundwater: An Assessment of Gujarat's Pioneering "Jyotigram" Scheme', International Water Management Institute.
11. Shah et al. 'Secret of Gujarat's Agrarian Miracle after 2000', *Economic and Political Weekly*, 26 December 2009, p.48.
12. *Express News Service*, Ahmedabad, published April 27, 2016.
13. Amarendra Jha, 'From plague ugly to khub-surat', *The Times of India*, 31 July 2005.
14. Surat Municipal Corporation, 'Project Overview Surat 2009'.
15. R. Jagannathan, 'Is the Gujarat growth story for real? Apparently, yes', *First Post*, 8 October 2012.
16. Jayati Ghosh. 'Gujarat model: The real story', *Frontline Magazine*, 22 August 2014.
17. Sebastian Morris. *'A Comparative Analysis of Gujarat's Economic Growth', Growth or Development-Which Way is Gujarat Going*, Oxford University Press, Sep. 2014.
18. Amita Shah and Itishree Pattnaik. *'High Growth Agriculture in Gujarat: An Enquiry into Inclusiveness and Sustainability'*, Oxford University Press, Sep. 2014, pp. 35-45.
19. Y. K. Alagh. *'Gujarat: Sifting Fact from Fiction', Mint Opinion*, 11 August 2013, pp. 45-56.
20. Darshini Mahadevia. *'Dynamics of Urbanization in Gujarat' Growth or Development-Which Way is Gujarat Going*, Oxford University Press, Sep. 2014.
21. P. K. Viswanathan and Jharna Pathak. *'Economic Growth and the State of Natural Resources and the Environment in Gujarat: A Critical Assessment', Growth or Development: Which Way is Gujarat Going*, Oxford University Press, Sep. 2014.

22. Bibek Debroy. 'Moral of the Gujarat Story', *India Today*, 21 Dec. 2012.
23. Dr. C.K. Gariyalli I.A.S. & Dr. S.K. Vettivel, Vetri. 'AMMA Model of Development in Tamil Nadu', New Delhi: Vetri Publishers, 2014, pp. 1-3.
24. *Tamil Arasu,* January 2013, English Edition, pp. 1-7.
25. Dr. C.K. Gariyalli I.A.S & Dr. S. K Vettivel, Vetri. 'AMMA Model of Development in Tamil Nadu', New Delhi: Vetri Publishers, 2014, pp. 15-19.
26. Policy Notes 2013-14 of Industrial Department, Government of Tamil Nadu.
27. Policy Note 2013-14, "MSME Department", *Government of Tamil Nadu.*
28. *"Policy Note 2013-14, Energy Department"*, Government of Tamil Nadu.
29. *Tamil Arasu,* January 2013, English edition, p. 52.
30. "Policy Notes 2013-14 of Health, Social Welfare, Social Education, Adi-Dravidar departments", Government of Tamil Nadu.
31. *Tamil Arasu,* January 2013, English edition, p. 31.
32. C.K. Gariyalli, S.K. Vettivel and Vetri. *"Amma Model of Development in Tamil Nadu"* New Delhi: Vetri Publishers, 2014. pp. 35-60.
33. "Policy Notes 2013-14 Health, Social Welfare, School Education, Adi Dravidar, Civil Supplies Departments", Government of Tamil Nadu.
34. "Policy Note 2013-14 School Education", Government of Tamil Nadu.
35. "Policy Notes 2013-14 Public, Home Departments", Government of Tamil Nadu.
36. "India's urban awakening building inclusive cities sustaining economic growth", McKenzie Global Institute, April 2010.
37. Abdul Kalam, A.P.J. & Srijan Pal Singh. *Target 3 Billion, PURA: Innovative Solutions towards Sustainable Development*, Penguin Books, pp. 13-18.
38. "Ministry of Rural Development', Annual Report 2002, PURA Implementation.
39. Abdul Kalam, A. P. J. & Srijan Pal Singh. *Target 3 Billion, PURA: Innovative Solutions towards Sustainable Development*, UK, 2011, pp. 56-87.
40. "Final Report of Working Group", *Ministry of Rural Development,* December 2013.
41. Indra Rajni Kant. PURA, Information & Analysis, https://sites.google.com/site/errajanikantissuediscussion/policy/pura
42. Yogima Seth Sharma. "Gujarat's 'Rurban Model' to Replace UPA's 'Providing Urban Amenities in Rural Areas' Plan, *ET Bureau,*15 July 2014.

4

Ex-Servicemen's Leadership: A Paragon for Rural Development

"We will form an army of poor, where every poor will be a soldier and we will win the war against poverty on behalf of their strength".

—Narendra Modi, Prime Minister of India

Introduction

The term "Development Administration" came into use in the 1950s to represent those aspects of public administration and those changes in public administration that were needed to carry out policies, projects, and programs to improve social and economic conditions. During a period of 15 years following the end of World War II in 1945, colony after colony threw off the imperial yoke. Country after country achieved independence and political autonomy. This new status gave a promise of freedom and liberty and self-determination in political systems of representative democracy. It gave hope of greater individual freedom and equality of treatment in society. Independence created hopes of higher national and per capita income, a rapid rise in standards of living, and an increase in individual opportunity. Even in countries which had not been colonies but had been administered by some other form of authoritarian government, this was a generation of rising and insistent expectations pressing for rapid political, social, and economic change. New governments and their bureaucracies, their administrative[1] agencies and processes, were expected to give reality to these anticipated fruits of independence and liberty. These new functions, these demands upon the administration system, were not only enormous in size and weight; they were novel and complex in character.

Every civilised society needs a good administrative system, and administration is as old as our ancient civilisation. Public administration is essential for executing government orders and functions. In the Indian administrative system of ancient times, different systems are found to have existed at different periods. The earliest reference can be traced to the Indus Valley civilisation. Governance in Mohenjo-Daro and Harappa was systematic. In the Indus Valley civilisation can be found planned roads and drainage which indicates that in cities there existed a municipal government which looked after the needs and made systematic arrangements for the cities. A deeper study of Indian history reveals the existence of such organisational administrative structures even in the time of the Mauryan dynasty, Cholas, and the Mughals. A brief account of them has been covered in the succeeding paragraphs.

Societal Organisation Structure & Administrative Setup (SOSAS) during 'Ashoka the Great's Period

During Ashoka's reign, the Mauryan territory was extended because of his military expeditions. To manage the administrative functions of a vast territory, Ashoka introduced several administrative reforms. With the help of such reforms, he continued to maintain a centralised administration and at the same time capably managed the provincial administration thereby ensuring social harmony. The structure of the Mauryan government was a centralised one.[2] Ashoka was at the helm of his administration with his brother, Tishya, as the deputy. The crown prince and the other kumaras in the sphere of provincial administration also assisted Ashoka. He appointed a group of trusted ministers who always helped him in matters of administrative policies. He introduced legal reforms like Danda Samahara and Vyavahara Samahara. Ashoka was the sovereign head of the Mauryan Empire in every inch, as the *Arthashastra* instructed him to be.

Administrative Reforms. Ashoka introduced several reforms in the sphere of provincial administration, which brought about many improvements in the existing system of provincial government. He retained the traditional administrative divisions of the empire in provinces or pradesas or districts. These provinces were again subdivided into aharas or vishyas or subdivisions and janapadas, which were further subdivided into villages. One of the important policies he adopted for the provincial administration was that he used to change the provincial governors from time to time. Moreover, Ashoka had appointed many functionaries and dharma mahamatas and dharma yutas to cope with the increasing burden of missionary work and welfare schemes. In the Ashokan regime, rajukas, yutas, and pradesikas were entrusted with special assignments in the sphere of provincial administration.

Role of Mahamatas. The mahamatas were invested with specific departments with specific titles. The dharma mahamatas appointed by him looked after the material and spiritual well-being of the people. The adhyaksha mahamatas were entrusted with the task of the well-being of women. The anta mahamatas were appointed for the general administration of the frontier provinces. The nagara mahamatas were in charge of cities and towns. They were often engaged in periodical tours in order to collect news about administrative and general affairs throughout the empire.

Management of Public Services. There was a group of special officers called vrajabhumikas in the public utility department. They supervised the execution of Ashokan welfare schemes like construction of roads, digging of wells, planting of shady mangroves, etc.

Implementation of Reforms. During the reign of Ashoka, officials called rajukas held a significant place. Ashoka, in his administrative policy, created the rajukas as the sole agency to execute his reforms.[3] Originally, the rajukas were in charge of measurement of land and settled disputes. Since they were connected with the land revenue department, they normally had a great influence in the rural areas. Ashoka, while implementing his administrative policies, enhanced their powers and position and made them the most important officers of janapadas. Gradually, the rajukas became key officers and were entrusted to execute most of Ashoka's welfare projects and administrative reforms.

Justice and Civic Life. In the sphere of justice and civic life, Ashoka introduced many reforms because of his humanitarian and paternal sentiments. He set up officials to execute justice properly and preach the principles of Dharma. Moreover, there were special groups of officials to organise charities, promote tolerance and reduce the punishment of criminals. Ashoka tried to promote the spiritual welfare of his subjects by preaching dharma and inculcating tolerance among his subjects; he aspired to have a social harmony.

Such a planned and balanced structure of government with effective administrative reforms, had established the Mauryan empire under Ashoka as one of the supreme powerful empires in India. During his time, the Mauryan empire experienced a fair civic and social life and was free of any sectarian revolts and internal chaos and anarchy. Owing to his effective administration, Ashoka is often considered one of the greatest monarchs of India.

'SOSAS' during Chola Dynasty

The administration of the Chola dynasty was essentially monarchical in character where the king was at the helm of the administration and all executive legislative and military powers rested with him. A council of ministers and other high officials were there to advise the king for administration of the Chola empire[4]. The empire, known as Rajyam or Rastrayam, was divided into several provinces or mandalams. The most important mandalams were placed under the charges of viceroys who were generally princes of royal blood or from noble families. The provinces or mandalams were subdivided into a number of divisions known as kottams/ valanadus. The next administrative subdivision of the Cholas were the districts (nadus), each of which again consisted of several autonomous villages, unions or groups of villages, playing a vital part in the Chola administration system.

The Chola Village Administration. The Chola village administration was very systematic and well developed. The village assemblies were called 'ur' and the 'sabha' or 'mahasabha', which were gatherings of adult male members of the community. The 'ur' was a gathering of local residents to discuss matters without any formal rule or procedure. However, the sabha or mahasabha was the assembly of the Brahmin settlement (agrahara) comprising a number of committees. The number of the committees and its members varied from village to village and no payment was made for their services. The members of the committee were called "variyapperumakkal" and the mahasabha was called "perunguri" and its members 'perumakkal."

The mahasabhas had autonomous functioning, wherein; they possessed the proprietorial rights over communal lands and controlled the private, forest and water areas within their jurisdiction. They cooperated with royal officials in estimating the products of the cultivated land and assessing the land revenue due from the village. They also enjoyed the power of taxation for purposes connected with the village, and of remission of such taxation for specific purposes. The committee was assisted by paid officials who detected crimes. The judicial committee, "nayattar" of the assembly settled disputes and awarded punishment to the guilty.[5]. The maintenance of roads and irrigation works including tanks, supervision of religions, medical and eleemosynary endowments by the dharmavariyam, making provisions for learning, etc., from its own limited resources were the duties of the mahasabha.

'SOSAS' during the Mughal Period

The administration during the Mughal dynasty[6] was carried out by incorporating certain elementary changes in the central administration structure in India. The Mughal emperors were all powerful in the administration. They accepted two primary duties for themselves, Jahanbani (protection of the state) and Jahangiri (extension of the empire). Besides, they tried to generate those conditions that were conducive to the economic and cultural progress of their subjects. The emperor was the head of the state. He was the lawmaker, the chief executive, the commander-in-chief of the army and the final dispenser of justice.

During the reign of Akbar, there were only four ministers, namely, Wakil, Diwan or Wazir, Mir Bakshi and Sadr-us-Sadur. The posts of Wakil and Wazir were combined later, and the holder of the post was called Vakil-i-Mutlaq. Primarily, the Diwan looked after the income and expenditure of the state. Thus, Vakil or Wazir or Prime Minister was the person next to the emperor in the administration. The Sadr-us-Sadur advised the emperor on religious matters. He looked after the religious education, distribution of jagirs to scholars and observance of the laws of the Islam by Muslims.

Land Administration under the Mughals. The empire was divided into subas or provinces. The state lands were divided into parganas for the purpose of evaluating taxation; the taxes were collected by amirs. When jagirs were initially awarded, the emperor retained the right to collect taxes, but later the jagirdars were allowed to levy taxes themselves and to keep a portion to maintain soldiers and horses. The peasants were pressurised to pay exorbitant taxes to get immediate returns, which usually went to finance the jagirdar's personal expenses, and the fertility of the land and condition of the peasants deteriorated.

Scribes in Mughal Administration. Several scribes were delegated to keep a record of the affairs of the court and the empire, to maintain a list of nominated officers, and to keep a record of their performance. The movements of dignitaries were also noted. Special scribes kept journals of the activities of the emperor and the royal family. There was a 'Diwan of Finances' to keep an account of all the expenses, and the magistrates were responsible for justice and religious affairs and for compiling centralised reports from all over the empire. The emperor was at the centre of this network of agents, functionaries, and spies, and he collected all the sifted information.

Transformational Movements for Establishing SOSAS in India: Post Independence

In order to bring about a transformation in the administrative, social and governance systems within the country, a number of movements have been initiated since Independence, namely, Acharya Vinova Bhave's 'Bhoodan Movement', Jayaprakash Narayan's 'Total Revolution' and the more recent Anna Hazare's 'Anti-Corruption Movement'. These leaders tried to transform Indian society; however, their efforts could not reach a conclusive end as each of these models had limitations to address total societal transformation. Let us analyse the reasons for failure of the most recent movement, that is, the 'Anna Hazare Movement'. History has shown that people who stood for a cause succeeded in bringing about a change. The whole world supported their cause because they were incorruptible. They could not be influenced nor deviated from their main cause. Such men and women had the support of the people which they utilised against people opposing their cause efficiently and brought about the change. Unfortunately, Anna deviated from his cause; Lokpal Bill was not seen as the primary priority[7] and the primary target became the Indian National Congress party. This one change in stand or deviation from stance caused the death of the Anna Hazare movement which had gained so much momentum. This resulted in a slight loss of confidence of the people.

Apart from the transformational movements, there have been instances of successful growth models in a few of the Indian states with Tamil Nadu and Gujarat being the front runners. Though the Gujarat model is essentially based on the economic reforms launched on an all-India level, it incorporates several modifications introduced by the Government of Gujarat in the context of the state's socio-economic and cultural conditions as well as the ruling party's political ideology under the dynamic leadership of its leader, Mr. Narendra Modi. Gujarat has, unlike many other states, followed the classical model of transition from agricultural development[8] to industry-led development before transforming into an economy dominated by the service sector. In the last decade, the state has seen an exceptionally large flow of industrial, especially large infrastructural, investment – both by the private sector and the government.

From the research, it emerges very clearly that success of a revolution/movement/model should manifest itself in total transformation, social revolution and empowerment of people which is further contingent upon the following important factors:

- **Emergence Phase**
  - Just/Legitimate Cause.
  - Common Goal/Shared Interests.
  - Dynamic and Transformational Leadership.
  - Mass Appeal.
- **Sustenance Phase**
  - Focused Approach.
  - Leadership.
  - Visible Changes.
- **Implementation Phase**
  - Acceptance by Government/Authority.
  - Formalising it through a legislation/bill/amendment.
  - Incorporating society in the change.

Efficient Governance towards Transformational Holistic Growth

Governance, in contemporary usage, goes beyond how government institutions function. It is seen in terms of partnerships and cooperation between governments, corporate sector and civil society. The United Nations' definition of governance includes specifically effective cooperation between the government and non-government actors to bring about solutions that are mutually beneficial.[9] This inclusive process is based on shared interests, where each partner contributes according to their respective resources, strengths and areas of expertise. Thus, governance is seen to go beyond the official government structure to include diverse ways through which civil society can demand, actualise and make more effective the required delivery of services by those in the government. It is also desired that governance be compatible with the principles of equality, justice and human rights.

Core Principles of Responsive Governance. A major and basic restructuring is essential to combat the evils of fragmentation, narrow departmentalism and micro-management at the higher levels which lead to inordinate delays and lack of accountability thereby impinging upon the holistic growth of the nation and society. The following core principles should govern the restructuring:

- **Coordinated Implementation**. Coordination is essential in implementation as in policy making. The proliferation of vertical departments makes this an impossible task except in cases where empowered commissions, statutory bodies, and autonomous societies have been created.[10]
- **Flatter Structures – Reducing the Number of Levels and Encouraging Teamwork.** The conventional approach of the Government of India has been to adopt uniform vertical hierarchies. There is a need to shift to flatter[11] organisations with greater emphasis on teamwork.
- **Separation of Policy Making Functions from Executive**. The ministries should give greater emphasis to the policy making functions while delegating the implementation functions to the operational units or independent organisations/agencies. This is even more necessary because implementation of the policies requires in-depth knowledge of the subject and managerial skills. It is this field of implementation which requires transformation leadership.
- **Well-Defined Accountability.** The present multi-layered organisational structure with fragmented decision-making leads to a culture of alibis for non-performance. A clearer demarcation of organisational responsibilities would help in developing a performance management system for individual functionaries.

Broad Framework for Improving Governance Capacity. Concerned about the failures of public administration in many states, especially the poorly developed states, the World Bank came out with a number of prescriptions for increasing governance capacity wherein it recommended that there should be a two-part strategy for increasing the effectiveness of the state.[12] Part one, requires narrowing the gap between the demands on a state and its capabilities to meet these demands, through greater selectivity in the state's priorities. The state should concentrate on priorities and offload the rest to civil society and the private sector. Outsourcing can be resorted to increase competition and innovation. Part two of the strategy of reform is strengthening the state's institutional capability by giving people a voice in the affairs and activities of the state, co-opting them on various advisory councils and involving the beneficiaries of government programmes in the planning and implementation of such programmes.[13]

Thus, it is very apparent from the above discussion that 'Core Principles' and 'Broad Framework' are necessary to bring about a transformational change in existing governance; implementation of various schemes and growth policies is possible only by co-opting civil society. The core issue that has been identified is not lack of planning but a planned road map for implementation of the thought process. The Indian bureaucracy is a haven of mental reforms. It still attracts many of the brightest students in the country, but despite their very high Intelligent Quotients (IQs), most bureaucrats fail as managers. Most Indian civil servants fail to plan their projects well, monitor them, or follow through on them: their performance failures mostly have to do with poor execution. This lack of transformational leadership is evident in the fields of public education, health, water and electricity services, delayed infrastructure projects and, above all, governance. The officers of the Armed Forces who retire between 45 and 58 years of age have a vast experience in the transformational leadership and can be rightly suited to head/part of the monitoring/execution agencies.

Transformational Leadership and Holistic Growth

In May 2008, the Commission on Growth & Development, World Bank, issued a report entitled 'The Growth Report'. In it, the commission attempted to distil what had been learned in the past two decades from experience and academics and policy research, about strategies and policies that produced a sustained high growth in developing countries. It became clear in the course of the work that politics, leadership and political economy were certainly important ingredients in the overall growth story. There is no one style of leadership that covers all the high-growth economics. Nor is leadership the only input. At best, one can venture that effective transformational leadership involves seizing opportunities created by the political-economic dynamics to institute change in strategy, structure and direction. Although transformational leadership seems an obvious component of growth to some, academic literature has not, until recently, been able to demonstrate the importance of the role of leaders in growth economics.

Transformational leadership is defined as a leadership approach that causes change in individuals and social systems. In its ideal form, it creates valuable and positive changes among its followers with the end goal of developing followers[14] into leaders. Enacted in its authentic form, transformational leadership enhances the motivation, morale and performance of followers through a variety of mechanisms. These include connecting the followers' sense of identity and self to the mission and collective identity of the organisation; being a role model for followers that inspires them; challenging followers to take greater ownership for their work, and understanding the strengths and weaknesses of followers, so that the leader can align followers with tasks that optimise their performance. History is full of instances where individuals have transformed the course of the future with their own charismatic manner and leadership style. Examples are many, both in the economic domain as well as on the battlefields, illustrious leaders, namely, Nelson Mandela, Steve Jobs, Mahatma Gandhi, Bill Gates, Field Marshal S.H.F.J. Manekshaw, General D. Eisenhower, to name just a few.

The leaders in the Armed Forces are a true epitome of transformational leadership as they lead their men from the front in the most difficult and life-threatening conditions by motivating them and getting the best out of their command in inhospitable and unfavourable conditions. However, it is an irony of our 'great nation' that these men in uniform are not being co-opted in nation building and holistic growth once they get superannuated from their respective services.

Recommending a SOSAS Paradigm for Holistic Growth

India's growth in the last decade, when compared with some of the Asian countries, shows that although India's growth since 2001 has been beneficial to the poor, India's achievements are fairly modest relative to the other Asian countries. This calls for a concentrated effort to make India's growth more holistic and inclusive in future. The first four parts of this paper have highlighted the flaws and opportunities in rural growth, existing public administration as impediment to growth, potency of retired personnel of the armed forces, a peek into our history as regards administrative structures and has also analyzed the various transformational movements/model's post-independence and the reasons for their failure. In order to ensure a holistic growth of the country from rural areas to the state, we need to evolve a successful model and give it life by incorporating all sections of our society.

National Level Strategic Planning Commission (NLSPC)

To ensure continuous improvement of the system towards holistic growth, a number of steps are required by a country for strengthening its strategic planning process and moving them in the direction of a sustainable development strategy. This entails identification, coordination and continuous improvement of mechanisms that help towards balancing the economic, social and environmental concerns of multiple stakeholders.

Figure 4.1. Essential Components of Strategic Planning Commission

The following steps apply in full to strategy development tasks, that is, those needed to flesh out and establish the strategy by building on existing mechanisms, and/or initiating new mechanisms if necessary. It should not be assumed[15] that subsequent steps be undertaken as a rigid sequence. In practice, many of them will need to be pursued in parallel and some might best make of opportunities as they arise:

- Define and seek agreement on the roles of stakeholders-private sector, civil society, national and local government, the secretariat.
- Develop or improve coherence and coordination between strategy frameworks at all levels from international to local; and between and within sectors.
- Ensure broad-based ownership by key ministries and agencies, civil society and the private sector.
- Establish and promote a schedule or broad-based calendar for the strategy process to determine activities, responsibilities, capabilities and resources needed, and their timings.

Government	**Government Supported Bodies**	**Civil Society**	**Private Sector**	**Regional & International Agencies**
✓Cabinet ✓Line ministries ✓Government agencies ✓Sub-national authorities at all levels	✓Research establishments ✓Educational institutes ✓Armed Forces ✓The judiciary ✓Parliament ✓Resource management authorities & agencies ✓Quasi autonomous NGOs	✓Independent academic & research institutions ✓Community groups ✓Private voluntary organisations ✓Political parties/groups ✓Resource user associations (farmers, fishermen, tourism operators, etc.) ✓Trade Unions ✓Women's groups ✓Campaign groups	✓Banking & financial institutions ✓Industry associations ✓Major companies ✓Chambers of Commerce ✓Business round tables ✓The media ✓Enterprise development agencies	✓Multilateral development banks ✓Bilateral development cooperation agencies ✓International NGOs ✓Regional aid organisations

Table 4.1. Checklist of Key Stakeholder Groups in a National Sustainable Development Strategy

- Establish or improve provisions for regular analysis, debate, communications, planning, implementation, monitoring and review; to ensure that all stakeholders are best able to play their part in the strategy. These processes are the 'heart' of the strategy.
- Establish or strengthen a secretariat or coordinating body acceptable to stakeholders, with sufficient authority and resources to coordinate.
- Establish or strengthen a steering committee with a broad balance of representation from government, the private sector and civil society.
- Identify the stakeholders[16] who will own the preparation and implementation of an integrated sustainable development strategy and encourage discussion of their roles.
- Mobilise the required resources, identify, secure and allocate in a timely and accountable manner, the required skills, management and financial resources.
- Promote the strategy as a unified concept. Possibly publish a prospectus for the strategy outlining all the above.
- Secure or confirm a mandate for the strategy.
- Seek or improve political commitment to the strategy preparation and implementation process from the highest level as well as all other levels.

RURAL AREAS PROGRESSIVE INTEGRATED DEVELOPMENT (RAPID): PROPOSED NEW STRATEGY

To ensure development of our rural areas, we need to evolve a strategy which should be holistic in nature and ensure creation of Rural Areas Progressive Integrated Development (RAPID) which must be guided by the following key elements:

- **Administration of RAPID Clusters**. To ensure holistic growth, a group of villages should be made into RAPID clusters, sharing basic economic and social assets, such as connecting roads, markets, advanced health-care services, higher education facilities and electronic connectivity. These clusters should be located close to each other, physically as well as culturally and linguistically, and may have some common elements in the resources they possess or the skills they have developed. India, taken as the entire country, needs around 10,000 RAPID clusters covering more than 600,000 villages.

- **Area Based Approach**. The RAPID areas should have some real local identity, rather than simply respect the old established administrative boundaries, and should not normally have more than 1 million inhabitants. These areas can cross village and district boundaries.
- **Bottoms-Up Approach**. It is imperative to place a high premium on the active participation of people living within the selected areas. This will necessitate formation of ad hoc 'Local Action Groups' to manage the programmes. It is here, where ex-servicemen who are settled in the villages/RAPID areas will get involved, enhance accountability, and hence can facilitate transformation and enforcement.

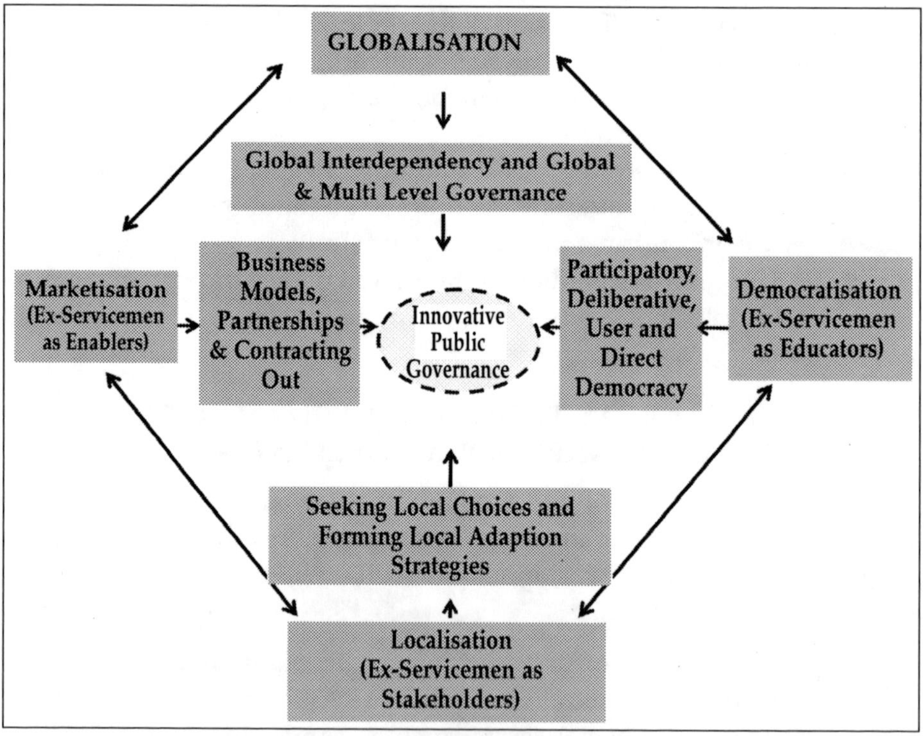

Figure 4.2. Contextual Factors Affecting New Forms of Governance[17]

- **Industry to Penetrate Rural India**. The growth story of Indian industry is that of a success; though all their products reach the rural areas and villages; however, the role of middlemen in the marketing of the produce end up in making the products more expensive for rural consumers. It is therefore imperative for the industry to develop distribution outlets and capabilities[18] in rural areas.

- **Distribution Planning**. The physical distribution system in rural markets includes transportation, storage, local delivery and sub-distribution. Reducing dead time between the points of production to the end user is of prime importance. Companies need to develop the 'barefoot' approach and train local talent to operate as 'barefoot salesmen'. Ex-servicemen from the logistics branches of the three services who are residing in these villages have skills of distribution management. Private industry has to tap this potential to penetrate the rural market in a more profitable and economical way.
- **District Administration**. At the district level, district collector (DC) along with the chief executive officer (CEO) execute the regulatory and development administration. While the district collector is from the civil administrative field, the CEO can be from the local population with a good reputation, entrepreneurs and investors, prominent public figures, etc. Keeping in view the organisational skills of high-ranking officers retiring from the three services, it will be a de-novo approach by appointing some of these retired officers as chief executive officers in the districts. The role of the CEO is more managerial and would pertain to implementation of schemes, which can be best executed by retired officers from the armed forces. The CEO can be placed under the DC but should report directly to the state secretary. The concept has also been applauded in the questionnaire that was forwarded to district collectors in Tamil Nadu.
- **Emphasis on Innovation**. Innovation will hold the key to test new ways of addressing rural problems in the hope that some would subsequently be 'mainstreamed'. It is imperative to have an innovative management approach at the local level. This will require adequate funding from the Centre/State.
- **Emphasis on Integration**. The final hallmark of the 'RAPID' approach will be conforming to the wish of the local people and their programmes, which are multi-sectoral, relating to vocational training, rural tourism and the promotion and marketing of rural products and are all genuinely integrated.

- **Improving Transparency and Accountability**. Transparency and outward accountability is essential for greater cerebral responsiveness to the needs of the public and thus improve service quality and prevent bogus and inflated reporting.[19] Departments such as Police and Revenue, which have more dealings with the people, should be assessed once in three years by an independent commission consisting of professionals such as journalists, retired judges, ex-servicemen, academicians, activists and retired government servants.
- **Local Partnership Approach**. This will require to consolidate the 'Local Action Groups' to devise and draw up local action plans to organise their work in local needs and resources, as also to determine how the limited funds available will be distributed between competing project applicants. This will require partnership by all living in the RAPID areas.
- **National Level**. The national institution for transforming India, the Niti Aayog, under the chairmanship of the prime minister has a vice-chairperson, two full-time and two part-time members, ex-officio members, and chief executive officer. At present, there is no representation from the armed forces. Among the two part-time members, one could be a retired officer with more than 25 years of experience from the uniformed forces. This member will ensure due exploitation of the capabilities of our ex-servicemen towards the overall objectives of this Aayog.
- **Physical Distribution Strategy**. Problems of warehousing and storage in the rural marketing context are well known. It is not possible to service interior outlets efficiently with the existing warehouses. Hence, rural warehousing corporations should be established with warehousing facilities in each of the RAPID cluster headquarters. Technical knowledge and expertise of ex-servicemen from the Engineers and MES branches of the three services should be exploited to construct and man these warehouses.
- **RAPID Management and Monitoring Bodies**. The concept of RAPID clusters is akin to the existing arrangement of tehsils. However while tehsil panchayats can be the execution organs, there is a requirement of separate RAPID management bodies to

supervise and monitor the progress of the development schemes. These bodies should be directly reporting to the state secretary and should have representation from civil society, civil administration and mid-rank retired uniformed forces officers.

- **State Administration**. In a state, there are a large number of planning and implementing bodies responsible for the execution of a particular scheme. All these bodies should have independent representatives from retired high officer ranks of the uniformed forces and civil society, whose task should be to ensure timely and 'graft free' implementation of projects. They should report directly to the chief secretary/chief minister of the state. This will put a cap on corruption by bringing in greater accountability of the state mechanism.
- **Tehsil and Village Level**. The existing concept of tehsils (groupings of 3-4 villages) needs to be made more responsive by having regulatory and monitoring mechanisms at the gram panchayat and block samiti levels. These two bodies have to incorporate retired Junior Commissioned Officers/Non-Commissioned Officers of the uniformed forces in their functioning. This will ensure greater efficiency, transparency, credibility and reduce corruption at the functional levels.

Ex-Servicemen: A Resource Untapped – Reality Check

Rural development has at last received recognition in India's nation building activity. After forty years of independence, the bureaucratic imprint of ineptitude has been strongly revealed at the village level. The bullock cart and cow dung are still the indeterminate core of economic ethos. The local level politician is steeped in age-old petty parochialism and greed. The arm of the law makes an occasional hazy, indeterminate appearance and judicial relief seems but an ever-lengthening shadow of unfulfilled hopes. The average citizen hemmed in from all sides by de-motivating forces seeks solace in the age-old philosophy of fatalism, which according to one interpretation, ends in accepting and indirectly eulogizing incompetence and failure as a preordained manifestation of Karma.

The nation's existing lifestyle cannot be wished away. The criminalisation of politics and the resultant systemic erosion of our institutions have made deep inroads into our age-old value system. At the village and higher functional levels, everyone demands his pound of flesh in a cascading pattern of a cost-benefit equation. Each functionary, instead of being a catalyst for national development, has an inborn instinct to thrust a millstone of parochial envy into the already indolent and non-accountable administrative system. Our suspicion-oriented, financial and bureaucratic rules and regulations act as cobwebs of frustration to speedy decision-making and modernisation.

Various statistics drawn up by the Planning Commission and similar government and private agencies reveal that of all the allocations made for the growth and development of the rural areas, not more than 5 per cent of the intended allocations reaches the actual beneficiary. This wholesale sieving of financial resources through mismanagement, through devious politico-bureaucratic design and through deep–rooted corruption, would put any upright nation or people to shame. Ours, of course, is a different ethos and this is condoned as is every other indiscretion, big or small. This has now become our way of life.[20]

Over the last six decades, there are some agencies of the government that have proved, time and again, their total dedication to national interests and their ability to execute assigned tasks with efficiency. One such organisation is the nation's armed forces, paramilitary forces and other uniformed organisations. About 60,000 officers and men retire from the armed forces every year; the men between the ages of 35 to 45 are essentially from a rural background and return to their villages where they get disoriented in the quagmire of despondency. Similar is the case with the uniformed personnel from paramilitary forces and others. This trained and disciplined manpower, which spans a large variety of disciplines, both at the conceptual and executive levels, is a major loss because it is not formally nursed and re-utilised for the overall development of the nation but allowed to dissipate.

Working on the availability of the past 10 years, we would probably have more than five lakh personnel available, of which, to begin with, about one lakh may be willing to join the rural development programme if formally structured at the national, state, regional, district and village levels. We need to create a national-level workforce to undertake the task of rural development. A disciplined and well-trained force is available to the nation. The nucleus of this force could be provided primarily by retired personnel from the uniformed forces of the nation. By doing so, the nation would benefit manifold.

Uniformed Services: A Reservoir of Trained and Experienced Human Resources. Approximately 60,000 personnel are released annually from the three armed forces. The analysis in this thesis has been done based on the data of personnel retiring only from the Indian Army. However, a similar number of trained and disciplined manpower retires every year from the Indian Air Force, Indian Navy, Border Security Force, CRPF, ITBP, State police departments, etc. Age-wise availability of skilled manpower is as under:

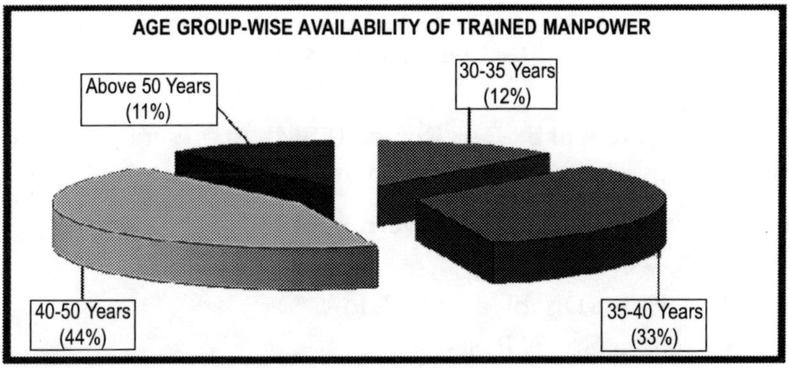

Figure 4.3. Age Group-wise Availability of Trained Manpower

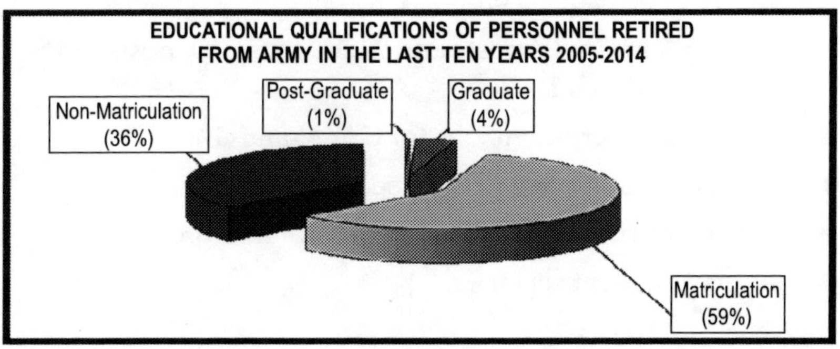

Figure 4.4. Educational Qualifications of Personnel Retired from Army in the Last Ten Years

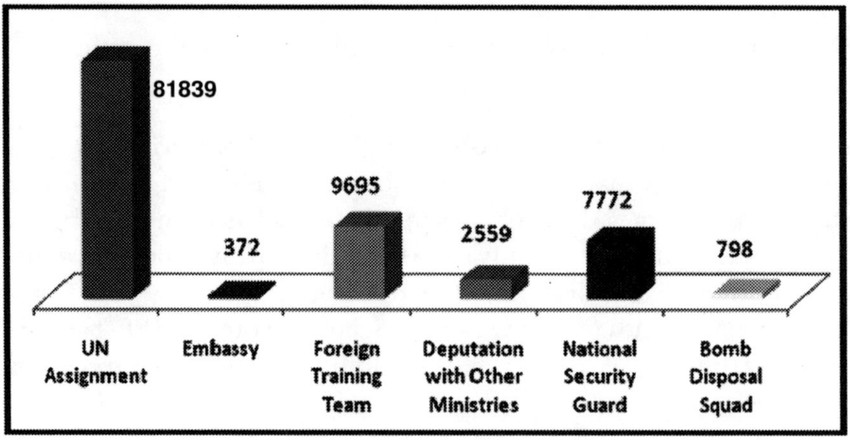

Figure 4.5. Service Experience of Army Personnel Retired in Last Ten Years (2005-14)

Existing Employment of Ex-Servicemen (ESM). At present, ex-servicemen are being employed in the following manner:

- **Reservation in Central Government Jobs**.
  - 10% in Gp 'C' Posts.
  - 4.5% for Disabled and Widows.
  - 20% in Gp 'D' Posts.
  - 10% Posts up to Asst. Commandant in Central Para-Military Forces.
  - 100% in Defence Service Corps.
  - 14.5% in Gp 'C' posts and 24.5% in Gp 'D' posts in PSUs and Nationalised Banks.
- Priority in government jobs for Gp 'A' and 'B'.
- Jobs in Corporate and Private sectors.
- Lateral absorption in Central Para Military Forces.
- Self-employment schemes.

Dept.		EXISTING				NEW RECRUITMENT			
	Reservation %	Overall Strength	ESM Auth	ESM Held	ESM Deficiency %	Total vacancies in the year 2013	ESM vacancies authorised	ESM Employe d	ESM Deficiency
GROUP 'B'									
CAPF	10	2689	269	7	262 (97%)	1007	101	0	101 (100%)
GROUP 'C'									
Bank	14.5	185006	26825	4767	21358	55430	8037	2166	5871
PSU	14.5	37965	5505	659	5846	3679	533	35	498
Central Govt.	10	662	66	5	61	303	30	0	30
CAPF	10	25776	2578	169	2409	25048	2505	127	2378
Total		249409	34974	8300	28674 (82%)	84460	11105	2328	8777 (79%)
GROUP 'D'									
Bank	24.5	88980	21800	9797	12003	19020	4660	901	3759
PSU	24.5	5911	1448	136	1312	171	42	2	40
Central Govt.	20	334	66	13	53	-	-	-	-
CAPF	20	-	-	-	-	-	-	-	-
Total		95225	23314	9946	13368 (57%)	19191	4702	903	3799 (80%)

Table 4.2. Employment of Ex-Servicemen in Government Jobs

STATE	GAZZETTED POSTS							
	GP A /CL I 1	RES (%) 2	AUTH ESM VAC 3	GP B/CL II 4	RES(%) 5	AUTH ESM VAC 6	TOTAL VACS 1+4	TOTAL ESM VACS 3+6
HARYANA	7950	05%	397	11130	05%	556	19080	953
KARNATAKA	20075	10%	2007	28105	10%	2810	48180	4817
PUNJAB	9150	13%	1189	12810	13%	1665	21960	2854
CHANDIGARH	750	13%	97	1050	13%	136	1800	223
GUJARAT	15175	01%	152	21245	01%	212	36420	364
HIMACHAL PRADESH	6175	15%	926	8645	15%	1297	14820	2223
MANIPUR	1700	-	-	2380	02%	48	4080	48
ORISSA	11050	-	-	15470	03%	464	26520	464
UTTRAKHAND	4000	08%	320	5600	08%	448	9600	768
TOTAL	76025		5088	106435		7636	182460	12724

Table 4.3. Employment of Ex-Servicemen in Gazetted Jobs[21]

State	Non-Gazeted Posts							
	GPB, C/CL III	RES (%)	Auth ESM VAC	GP D/CL IV	RES (%)	Auth ESM VAC	Total VACS	Total ESM VAC
Assam	279720	02	5594	75600	02	1512	355320	7106
Chhattisgarh	113220	10	11322	30600	20	6120	143820	17442
Goa	46620	02	932	12600	02	252	59220	1184
Haryana	235320	14	32945	63600	14	8904	298920	41849
Delhi	185000	10	18500	50000	20	10000	235000	28500
Karnataka	594220	10	59422	160600	10	16060	754820	75482
Madhya Pradesh	428460	10	42846	115800	20	23160	544260	66006
Chandigarh	22200	10	2220	6000	20	1200	28200	3420
Mizoram	8880	10	888	2400	20	480	11280	1368
Nagaland	47360	5	6157	12800	5	640	60160	6797
Punjab	270840	13	35209	73200	13	9516	344040	44725
Rajasthan	564620	12.5	70577	152600	15	22890	717220	93467
Puducherry	18500	10	1850	5000	20	1000	23500	2850
Himachal Pradesh	182780	15	27417	49400	15	7410	232180	34827
West Bengal	396640	05	19832	107200	10	10720	503840	30522
Andhra Pradesh	677100	02	13542	183000	02	3660	860100	17202
Gujarat	449180	10	44918	121400	20	24280	570580	69198
J & K	120620	06	7237	32600	06	1956	153220	9193
Odisha	327080	03	9812	88400	03	2652	415480	12462
UP	842860	05	42143	227800	05	11390	1070660	53533
Uttarakhand	118400	5	5920	32000	05	1600	150400	7520
Tamilnadu	770340	05	38517	208200	10	20820	978540	59337
Manipur	50320	03	1510	13600	05	680	63920	2190
Tripura	97680	02	1954	26400	02	528	124080	2482
Maharashtra	1036000	15	155400	280000	15	42000	1316000	197400
Total	7883960		656664	2130800		228222	10014760	884886

Table 4.4. State-wise Employment of Ex-Servicemen in Non-Gazetted Posts (Gps C&D)

Aspirations and Reality Check. To analyze the research topic in greater detail, a study was undertaken by the Directorate-General of Resettlement, IHQ of MoD (Army) and feedback obtained from the environment regarding the aspirations of retiring personnel of the three services. A summary of the study is as under:

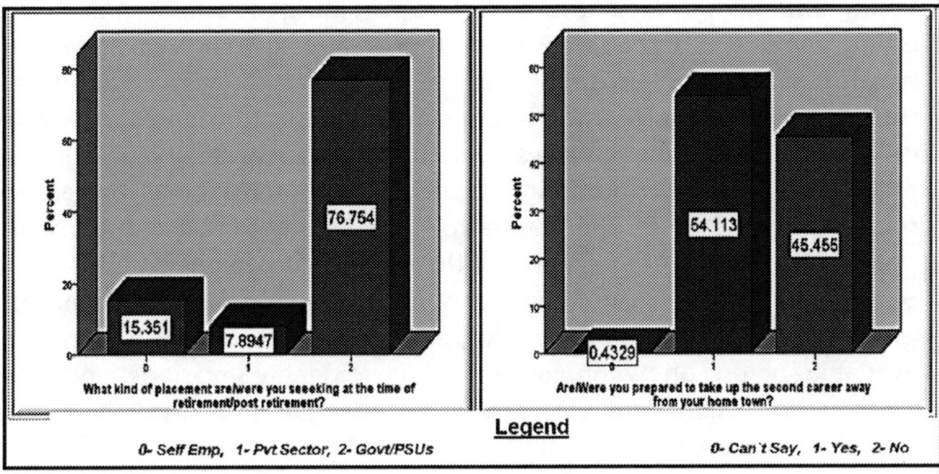

Figure 4.6. Aspirations of Retired Personnel

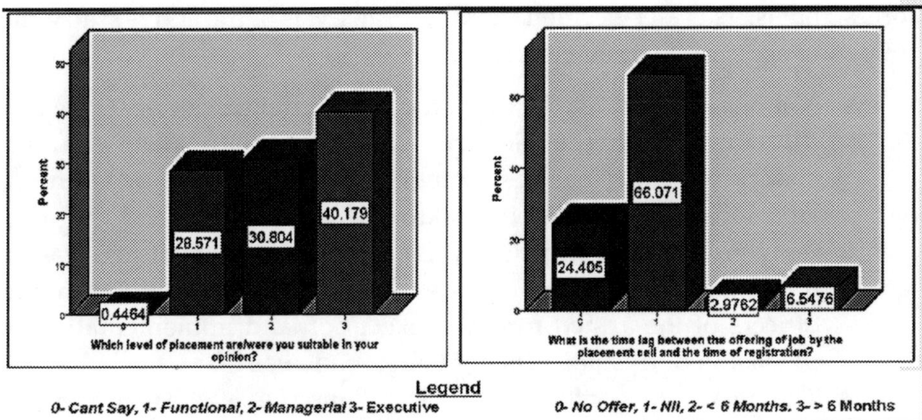

Figure 4.7. Status of Jobs Expected

Existing Dynamics: Analysis

The emergence of a welfare state, primarily because of industrial revolution, witnessed the state being gradually forced to take up the responsibilities of the well-being of its citizens. Ensuring full employment of its people till the age of 60 has now become one of the major welfare objectives of every state, irrespective of its nature or type. The Directive Principles of State

Policy of the Indian Constitution declare providing full employment to all its citizens as one of the state's most important goals. The goal so far has hardly been realised. No doubt, with the slow but impressive agricultural transformation, gradual accelerating industrialisation and large-scale deliberate expansion in services; there has been a marked increase in the number of vacancies and the employment potential has increased multifold.[22] However, the generation of seemingly vast employment potential has always fallen short of the number of persons wanting jobs, primarily because of the fast-multiplying population and tremendous growth in educated manpower. The gap between the number of vacancies available and persons wanting jobs has been widening since independence. The situation becomes more precarious because of the inability of the nation to tap the vast potential of skilled and experienced manpower already available in terms of its ex-servicemen.

The above study revealed certain glaring facets about the non-exploitation of trained, organised, and disciplined domain of the armed forces, that is, its ex-servicemen (ESM). On analysis of the above study, the following aspects emerged clearly:

- Neither is there any policy on the subject matter nor are there any directions from the Government of India to ensure lateral absorption and seamless integration of this pool of talented, laborious and disciplined workforce.
- Only nine states (including UTs) provide any sort of reservation for gazetted posts. The experience of the mid- and high-ranking officers of the armed forces in execution and implementation of the vision of the nation is not being made use of.
- The bulk of reservations is in Gp 'C' and 'D', whereas the Gp 'D' category has been abolished with effect from the 6th Pay Commission.
- The country has 22.5 lakh defence pensioners and the number increases by about 60,000 each year and less than 50 per cent are being engaged in the growth story of this great nation.
- The Government Sector (Central Armed Police Force (CAPF)/ ministries/departments/banks/PSUs) should be the largest employer. However, less than 20 per cent jobs earmarked for the ESM are utilised.
- There is no central data bank on the number of personnel

superannuating, their capabilities/expertise and corresponding link with the industry to ensure automatic absorption or follow the dictum of 'Right Man for The Right Job'.

- There is no Law/Bill/Act like ESM empowerment legislation and ESM Empowerment Act existing which formalises the involvement of ESM in nation building to include them both at the execution as well as governance levels. There is, therefore, a need to get a resolution passed which could address this critical issue.

Recommendations: Village to State Holistic Socio-Economic Growth

There are approximately 60,000 personnel who retire every year from the defence forces. About 44 per cent of the pensioners are in the age group of 40-50, 33 per cent in the 35–40-year age bracket, while 12 per cent of the people who leave the services are in the age group of 30-35 years. Optimal utilisation of this well-trained and young workforce exiting the services can yield multiple benefits. Firstly, it will exponentially raise the morale of Indian soldiers, Secondly, both private and public sectors can benefit by absorbing a skilled and disciplined workforce, and thirdly, employing ex-servicemen is cheaper for the government as compared to fresh recruitments they would be paid only the difference between their entitled emoluments and the pension being drawn by them.

About 80 per cent of ex-servicemen of the rank of JCOs and NCOs post retirement are settled in their villages. Investments incurred in the specialised training of ex-servicemen while in service should not be allowed to go waste or unutilised. It requires some time and money to make a man culturally rich to enable him to understand the importance of hard work, discipline, sincerity towards work, honesty in one's dealings, etc. Therefore, the training acquired in the army, both technical and moral, should not be allowed to go waste in order to ensure holistic growth from the grass root level up to the highest level in Indian states. The same also finds a mention in the questionnaire as replied to by Dr. P. Sankar, IAS, District Collector, Nilgiris, "The services of the ex-servicemen can be utilised not only in the RAPID model but also in various government sectors such as highways & road transport, ports & shipping, aviation, health, disaster relief, public works and infrastructure, supply chain management, e-Governance, transport, etc".

Measures for National Rural Socio-Economic Transformation. The following measures based on a detailed critical analysis, deep study and intensive interactions are recommended for holistic growth of our rural areas:

- **Impetus to Self-Employment**. The state government must encourage agro-industry based self-employment. This will involve the following:
    - A recent study by the Directorate-General of Resettlement, New Delhi, has revealed that most of the self-employed ex-servicemen in the villages are engaged in the agriculture sector. Support should be extended to the villagers (including retired defence personnel) to set up small industries like dairy farming, poultry, piggery, sheep and goat breeding, beekeeping, sericulture, etc.
    - Anti-poverty strategies, like assistance to rural poor families to raise them above the poverty line through the process of social mobilisation, training and capacity building.
    - Using science and technology for inclusive rural growth to include e-health care, distance education and. promoting e-governance in villages.
    - Infrastructure development through gram panchayats.
- **Industry to Penetrate Rural India**. The growth story of Indian industry is that of a success. Though all their products do reach rural areas and villages, the role of middlemen in the marketing of the produce end up making the products more expensive for rural consumers. It is therefore imperative for the industry to develop distribution capabilities in rural areas by:
    - **Distribution Planning**. The physical distribution system in rural markets includes transportation, storage, local delivery and sub-distribution. Reducing dead time between the points of production to the end user is of prime importance. Companies need to develop a barefoot approach and train local talent to operate as 'barefoot salesmen'. Ex-servicemen from the logistics branches of the three services who are residing in these villages have a knack for distribution management. Private industry has to tap this potential to penetrate the rural market in a more profitable and economical way.

- ❖ **Physical Distribution Strategy**. Problems of warehousing and storage in the rural marketing context are well known. It is not possible to service the interior outlets efficiently with the existing warehouses. Hence, rural warehousing corporations should be established with warehousing facilities in each of the RAID (Rural Area Integrated Development) cluster headquarters. The technical knowledge and expertise of ex-servicemen from the Engineers and MES branches of the three services should be exploited to construct and man these warehouse.[23]

- **Impetus by the Government**. To ensure holistic growth by involving ex-servicemen towards nation building, the government should undertake the following:
  - ❖ **Employment in Government Sectors**. Exploiting the technical expertise and capabilities of retiring personnel of the armed forces by employing them in the following government sectors:

Sl. No.	Government Sector	Field of Retired Defence Personnel
1.	Highways & Road Transport	Engineers of three services
2.	Port & Shipping	Navy
3.	Aviation	Air Force, Army Aviation
4.	Health	Medical Corps
5.	Disaster Relief	Engineers, Medical
6.	Public Works & Infrastructure	MES, Engineers
7.	Supply Chain Management	Logistic Branch
8.	E-Governance	Signals and Communication Experts
9.	Transport	EME & Vehicle Mechanics

Table 4.5. Field of Retired Defence Personnel

  - ❖ **Employment with Ministry of Defence (MoD)**. The MoD is a major employer of the civilian workforce. Organisations including ordnance factories (OFs), defence public sector undertakings (PSUs), defence research & development organisations (DRDO), Directorate-General of Quality Assurance (DGQA), defence think-tanks, Canteen Stores Department and hospitals employ several hundred thousand civilians. Absorption of ex-servicemen in such organisations will increase overall synergy, reduce defence expenditure and increase the satisfaction levels of ex-servicemen.

- **Tax Concessions to India Inc**. India Inc. can effectively employ our ex-servicemen across functions, be it security, HR or procurement. However, the sad reality is that the bottom-line matters even for companies with a large heart. India should take a cue from the tax credit mechanism that was available in the USA for employers who hired veterans (ex-servicemen). For a US corporate employer, the tax credit can be as high as $ 9,660 for every qualified veteran hired. A similar model could be adopted by our Finance Ministry to provide tax concessions to companies that hire retired, or ex-servicemen based on their skill requirements. It is time to have a more cerebral approach and understand business realities. Further, there is a need to institutionalise this and make it a mandatory (rather than obligatory) provision under Corporate Social Responsibility (CSR).
- **Self-Employment Schemes**. The Department of Ex-Servicemen's Welfare offers a host of self-employment schemes but the demand which exists is far more than the availability. The government needs to create a climate which brings together industry as the franchisor, ex-servicemen as the franchisee and MoD as the facilitator, with the final aim of forging a win-win partnership which can boost the national economy.
- **Raising of Environmental Battalions**. The 'Swachh Bharat Abhiyan' and 'Ganga Rejuvenation Plan' are today national missions which can be best implemented by raising environment battalions staffed and manned by ex-servicemen from eco-battalions.[24]
- **Exploiting Pan-India Presence**. Perhaps one of the most important untapped advantages that ex-servicemen have is their presence across the length and breadth of the country. They are, therefore, the best candidates when it comes to Pan-India requirements. With the government planning to construct SEZs and associated infrastructure in terms of highways to connect them, there exists a scope to have a Welcom-Spot at every 50/100 km. These places can be hubs for refreshment, refuelling, repair, ATM services with ex-servicemen providing the nucleus of the staff. This is an example of just one of the many such opportunities that exist.

- **Rural Area Progressive Integrated Development (RAPID) Clusters**. The concept, staffing details, and methodology of RAPID has already been discussed at earlier. For ease of comprehension and clarity of thought on its evolution, paradigmatic changes and implementation pragmatism, the essential aspects of the same can be summarised diagrammatically as under:

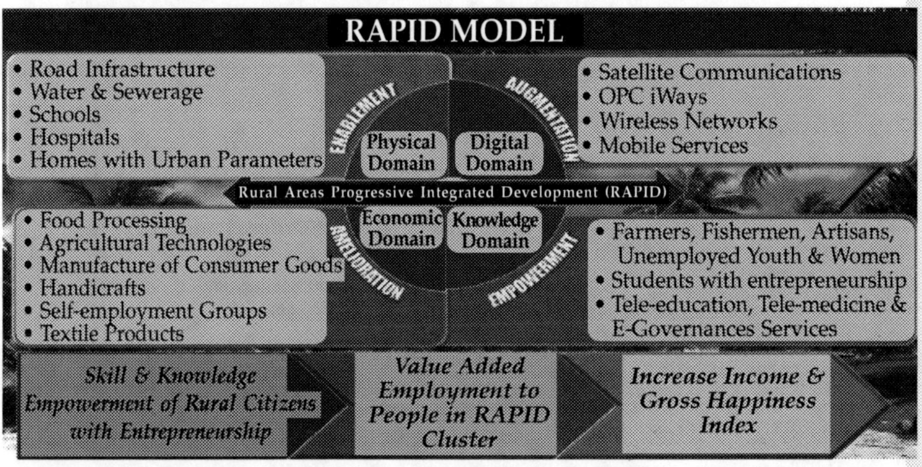

Figure 4.8. Structure: Rural Areas Progressive Integrated Development (RAPID) Model

APPROACH	• Area Based - geographical iden tity • Bottom-Up - local action groups to manage programmes • People-Public-Private-Partnership
EMPHASIS	• Innovation • Integration - multi-sectoral • Industry Participation - CSR
DISTRIBUTION	• Developing Supply Chains • Eliminating Middlemen • Technology Enabled
ADMINISTRATION	• RAPID Clusters • Management & Monitoring • Tehsil & Village Level - to include mid-level officers • District & State Level - to include Chief Exec Officer

Figure 4.9. Structure: (RAPID) Model: Implementation

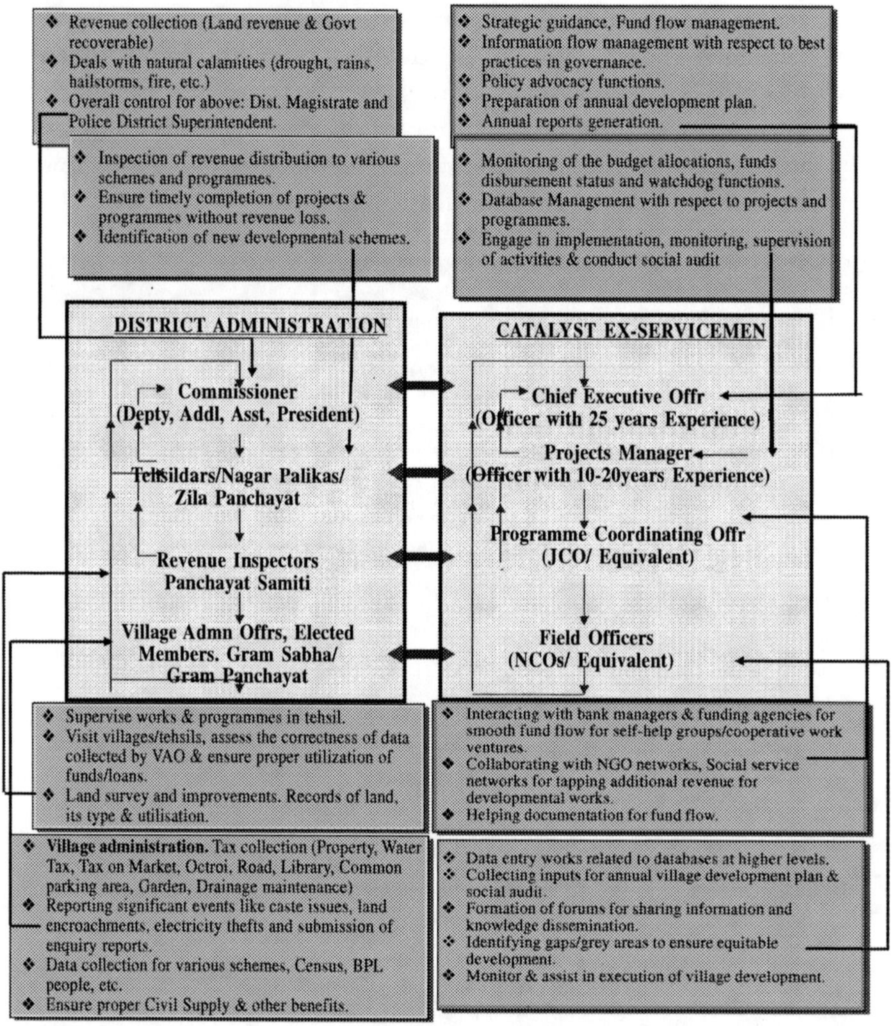

Figure 4.10. National Rural Socio-Economic Transformation Model through Civil

The above recommended model will ensure that the following numbers of retired uniformed personnel are incorporated into the overall growth story of the country through the grass root levels, thereby ensuring holistic growth of rural areas. The dream of creating a Smart/Ideal Village will soon become a reality.

S. No.	Body	Number	Recommended Number of Retired Uniformed Personnel	Total
1.	RAPID Clusters	10,000	1 x JCO/Equivalent 1 x NCO/Equivalent	20,000
2.	Gram Panchayats	239,582 (Census 2013)	1 x JCO/NCO (Equivalent)	239,582
3.	Tehsildars/Zila Panchayats	6,612	1 x Officer (10-15 Years' Experience)	6,612
4.	District Administration	676	CEO (25 Years' Experience)	676
5.	State Administration (Governing Bodies)	160 (Average of 5 per state and 2 per UT)	1 x Officer (30 Years' Experience)	160
6.	National Level	1	1 x 3/ 4 Star Officer	1

Table 4.6. Scope for Incorporating Retired Uniformed Personnel in Socio-Economic Transformation of Rural Areas

- **Resolution in the Constitution**. To ensure holistic growth of the nation by incorporating the retired uniformed personnel, it is imperative that the recommendations given above should be tabled in Parliament for passage of suitable legislation/resolution by the government for its implementation in entirety.

Implementation Methodology. The recommended model can be trial evaluated as a pilot project in the state having the largest number of districts and gram panchayats, followed by tabling a resolution/legislation in Parliament and its implementation in the rest of the country. It could be

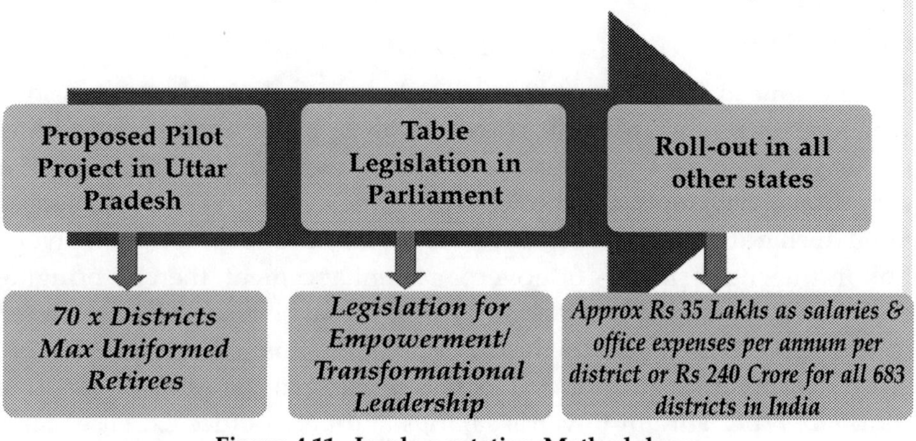

Figure 4.11. Implementation Methodology

The following thus far emerges from the above detailed enunciation in support of ex-servicemen and leadership, a paragon for rural development:

- There are many sensible steps that can be taken to improve governance. Focusing on outcomes rather than internal procedures would help, as would delegation of responsibilities. Retired officers of the armed forces are a highly experienced pool available in civil society, which if dovetailed into the planning and monitoring process of the various government schemes, will pay extremely rich dividends. The officers of this sector, because of their expertise in transformational leadership, not only have relatively better ability to perceive and plan things, but most importantly, their ability to lead from the front and complete assigned tasks with diligence. It is often said 'Growth of society will have to come from society itself', but rarely is this implemented. Hence, it is prudent to state that there is a need for delegation of responsibilities amongst various stakeholders, including ex-servicemen.
- The level of diversification in rural livelihoods in the last decade in rural India has undergone a drastic change. Rural enterprises and the rural non-agricultural sector are expanding more than agricultural enterprises. The number of non-agricultural establishments are growing in rural areas. Thus, there exist vast resources to be tapped in our rural areas if we want to ensure inclusive growth and follow the path of rapid development in the near future. Hence, there also exists the feasibility of an 'Alternative Rural Development Model' necessitated by new rural opportunities.

Conclusion

There is a need for 'Governance through Augmentation & Progression', which can be brought about at grassroots levels by ex-servicemen residing in villages, who, given their sense of commitment and ability to monitor execution of developmental projects, can mitigate the gravity of challenges faced during attainment of objectives. Thus, they can be the common pivotal link in the entire process of governance enhancement, thereby bringing about 'wholesome transformation'. The proposal given above, as reflected in Figure 3.12, highlights the broad issue of the financial effect of Rs. 240 crore incorporating the proposal for 683 districts, considering the aspect of Rs. 35 lakh per annum towards salaries and allied office expenses for a district. There could be a difference in all the given retrospective empirical data given above, as worked out a few years ago. However, the primary issue which requires cognitive action is that parliamentary legislation is deemed essential to institutionalise this concept, thereby giving validity and corresponding empowerment to ex-servicemen selected by identified rigorous processes to execute projects and alleviate conditions in rural areas with greater expediency for a 'Developed India'.

NOTES

1. George F. Gant. *The Concept of Development Administration*, Emerald Group Publishing Limited, 2006, pp. 257-285.
2. Keuning Wyte. *Ashoka The Great*, Rupa Publications, 2011, pp. 245-298.
3. Radhakumund Mookerji. *ASHOKA*, Motilal Banarsidas Publishers Pvt. Ltd., 2007, pp. 47-59.
4. Y. Subbarayalu. *South India Under The Cholas*, Oxford University Press, Dec. 2011, pp. 133-145.
5. Noboru Karashima. *A Concise History of South India: Issues and Interpretations*, Oxford University Press, Sept. 2014, pp. 87-91.
6. Ishtiaq Husain Qureshi. *Administration of the Mughal Empire*, Majestic Books, Dec. 2004, pp. 212-245.
7. Priyankan Goswami. 'Indian Democracy, Where Anna Hazare Failed', *Times of Assam*, Dec. 13, 2011.
8. Indira Hirway & Amrita Shah. *Growth or Development: Which Way Gujarat is Going*? OUP, Aug. 2014.
9. United Nations Development Programme, Human Development Report, United Nations, New York, 2004, p. 103.
10. Mark Turner & David Hulme. *Governance, Administration and Development*, London, MacMillan Press, 1997, pp. 24.
11. Dev J. Int & Harmut Schneider. 'Participatory Governance for Poverty Reduction', *Journal of International Development*, 1999, pp. 221-234.
12. Increasing Governance Capacity, *World Bank Report*, 1997.
13. A. Anttiroiko and Bailey, S. J. *Innovations in Public Governance*, IOS Press, May 2011, pp. 3-4
14. I. Kotlyar & L. Karakowsky. 'Falling Over Ourselves to Follow the Leader', *Journal of Leadership & Organisational Studies*, vol. 14, 2007, pp. 38-47.
15. Dalal Clayton & D. B. Bass. *Sustainable Development Strategies: A Resource Book*, Earthscan, Canada, Oct. 2002, pp. 78-80.
16. Ibid, pp. 85-92.
17. V. Anttiroika and Bailey S. J.. *Innovations in Public Governance*, IOS Press, New York, 2011, p. 6.
18. Awadesh K. Singh. 'Rural Marketing: Indian Perspective', *New Age International*, 2005, pp. 205-207.

19. Singh, P. K. and Sandeep Deewan, *Comprehensive National Power: A Model for India*, Vij Books, New Delhi, 2013, pp. 177-179.
20. Rear Admiral Sattyindra Singh, AVSM. 'Ex Servicemen as an Instrument of National Development'.
21. Data collected from Directorate-General Resettlement, IHQ of MoD (Army) in May 2015.
22. Satyendra Kishore. *Re-Settlement of Ex-Servicemen in India: Problems, Patterns and Prospects*, Concept Publishing Company, New Delhi, 1991, pp. 22-26.
23. Awadesh Kumar Singh. *Rural Marketing: Indian Perspective*, New Age International, 2005, pp. 205-207.
24. Sanjay Sethi. "Initiatives for Exploiting the Potential of Ex-Servicemen", *CLAWS*, April 2015, pp. 2-3.

5

A Citizens-First Approach: Insights into Good Governance

"Poverty is multidimensional. It extends beyond money incomes to education and healthcare, political participation and advancement of one's own culture and social organisation".

—Atal Bihari Vajpayee, Bharat Ratna

Introduction

On 25 December 2014, the Honourable Prime Minister, Shri Narendra Modi, on the occasion of the birth anniversary of former Prime Minister Shri Atal Bihar Vajpayee enunciated a very prudent Vision for Good Governance, namely, "Citizen First" as the mantra and the guiding principles, Simplification of procedures and processes in the government to make the entire system transparent and faster, Re-engineering government process, Redress of public grievances by ensuring responsive administration, Harnessing technology to bridge the divide between the government and the citizens, 'Digital India' aims to transform the country into a digitally empowered society and knowledge economy and Open and accountable administration and focus should be on 'Minimum Government but Maximum Governance'. The UNDP definition of good governance "encompasses three key words 'transparency, accountability, and participation'. Transparency is the scrupulous functioning of government and all institutions, ensuring the sharing of information with the entire population, public engagements for decisions, directions, and implementable policies and accountability. Government is accountable to the citizens of the country on agreed principles of constitutional rights and duties to ensure proper audit, accountability, monitoring, and enforcement through guidelines & strict legal action against defaulters. Thereafter, it is participation, which encompasses aspects of sound and timely decision-making, deliberations on good governance and getting citizens closer to the government contributing to progression with the desired functional ethos.

Comprehensive critical issues have been elucidated in the succeeding paragraphs which, if implemented and concluded in the correct perspective, would enhance the 'Good Governance' threshold in the country in urban and rural areas wherein ex-servicemen ofall ranks must be used in a very judicious and astute manner, for their valuable services contributing to the development of infrastructural projects and sustainable growth of the areas.

Long-Term Strategy

The national 'Gati Shakti' master plan synergises 16 ministries and seven core sectors, by incorporating infrastructure schemes of state governments like Bharatmala, Sagarmala, inland waterways, varied ports, UDAN, etc., which mandates implementation by a special committee, with a proposed 'Civil-Military Fusion' towards fast track conclusions, such that economic zones like textile clusters, pharmaceutical clusters, defence corridors, electronic parks, industrial corridors, fishing clusters, and agriculture zones are covered adequately to improve connectivity and make Indian businesses highly successful. Also, building and consolidating 'core strengths' in all ministries, resonating with the Niti Aayog and in keeping with national interests.

Creation of a suggested 'National Strategic Communications Authority of India' to essentially obviate equivocation of national issues and build cogent responsive mechanisms in conformity with the national agenda cleared by the PMO. Ministry of Information and Broadcasting (MIB), Ministry of Defence (MoD), Ministry of Culture Ministry of Home, certain dedicated NGOs, members of the FICCI, and select veterans of the Armed Forces.

Implementation of the 'Naresh Chandra Task Force Committee'[1] report and the recommendations thereof which would be extremely beneficial for the future security and governance of the country.

Establishment of Indian 'Think Tanks' in the important capitals of the 195 countries of the world, with whom we have significant strategic outcomes. On priority, these must be established in Washington DC, Moscow, Paris, London, Amsterdam, Berlin, Madrid, Tokyo, Canberra, Singapore, South Africa, Nigeria, Egypt, Israel, Brazil, etc. This contributes exponentially towards growth-oriented development as a strategic knowledge base to be used optimally by visiting Indian political and ministerial officials, dignitaries and eminent personalities.

Strategic Autonomy must be the edifice of our foreign policy and greater coherence mandated on strategic dialogues and concerned issues. Consistency, obligatory and continuity ensured as related to mutual respect for each other's territorial integrity and sovereignty, non-aggression against each other, non-interference in each other's internal affairs, equality and mutual benefit.

Maximising opportunities for economic resurgence, enhancing GDP, foreign exchange reserves (FOREX) and well-being of all citizens most essential, by adopting and sustaining a prudent policy response to global spillovers. Despite the Eurasian war, India must continue to navigate global and domestic challenges. Furthering the globalisation process in coming decades, concomitantly addressing domestic inequalities with commitment of resources for Social Welfare programmes for the disadvantaged.

The Indian Green Building Council (IGBC), the beacon for the green building movement in the country, emphasises use of less water, optimises energy efficiency, conserves natural resources, generates less waste and provides healthier spaces for occupants, as compared to a conventional building. Comprehensive 'Green Housing' schemes for medium income group (MIG), low income group (LIG), educational institutes, schools, and hospitals (including multi/super specialty), and multiplexes for healthier living standards of all strata of people. Slum areas to be demolished in the nation and people re-located in LIG housing. Improved connectivity to all residential housing with compulsory arboriculture layout.

Indian agriculture reforms to be initiated and implemented in three years with an agricultural development strategy after appropriate all-party meetings, consensus and consequently parliamentary legislation. This would further increase agricultural productivity and household income for smallholder farmers, enabling equitable consumption of safe, affordable, and nutritious diet for the people.

India's National Water Development Agency, Ministry of Jal Shakti, has prepared reports on 67 inter-link projects for the Himalayan component, the peninsular component and intra-state river-linking projects. Interlinking of rivers, canals and distributaries in our country requires to be acclerated to cater for basic necessities of drinking water, irrigation and prevent droughts and floods. The respective states with contentious water quota problems should not prevaricate over the process but settle the criticality with bilateral dialogues in timelines.

Thrust on Collective Citizenry Responsibility approach to ensure India becomes a developed country in the next two decades. In addition to the intrinsic democratic value, participation is an instrumental driver of democratic and socio-economic change, and a fundamental way to empower citizens.

Veterans and ex-servicemen are a patriotic force nurturing progressive ideology and are constantly involved in strategised planning catering for contingencies whilst in their military careers. They are excellent assets as guarantors of optimised outcomes in various government/non-government organisations and civil enterprises. Suitable positions could be tenanted by ex-servicemen, thereby mitigating security hazards and improved productivity.

National Security

- Conceptualisation and finalisation of the document mandated on 'National Security Strategy' in concert with ministries by a designated committee authorised by the National Security Advisor (NSA), towards strengthening military capabilities, internationally benchmarked strategic institutions, meeting security challenges and development of the economy. The Indian strategic community to assist the government multi-disciplinary thinking on global futures, the nuclear posture and national security strategy, instead of governmental furtive secrecy.

- Concerted emphasis on human security to secure the country from both external and internal threats. India is the second largest consumer of petroleum products after China. To sustain the present growth rate, the energy requirement would increase by two times.
    - ❖ Need to have major understanding with energy-rich countries in West Asia, Africa, Central Asian Region, and Southeast Asian countries and develop pipelines through MOUs in the next five years, bypassing Pakistan.
    - ❖ Develop strategic partnerships based on mutual economic interests with countries in these regions and all five Central Asian Republics (CARs).
    - ❖ Invest in renewable energy resources, namely, wind, biomass, solar and small hydro, to revolutionise electrification of hamlets, smart villages, and cities in our country.
- Integration of National Security apparatus at the apex level to ensure maximum accountability and high-level synergy. This should include integration of the multi-intelligence agencies, armed forces, CPMF and state police.
- Shaping of strategic military dialogues with friendly foreign countries, promotion of politico-military diplomacy.
- Security being the 'sine qua non' of a advanced, secure democratic society, it is suggested that multi-agencies of intelligence could enrol ex-servicemen for cohesive and result based efficient outfits at the state and national level. Likewise, veteran officers could be suitably positioned in the intelligence/security matrix of the nation for enhanced role in leadership positions.

Containing Threat of Left-Wing Extremism

Left-wing extremism, also known by various other names such as Naxalism and Maoism, is a form of armed insurgency against the state motivated by leftist ideologies. Need to create enhanced confidence building measures (CBMs) and sensitisation of government machinery.

- Advanced weapon systems, sensors, night vision devices, helicopters, UAVs and equipment for the Central Armed Police Forces (CAPFs); sanction of India Reserve (IR) battalions, setting up of counterinsurgency and anti-terrorism (CIAT) schools; modernisation and upgradation of the state police and their intelligence apparatus.

- Empowerment of tribals by respecting their culture and traditions and including them in the governance of the tribal areas with popular moderate leaders. Educate youth on advantages of peace and development in the region.
- If the 'Peace Accord' fails, then conduct one-time strategised application of joint special forces (SF) and well-planned paramilitary forces in 22 districts (Naxal corridors in nine states of the country) infested by the Naxal menace, with assistance of the Army and Air Force.
- In consonance with the government policy, it is imperative that MHA should employ suitably qualified outstanding ex-servicemen in all the nine states affected by LWE (as selected by DGR) to effectively train CAPs at designated 'Centres of Excellence' to neutralise the Naxals. The local ex-servicemen soldiers and veterans would act as force multipliers in imparting contemporary counterinsurgency fighting mechanisms towards meaningful outcomes.
- Initiate a 'Peace Accord' with tribal leaders for sustained stability and prosperity (akin to the Mizoram Accord) through incentivised policies. Surrender policy imperative in Naxal-affected states. Government must offer lucrative money to surrendered Naxalites, a monthly allowance, agricultural land, and educational and health benefits to their children.
- Making the locals of the region part of growth and development programmes.
- Optimise the 'Greyhounds' operations (elite commando force of Andhra Pradesh created to combat left-wing extremists) in synergy with CAPFs. It is considered the best anti-Naxalite force in the country, an effective organisation and recruits the best personnel from Andhra Pradesh Police.
- Socio-economic development, education, healthcare, more employment opportunities and infrastructural facilities in affected tribal areas on priority through a GOI policy on the subject.

Rule of Law

- **Judicial Reforms.** "The Three Pillars of Democracy" in the Constitution, are Legislature, Executive and Judiciary. Judicial reform is the complete or partial political reform of a country's judiciary, often done as part of a wider reform of the country's political system or a legal reform.

- ❖ Multispectral areas of judicial reform are codification of law instead of common law, moving from an inquisitorial system to an adversarial system, establishing stronger judicial independence with judicial councils or changes to appointment procedure, establishing mandatory retirement age for judges or enhancing independence of prosecution. These must be in vogue with transparency.
- ❖ The judges need to adapt to various reforms, including administrative reforms to overcome the lingering gap in the number of cases in the Indian judiciary. Also, there is a large vacancy in the number of judges resulting in delays in cases, which has slowed the country's justice system. Removal of judicial backlog of GOI cases/others will increase accessibility of justice for a common man, through 'Fast Track' Tribunals, incentivized by the GOI.
- ❖ The apex judiciary body, namely, the Supreme Court of India, to analyse and in consultation with Central Government and State high courts adopt a prioritised 'Fast Disposal' concept of all pending judicial cases. Time bound trials, the concept of time frame, should be followed.
- ❖ The collegium system and judges' appointment is mandatory to maintain transparency. Selection of high court judges should be through a obvious and public mechanism so that the right candidate is chosen to sit in the constitutional courts. Pro bono cases by 20 per cent advocates is suggested for the poor who can ill afford the legal expenses.
- ❖ Live hearings of PILs refers to litigation undertaken to secure public interests and demonstrate the availability of justice to socially disadvantaged parties. Revenue courts specifically deal with matters related to land revenue where the sufferers are poor farmers; hence, to regulate them, the state should provide them with proper resources and infrastructure to work effectively.

- **Police Reforms.** Police reform aims to transform the old cultures, policies and practices of the police organisation so that they optimise performance with respect of democratic values, human rights and rule of law. Police reform aims to maintain law and order in the state with better audit, accountability, monitoring, enforcement and transparency in the work.

- ❖ Implementation of the Supreme Court ruling of 22 September 2006 to make the police more 'people-centric' rather than 'ruler-centric' to be encouraged. Improving the ratio of providing security policemen for the protection of citizens of India.
- ❖ Establishing a staff security commission (SSC), as directed by the Supreme Court in 2006 to act as a watchdog with members from the government, judiciary, and civil society to ensure that 'state governments do not exercise unwarranted influence using pressure on the state police'.
- ❖ Modernised weapon systems, equipment with AI equipment, machine learning, unmanned aerial vehicles (UAVs) and training of police forces (like armed forces) to make them an effective and credible force. Impressive police uniforms, headgear and footwear.
- ❖ Judicial inquiry imperative for custodial rapes, deaths, injuries and deaths in police firings. Political interference in police work to be mitigated. Recommended measures to make the police more sensitive to the needs and complaints of the marginalised sections of society.

Policy on Empowerment

There are basically three dimensions of empowerment: self-empowerment through individual action, mutual empowerment that is interpersonal and social empowerment as the outcomes of social action. The fundamental aim is to to restore meaning to work, based on a clear vision, mission and set of goals and foster a team spirit while encouraging initiative and risk-taking:

- **Educational Opportunities**. Enhance educational opportunities for poor students. We should channelise education towards skill development and upgrade the merit of poor students. We could work on a policy of provision of 'long term' credit to poor students through public sector and cooperative credit institutions.

- **Galvanising Youth**
  - Build capacities through technical assistance and training of youth, youth organisations and institutes, through the Ministry of Youth Affairs.
  - Enable open, non-judgemental, and diverse forums for the young to learn skills, attitudes, behaviours, and values associated with active citizenship.
  - Imperative to enhance opportunities for direct youth engagement in social action for development activities.
  - Youth programs need to develop political and social awareness and perspectives among the young according to social justice values. The GOI must make sure that India's youth are prepared to take on industry, develop social enterprise, invent, innovate, work hard, and build a more prosperous nation.
- **Poverty Alleviation.** Need to identify persons below the poverty line correctly and make their 'data base'. This could be best achieved through the 'Aadhaar Card'[2] as well. Socio-economic transformation of all villages through civil administration, ex-servicemen/CPMF (retired) leadership ensuring progressive villages, as suggested in the earlier chapters of this book.
- **Reservation**. A committee formed by the GOI, should focus on primarilybenefitting society, and educationally and economically backward people and bring them at par so that the nation-state is able to harness most suitable talent through good education, skill development, and employment of youth. Reservation on castes should not be the criteria, but poverty mitigation should, on the contrary, be paramount consideration for privileges.
- **Women Empowerment**. Women's empowerment refers to the process of increasing women's access to control over the strategic life choices that affect them and access to opportunities that allow them to fully realise their capacities; it can be defined in five separate categories, namely, social, educational, economic, political, and psychological. Social empowerment might be one of the most prominent forms of empowerment as it strengthens women's social relations and their position in social structures outside of the home, incorporating success tenets of learning, labour and leadership.

Generation of Employment

The Centre for Monitoring Indian Economy (CMIE), a private organisation, estimates India's unemployment rate in India at around 8.3 per cent at present. It is 10.09 per cent in urban India whereas it is only 7.44 per cent in rural India. To generate employment, it is important to have better education, which forms the human capital leading to economic growth and development.

Industries, MNCs and establishment of domestic industries increases job opportunities and improves the standard of living.

- In view of the Youth Bulge, that is, the 15-59 age group in the next decade, the focus of the GOI should be on providing education that enhances youth with vocational skills. The average age will be 29 years in India by 2020, dynamically changing in the years thereafter.
- Send a mix of skilled and unskilled youth labour to foreign countries for execution of medium- and long-term projects, akin to China's overseas exploratory and exploitation processes, which has been highly beneficial in providing employment and settling their people abroad, with consequent remuneration to the nation, thereby improving the GDP and economy in perspective.
- The GOI must ensure employment opportunities in agriculture, R&D, biodiversity of eco systems, afforestation, and employ a large number of youth and technically qualified women in national projects and schemes. Foreign companies in India to employ youth for improving their enterprises and the Indian economy.
- There is a need to expand coverage of MNREGA[3] and accelerate the pace of implementation of the 'Bharat Nirman'[4] Scheme. Encourage public-private sector partnerships and self-help groups and micro-financing institutions.
- The government could consider cutting taxes to businesses, enabling them to hire more workers, increase the ability of businesses to take loans from them to employ more workers, use public works projects to put more people to work and improve the infrastructure of the nation. Lastly, it can maximise programmes of 'Skill India', 'Make in India' and 'Digital India' to progress towards superpower status.

Balanced Regional Diversity

It is extremely significant for developmental progression to ensure that certain issues are borne in mind to obviate regional diversity in the country. These are, namely, Historical factor, Geographical factors, Location specific advantages, Early mover advantage, Failure of planning mechanism, Restricted success of Green Revolution, Law and order problem and Higher resource transfers from the Centre to backward states.

- Focus on high quality of corrupt-free governance and efficient administration with very proficient and ethical leadership provided by topline management.
- High level of investment in northern, north-eastern and eastern states of India through industrialisation, agriculture reforms and planned modern infrastructure development.
- Generation of employment among youth in rural areas in northern, north-eastern and eastern states through corporate and GOI services sector.
- It is advisable to strengthen local governments and make them responsible and accountable and a system of rewarding respective states (including developed states) achieving significant reduction in intra-state disparities could be introduced.
- Public enterprises to be set up by the government to provide industrial growth in those regions that have the least industrial activities. They could also be in collaborative form with foreign companies, which helps to accelerate economic development, provide employment to the work force and thereafter develop a huge industrial base. In this manner, the government could maintain the desired regional balance in the country.

Delivery of Services in Social Sector

Social services are a spectrum of public services providing support and assistance towards specific groups, which commonly include the disadvantaged. They may be provided by individuals, private and independent organisations, or administered by a government agency. Social services relate to the concept of welfare and the welfare state, as countries with large welfare programs often provide a wide range of social services. Social services are employed to address the wide range of needs of a society. Prior to industrialisation, the provision of social services was largely confined to private organisations and charities, with the extent of its coverage limited. Social services are regarded globally as a 'necessary function' of society and a mechanism through which governments may address vital societal issues. There could be disproportionate and unprecedented positive dividends by enrolment of ex-servicemen and veterans in specific positions, coveted and otherwise, ensuring commensurate gains, in keeping with their eligibility criteria.

- Encouraging the judiciary, media, and civil society is necessary for ensuring better accountability from the systems and structures entrusted, with delivery of services towards social upliftment. They consist of facilities and services such as: public education, welfare, infrastructure, mail, libraries, social work, food banks, universal health care, police, fire services, public transportation and public housing. There should be a focused pragmatic approach by the municipalities, commissioners and all administrators to upgrade and modernise facilities for the citizenry.
- Implement the model of 'One-Day Governance' and 'Non-One day Governance' nationwide, which will have a positive impact on society and nation building. Implement SWAGAT (State-wide Attention on Public Grievances by Application of Technology) effectively in all states/UTs.
- Social services played a central role in the global response to the COVID-19 pandemic. Healthcare workers, public officials, teachers, social welfare officers and other public servants have provided critical services in containing the pandemic and ensuring that society functions. The impact of the pandemic was compounded by the shortage of social services globally, with the world requiring millions of more nurses and midwives to achieve the goals set by the Sustainable Development Goals at the time of the outbreak of COVID-19.
- Social services, such as education, adopted the 'online' model of education and 'online' healthcare services with telemedicine, established polyclinics for vaccinations to billions in India and vaccine diplomacy by sending Indian vaccines abroad to many nations was eulogised by the UN leadership. Social services have expanded worldwide through the introduction of economic stimulus packages, with governments globally committing billions

in funding in 2020 to manage the pandemic. Permanent solutions and structures to be in place by the government.

- 'Swachhta' campaign launched by the Prime Minister of India had a positive impact on society and 'climate change' benefitted tremendously with the movement. States must continue to incentivise people and organisations to maintain hygiene, sanitation and cleanliness as partof the mission to become a developed nation by 2047.

Urban Planning

Planning was first initiated in India in 1938 by Congress President and Indian National Army supreme leader Netaji Subhash Chandra Bose. Later, Jawaharlal Nehru was made head of the National Planning Committee. In this millennium, urban planning greatly affects our transportation system, infrastructure, layout, and prescribed densities of our residential, commercial, and industrial areas and more, than in the retrospective sense. It is significant for ex-servicemen and specialised veterans to be absorbed in various urban planning committees and at the execution level for expediency in completion of envisaged projects by judiciously utilising financial resources in areas of poverty mitigation, employment generation, water conservation, energy utilisation, transportation, environment etc.

- Due consideration for green areas and regeneration and renewal/ of neglected historic districts and derelict inner-city areas. All the 'dead zones' identified in the cities/townships, whether out of litigation, no legal claimant, or impounded properties must be examined by mayors and councillors and within timelines to be auctioned by the government for implementation of developmental schemes.
- Ensuring a fixed viable tenure for district magistrates/collectors/ commissioners and project planning directions given for suitable monitoring and time-bound completion of development projects.
- Focus on making land available and affordable housing including finance for low-income population with infrastructure and desired service delivery, preventing slum areas and encroachments. The public sector offers opportunities to explore policymaking, infrastructure development, public housing, real estate development, etc. The prerogative lies with the government and Niti Aayog, Ministry of Housing and Urban Affairs (MoHUA) with

executive authority over the formulation and administration of the rules and regulations and laws relating to housing and urban development in India.

- Integrated city/township planning for land use and transportation. Development of smart cities along growth corridors in a framework of transit orientation and related land use planning. Encourage growth of smart villages, as philosophised in the earlier chapters of this book.
- Reform-oriented political leadership to give priority to urban planners in the country to establish modern environmentally friendly infrastructures and sustainable systems, conforming to a holistic concept of climate change dynamics.
- Urban planning must ensure that cities modernise with growth and hyper trajectory developmental facilities, and should have a positive impact on the economy, improve the lifestyle of people and living standards, incorporating simpler bureaucratic procedures to enables civil society to navigate the system timely and ensure quality delivery of services.

Capacity Building of the Nation

Capacity-building is defined as the process of developing and strengthening skills, instincts, abilities, processes and resources that organisations and communities need to survive, adapt, and thrive in a fast-changing world. The UN system applies it in almost every sector, including several of the Sustainable Development Goals to be achieved by 2030. For example, Sustainable Development Goal 17 advocates enhanced international support for capacity building in developing countries to support national plans to implement the 2030 Agenda.

Professionalism of the Civil Service

- Access to information, participation, innovation, and accountability, thereby ensuring progression in multifaceted domains. Avoid 'Status Quoist' concepts and stagnation emerging from 'comfort zones' of those mediocrities who do not allow organisations to develop by innovating and enterprising employees.
- Good leadership (young generation) towards improving the organisation culture with enhanced professional and intellectual abilities to attain objectives.

- Professionalisation of the civil service, based on principles of meritocracy, efficiency, effectiveness, transparency and accountability with a keen sense of propriety and commitment to the department and society is an important factor in ensuring the competitiveness of public administration and the provision of public services quality.
- Subordinate staff to behave responsibly with good morals and high integrity and produce desired results, as envisioned by the department. Must follow the desired code of conduct and adopt sterling qualities that characterise accepted practices in the organisation alongwith good demeanour and deportment.

Decentralisation of Power/Empowerment of Local Levels of Administration

In essence, administrative decentralisation involves the transfer of decision making authority, resources and responsibilities for the delivery of selected public services from the central government to lower levels of government, agencies, and field offices of central government line agencies.

- Administrative decentralisation seeks to redistribute authority, responsibility and financial resources for providing public services among different levels of government. A collegiate effort would ensure better accounting, monitoring and progressive working ethics for the benefit of the citizenry in all domains of political, economic, finance, etc.
- Problem manifestation determines the decision for decentralisation, namely, the size and complexity of the organisation, dispersal of operations, degree of diversification, availability of competent personnel, outlook of the top management, nature of functions of the organisation, communications system, planning and control procedures.
- The advantages of decentralisation are that a large number of problems and issues are best settled at the local level. People have a better knowledge of their local problems, better management of functions in an efficient manner, not with profligacy, and they participate directly in decision-making and progressive mode of functioning. Decentralised decision-making promotes innovation, creativity and entrepreneurship and improves employee engagement and multiplies productivity.

Optimisation of Human Resources

The new approach is referred to as "Human Resource Optimisation" (HRO). It means understanding the skills required for a job, understanding an employee's strengths and weaknesses, and then finding a way to leverage the strengths and minimise the weaknesses to get the job done effectively. ***'WORKPLACE should be called GROWTH PLACE'***.

- Focal areas should be consistent with talent management, compensation and employee benefits, training and development, compliance and workplace safety for greater and more meaningful gains.
- Improve HR effectiveness by proper selection of resources by exploiting the strengths and competency of individuals in leadership positions or otherwise, improve organisational communication, develop an effective training program, provide more regular feedback to employees, build a company's cultural vision, harness available technology and take advantage of a database and its proliferation.
- Workforce optimisation is a management practice and is strategically imperative to focus on improving the efficiency, productivity and performance of a company's employees. The overall goal is eternally to improve organisational success, attaining pinnacles of excellence. Workforce optimisation is firmly rooted in IT and human resource centres.

INFRASTRUCTURE DEVELOPMENT

The versatility of an ex-servicemen is indubitably established during his military career; therefore their skills should be exploited in multifaceted areas of communication networks, farming & agriculture, water energy, engineering projects, science & technology, education, renewable energy sector, research & development, social security, thereby contributing in a holistic dimension to the national economy. This optimised employability of ex-servicemen must be coordinated by the DGR and respective Placement Cells of tri-services with the ministries through department of ex-servicemen welfare, Ministry of Defence (MoD). It basically involves improvement of the quality of the various components of infrastructure, such as roads, power, ICT, water and sanitation. Infrastructure can also mitigate costs of delivered goods, facilitate the physical mobility of people and products, remove productivity constraints, and increase competitiveness. The following impetus can be given in infrastructure development for enhancing commercial activities:

Road-Rail-Air-Waterways Communication Network

- Construction of international airports in major industrial, educational and military centres of the country, for developing better civil-military fusion. Clean energy and public transit can reduce emissions of greenhouse gases. This same economics logic applies to broadband networks, water systems and energy production and distribution
- Dedicated road-rail corridors matrix for commercial movement, incorporating latest high-end technologies. Increasing the inland waterway capability in northern and eastern states for greater mobility and quality communication systems.
- Linkages of international airports, ports, rail and roads to increase the flexibility of transportation. Aviation is most critically important. Telecommunications, bridges across major rivers/gorges in mountainous regions, especially for military purposes, power and energy resources, railways, roadways and waterways, and waste management assume due importance.
- Road-rail link connectivity to all important manufacturing hubs and raw material centres for movement of bulk resources. Connecting SEZs with main links to ensure faster movement of resources through multimodal transportation systems.
- Waterways are the cheapest means of transport. They are most suitable for carrying heavy and bulky goods. It is a fuel-efficient and environment-friendly mode of transport. India has inland navigation waterways of 14,500 km in length. Waterways act as refuges for terrestrial fauna species during times of drought and as corridors for dispersal; they also support a wide variety of aquatic and terrestrial flora species and vegetation communities.

Commerce and Industry

Industry is concerned with the processing of materials and production of goods, whereas commerce is concerned with the distribution of those materials and goods. The chambers of commerce comprising cerebral business owners and entrepreneurs should perpetually promote the interests of the local business community. Chambers of commerce must optimise access to valuable resources, discounts, and relationships that help businesses save money and market their products with profitability, thus contributing to the economy.

- Develop strategic partnerships based on mutual economic interests with countries in these regions and all five Central Asian Republics (CARs).
- E-commerce is a highly beneficial trend and must be capitalised, namely AI enhances the reality of online shopping, AI helps shops strategise and learn about shoppers, big data plays a vital part in creating personalised experiences, Chatbots improve the shopping experience, mobile shopping and headless and API-driven ecommerce allow continued innovation, better customer responsiveness to videos. Sustainability is becoming more important. Businesses should optimise digital strategy for conversion.
- Encourage 'Start-up India', 'Make in India' and 'Digital India' programmes in a revolution throughout the country.
- Focus on core industries like steel, pharma, automobile, shipping, and agriculture machinery. Exploit IT base service industries.
- Focus on multi-enterprise partnerships combining their strengths in product design, production, after-sales support and customer service. To support effective partnerships, focus on integrating design, planning, production, and decision-making process.
- India is the second-largest consumer of petroleum products after China. To sustain the present growth rate, the energy requirement would increase by two times. Cheap prices for oil and gas imports ensure domestic satisfaction and contribute to industry and economy of the nation.
- Invest in renewable energy resources, namely, wind, biomass, solar and small hydro projects to revolutionise electrification of hamlets, smart villages and cities.
- Need to have major understanding with energy-rich countries in West Asia, Africa, Central Asian Region, and Southeast Asian countries and develop pipelines through MOUs in the next five years, bypassing Pakistan.

- Rapid response to market needs incorporating new designs and ability to manufacture high quality goods in adequate quantity at competitive prices.

Agriculture Reforms

The MSP, introduced in the 1960s to prevent economic exploitation of farmers, has to be reformed. Intervention by the government as an intermediary customer ensures the balance of prices of agricultural crops, and the MSP ensures that farmers get enough profit for their crops. The Pradhan Mantri Fasal Bima Yojana (PMFBY) aims to stabilise the income of farmers to ensure their continuance in farming. It encourages farmers to adopt innovative and modern agricultural practices. A uniform premium of only 2 per cent to be paid by farmers for all kharif crops and 1.5 per cent for all rabi crops.

- Investment development of irrigation facilities and focus on mechanised farming. Focus on post-harvest technology, namely, market infrastructure and storage facilities, particularly in rural areas.
- Making available adequate timely credit for the agriculture sector and rectify inflexibility in credit closing and security-based ending system.
- Making available agriculture infrastructure and its skilful utilisation to maximise benefits for farmers.
- Need to relook at tenancy legislation which restricts participation of the private sector in agriculture.
- Provision of knowledge base and advice for correct crop configuration based on crop mapping and suitability of the land.
- Safeguarding arable land by enforcing strict regulations on development activities on it. Ushering agri reforms (as China has implemented).
- 'Stubble burning' to be stopped with legal provisions. Innovative scientific solutions to be implemented on a priority basis by GOI.
- Viable crop insurance plan to help farmers and prevent farmer suicides at all costs—No Farmer Suicides.

Management of Water Resources

The amount of water available for use in India is estimated as 1,900 billion cubic metres per year. About 86 per cent of this is the surface run-off in streams, rivers, lakes and ponds. In fact, these are the major sources of water in our country. The Central Ground Water Authority (CGWA) came into being in January 1997 with the objective to regulate and control development and management of groundwater with jurisdiction in whole of the country.

- GOI one-time incentives to farmers for providing 'State-of-the-Art' irrigation method technology.
- Improvised irrigation method as being done in Israel to ensure optimum utilisation of water—drip irrigation.
- More than half of the districts are threatened by groundwater depletion and contamination. However, constantly improve access to water on dry rain-fed lands through linking of rivers/canals, increase water catchment areas in monsoons and enhance dam safety in India.
- Recycling of wastewater for irrigation projects provide drinking water to rural areas, India is now the largest user of groundwater worldwide, pumping out 25 per cent of all the groundwater extracted in the world.
- **River Linking Project**. Formulate a coherent strategy to address environmental costs, rehabilitation, social unrest, and management of relationships with neighbouring countries (where applicable). We have bountiful water resources, but most are perennial in nature, and often wreak havoc during monsoons.
  - The 'River Linking' national project would address the challenge of uneven distribution of water volumes, both in terms of regional availability and spatially.
  - It would enable harnessing of renewable and environmentally sustainable method of energy generation with captive hydropower. It would facilitate transport corridors with inland water carriage capacity.
  - Importantly, it will prevent droughts and floods, thus saving billions of GOI expenditure.

Green Revolution and White Revolution

The Green Revolution started in 1965. It was the first time that high-yield seeds were introduced in Indian agriculture. The main aim of the Green

Revolution was to make India self- sufficient when it came to food grains. During 1964-1965, the Intensive Cattle Development Programme was introduced in India in which cattle owners were provided with a package of improved animal husbandry for promoting the white revolution in the country. Later, the National Dairy Development Board introduced a new programme named "Operation Flood" to increase the speed of the white revolution in the country.

- The availability of water for irrigation ensures the use of higher doses of fertilisers which, in turn, reduces the extent of fallow land. Quick-ripening varieties of seeds help in getting more than one crop from the same field in one agricultural year. Constant experimentation, R&D, new technologies and imported seeds of high yield must be obtained and tried out.
- The main factors influencing intensity of cropping are irrigation, fertilisers, early maturing high-yielding varieties of seeds, mechanisation of agriculture and plant protection measures using insecticides, pesticides and weedicides.
- The White Revolution is adopting new methods for animal husbandry and altering the composition of feed ingredients in different proportions. The objectives being that village milk producers' cooperatives make optimum use of modern technology and management, procure milk and provide the services. Creating a surplus of milk by increased production and enhancing the quality of fodder, better husbandry facilities, new innovative techniques for enhancing milk quality and yield. The government must persistently provide high-yielding seeds, fertilisers, pesticides and better irrigation at highly subsidised prices and concomitantly guarantee to buy the products of the farmers at a given price. Adequate credit facilities should be available to small and marginal farmers to purchase necessary inputs like seeds, and fertilisers and they should be encouraged to join cooperatives to avail the best use of new farm technology.
- There has been overall shortage of rainfall in the last decade and increasing pressure on water resources due to urbanisation. To offset this crisis, we need to take the following measures, namely, going in for genetically modified (GM) crops which require less water and interlinking of rivers by link canals, the way it has been done

in Pakistan (largest canal network in the world). The Amul Cooperative Society had shown the way for a viable 'White Revolution'. However, the same could not be replicated in other states. There is a need to undertake such projects in a scientific manner nationwide based on detailed mapping of animal husbandry through Niti Aayog and the concerned ministry in the Government of India.

Blue Revolution

Envisages transformation through a 'Blue Economy',[5] encompassing the fisheries sector with increased investment, better training, and development of the optimised infrastructure. It has the vision to achieve economic prosperity of the country and fish farmers as well as contribute towards food and nutritional security through full potential utilisation of water resources for fisheries development in a sustainable manner, keeping in view bio-security and environmental dynamics. Advantageous in creation of jobs, spurs economic growth, mitigates the impact of climate change and helps meet the sea food needs of a growing global population. From sustainable fisheries to maritime renewable energies, there are five crucial areas where the G20 would benefit from investing in the ocean and India being the chairman of G20 assumes critical significance.

The following roadmap can be followed:

- Augmentation and transformation of the 'Sagarmala'[6] programme by the GOI in the coastal areas of India (7,500 km of coastline).
- Breeding of colourful ornamental fish. Need to focus on construction of new fishing harbours, modernisation of fishing boat and processing industry. Need for training of fishermen, and above all promoting fishing as a self-employment activity. Need to encourage fishery as a subject in major universities.
- Investment in deep sea fishing including incentives to public-private partnerships, namely, PPP model and collaborating with foreign partners, who are major fish producers in the world.
- Projects namely comprise the Strengthening of database and geographical information system of the fisheries sector, Institutional arrangement for the fisheries sector and Monitoring, control and surveillance (MCS) and other need-based interventions shall be implemented with 100 per cent central funding. Individual

beneficiaries, entrepreneurs and cooperatives/collectives of the Union Territories shall also be provided central financial assistance at par and equal to such beneficiaries in general states. These must continue.

Digital India

The GOI has taken the initiative of reaching the remotest parts of the country through digital technology. Digital infrastructure creation, Digital delivery of services, and Digital literacy are the three main components of the Digital India initiative. Progress is visible in salient aspects, but more great improvements have to be undertaken including broadband highways, universal access to mobile connectivity, public internet access programme, e-governance: reforming government through technology, e-Kranti-electronic delivery of services, information for all, electronics manufacturing and IT for jobs.

- Connecting each panchayat with OFC and ensuring E-governance. We can follow the model of 'E-chauppal' by ITC. Ex-servicemen in villages can take the initiative and ensure foolproof communications.
- Financial inclusion with digitisation of payments through social services and national welfare schemes like MNREGA, RSBY, JSY, and so on will benefit the people considerably.
- Incorporation of information and communication services, with digital access via internet and mobiles.
- The 'Digital India'[7] mission, along with the existing common service centres and village level entrepreneurs can provide last-mile connectivity.
- The latest digital transformation trends certainly include artificial intelligence (AI) and machine learning (ML), Cloud and everything as a service (XaaS), hybrid work, automation, cyber-security, customer data platforms, robotic process automation (RPA) and edge computing. Curriculum of universities are all-inclusive of the above in the engineering and technology domains.
- Using information technology and digitisation of governance services, government can progressively reach people's doorsteps.

Science and Technology

Focus on understanding integrated natural systems on multiple time and space scales to address problems being faced by our populace. IT, biotechnology, aerospace, nuclear science, manufacturing technology, automobile engineering, chemical engineering, ship-building, space science, electronics, computer science and other medical science related research and development are taking place on a large scale in the country. Scientists and scientific institutions should address the following:

- Fully exploit the predictive power of science to serve social needs with candid awareness of the limitations of scientific predictions. Encourage the creation of science coordination mechanisms.
- It must be favourably considered to open a national institute of defence technology and colleges with degree programmes in defence technology in concert with DRDO to encourage youth to undertake innovative research in disruptive technologies and contribute to India becoming a technology superpower by 2030.
- Need to promote a vision for development of sustainable closed systems production and consumption compatible with the recycling behaviour and equilibrium of natural systems. Must ensure that systems for evaluating and funding project proposals are fair, objective and transparent.
- Policy makers must incorporate science/R&D for long-term social development. Decisions must not be based on political expediency. Greater spending on R&D will be beneficial to the nation for promotion of its defence Corridors and military industrial complexes for export of weapon systems.
- Promote multidisciplinary approaches to research, encourage cooperation between social and natural sciences and draw lessons from humanity.

Space Exploration

Provide impetus to space exploration and associated R&D by focusing on indigenous satellite fabrication and launch technologies for economic resurgence, national security, and technological superiority through the government policy of 'Atma Nirbharta'. Collaboration with French counterparts has been very productive. The Indian Space Research Organisation (ISRO) is the national space agency of India, headquartered in Bengaluru, which operates under the Department of Space (DOS) directly overseen by the Prime Minister of India, while the Chairman of ISRO acts as the executive of DOS as well. ISRO is India's primary agency for performing tasks related to space-based applications, space exploration and development of related technologies. It is one of six government space agencies in the world which possess full launch capabilities, deploy cryogenic engines, launch extra-terrestrial missions and operate large fleets of artificial satellites.

- A new dimension is the militarisation of space for effective C4ISR, which will strengthen not only defence preparedness and strategic planning processes, safeguards for space assets by developing requisite defensive counter space technologies, plans and resources to be worked out for weaponising space for offensive space operations to deter adversaries from initiating attacks against our space assets and finally interactions with the UN and other nations to ensure strong lobbying for early formulation of an appropriate treaty for a new regime of "Weapon Free Space".
- India's economic progress has made its space programme more visible and active as the country aims for greater self-reliance in space technology. In 2008, India launched as many as 11 satellites, including nine from other countries, and went on to become the first nation to launch 10 satellites on one rocket. ISRO has put into operation two major satellite systems: the Indian National Satellite System (INSAT) for communication services, and the Indian Remote Sensing Programme (IRS) satellites for management of natural resources.
- ISRO's programmes have played a significant role in the socio-economic development of India and have regularly supported both civilian and military domains in various aspects including disaster management, telemedicine and navigation and reconnaissance missions. ISRO's spin-off technologies also have founded many crucial innovations for India's engineering and medical industries.
- ISRO requires to replicate its institutes of space technology in select three states of India, thereby producing more intellectuals in the science and technology domain.

Renewable Energy Resources

By 2020, one third of the world's energy will need to come from solar, wind, and other renewable sources. In India, coal-fired generation currently provides two-thirds and hydropower supplies the rest of our energy needs. Nuclear energy collaboration with Russia, France, USA, Kazakhstan, Australia, etc., must be progressively pursued to enhance nuclear power generation by commissioning nuclear plants with timelines to cater for resurgence of the industry, manufacturing and services sectors. Technical potential of renewable energy in solar, wind, biomass and small hydro exceeds the present installed generation capacity. A transition to clean energy is a huge economic opportunity. India is particularly well placed to become a global leader in renewable batteries and green hydrogen. These and other low-carbon technologies could create a market worth up to $ 80 billion in India by 2030. Over 80 per cent of India's energy needs are met by three fuels: coal, oil and solid biomass. Cheap electricity from renewable sources could provide 65 per cent of the world's total electricity supply by 2030. The development and deployment of renewable energy, products and services is driven by the need to:

- Advantages of renewable energy resources are, namely, fuel supply that never runs out, zero carbon emissions, cleaner air and water, cheaper form of electricity, renewable energy creating new jobs, less global warming, improved public health, inexhaustible energy with greater reliability and resilience.
- Attempt to decrease dependence and mitigate bills for energy imports.
- Conversion to renewable energy to be undertaken on priority by the Ministry of New and Renewable Energy and states must consequently assist people in establishing a reliable cost-effective grid.
- Expand cost effective energy supply through modern power grids in all the states of the country. Augmenting energy supply to remote and deficient areas to provide normative consumption levels to all sections of the population across the country.
- Sustained accelerated deployment of renewable energy systems and devices through 'Make in India' programmes.
- Switch fuels through new and renewable system/device deployment. India is blessed with over 150,000 MW of exploitable renewable energy including wind, solar, biomass, etc.

Education Reforms

Accessibility

The New Education Policy (NEP) is based on four pillars which are Access, Equity, Quality, and Accountability. In this new policy, there will be a 5+3+3+4 structure which comprises 12 years of school and three years of anganwadi/pre-school replacing the old 10+2 structure. The policy also has emphasised the promotion of online as well as open and distance education. It seeks to make education more inclusive, equitable, and accessible for all, with particular focus on marginalised communities and emphasises the development of 21st-century skills like creativity, critical thinking, and problem-solving. Additionally, the policy provides for the establishment of new institutions, such as digital universities, and the use of technology to facilitate learning. We need to focus on the following and imbibe the NEP programme for mass education of the entire population of the younger generation of the country.

- Encourage the establishment of 100 sainik schools (inclusive of girls sainik schools) concept initiated by the GOI, Sainik School Society, MoD. Every state to have five where 'Modernity blends with Talent' for children, in the ratio of 4:1 for male and female students. Later, it can be incrementally increased to 1,000 sainik schools and gradually to 5,000.
- Focus on rural education as an agenda, that could be relatively free from bureaucratic backlog and general stagnation: encourage "Beti Bachao, Beti Padhao8" campaign – as a revolution in the nation.
- Invest large resources in school buildings, infrastructure and in the preparation and distribution of education materials/resources.
- Metaverse programmes and their better accessibility by schools in our country facilitating an immersive campus life, where learners wearing VR headsets enter the virtual campus or university to learn, explore, and socialise.
- Metaverse refers to a virtual-reality space that is collective and shared, and in which users can interact with computer-generated environments, objects, and other users' avatars. Metaverse is usually referred to as a unique technology; this virtual world would not be able to exist without employing a wide range of emerging

technologies, which includes Blockchain, Cryptography, 3-D reconstruction, Cryptocurrency, Artificial intelligence (AI), Augmented reality (AR), Virtual reality (VR), and Internet of Things (IoT).

- Opportunities for higher education, in terms of the number of places in universities. The primary focus should be an expansion programme, excellence, and inclusion. NCC to be compulsory in all schools of the country to build a spirit of nationalism and patriotism.

Affordability of Education

We have taken many steps in this direction by various flagship schemes like Education for all, Sarva Shiksha Abhiyan, infrastructure development in minority institutions, Saakshar Bharat (Adult education), Natural programme for education of girls at elementary level. We now need to focus on secondary education for children in the age bracket of 14-18 years. The secondary education affordability should be towards profession-based vocational training to help students attain skills for finding a vocation of their choosing.

- The government must attempt to make education for children free up to secondary education; it must be made compulsory and relatively cheaper, elitism must be curbed, and Corporate social responsibility (CSR) must be undertaken to educate underprivileged children of society.
- Tuition fees should be reviewed in all government and private schools by the Ministry of Education and largely mitigated with more scholarship schemes for the lower strata of society.

Quality of Education

Formal education tends, unfortunately, to restrict the mind to traditional careers and resist change and innovation. We need to break free and redefine the purpose of education. The tasks before educational institutions and emerging role of teachers be reconsidered. The following measures could be undertaken to improve quality:

- Classrooms must be lit adequately, ergonomic furniture for writing desks and seating of students, blackboards/modern fibreglass sliding boards and writing materials with overhead projectors for presentations. Metaverse infrastructure to be introduced in all schools of the country.

- Comprehensive and continual assessment of a hierarchy of knowledge, skills, and attitudes through a variety of test and non-test techniques in an internationally accredited framework.
- Education must assist youth in development of learning skills for successful transition between learning and work.
- Faculty/teachers/headmasters and principals should be properly selected through stringent procedures. They must be highly qualified with good behavioural attitude and empathetic to students, whilst maintaining highest academic standards and scholastic excellence.
- Regular and in-time feedback to all stakeholders to ensure qualitative threshold is maintained strictly, as per guidelines.
- Seamless, low-cost, and high-quality internet connectivity for newer forms of learning as also life-long learning and innovation. Investment in education must go beyond the government to new learning providers to ensure partnership in a constant innovation process.

Accountability in Education

Implementation of initiatives is a key to success. We should understand that walls, windows, doors, and teachers will not make a school till we have hungry children who avoid academics (fear of studies) and wish to work in the fields and factories to earn their early livelihood. The following can be enforced:

- Education for the masses is a massive task. It would need single-minded focus of the state to implement this programme. Reform in education is a cultural, political, financial, and administrative challenge, which should have the tenets of academic excellence and perpetuity.
- Ensure proper utilisation of planned expenditure on education, which must be contemporary and have the pre-requisites of modern educational norms.
- Feedback forms for parents and parent-teacher meetings are mandatory for student progression to be monitored and improved.
- The vision and mission of education for all will have to inculcate, in one and all, leaders, and followers that for every child born poor

and needy, there will have to be well drawn plan, to ensure that she/he does not remain so.

Research & Development

With a very low level of PhD enrolment, India does not have enough high-quality researchers. There are few opportunities for interdisciplinary and multidisciplinary working with lack of early-stage research experience, a weak ecosystem for innovation, and low levels of industry engagement. The following is recommended:

- Engagement with industry in the development of science parks, incubation centres and technology transfer units.
- Increasing internationalism in research and teaching to develop India's capacity in research and innovation. Enhance R&D sector in India.
- International collaboration for good quality research proposals through professional networking and specific skills.
- International funding for state universities especially in the areas of capacity-building in teaching and research and in developing research networks.
- Move towards international credit recognition to enable more international student mobility.
- Nurturing the next generation of Indian researchers, through providing early-stage research experience and international networking; analysis and problem-solving skills; research student exchanges and international research student workshops and conferences.

Higher Education

Higher education policy refers to education policy for higher education institutions such as universities, specifically, how they are organised, funded, and operated in society. Higher education, any of the various types of education given in post-secondary institutions of learning and usually affording, at the end of a course of study, a degree, diploma, or certificate of higher studies.

- Foreign universities, internationally reputed in the first 50, should be encouraged to open their campuses in India and undertake dual-degree programmes, approved by the UGC.

- Grant for development of more universities and colleges in the country, especially in the Northeast region to bring them into the mainstream of Indian pedagogy.
- Increased access to technical education by incorporating equity and excellence.
- Increasing the scope for the 'Central Sector Scholarship Scheme' for college and university students.
- Promoting distance and online education to facilitate a larger literacy base for students in very remote areas of the country/incapacitated/special children.
- Scheme to provide interest-subsidy for students on educational loans for professional courses/programmes.
- Special grants for construction of hostels for women.

Financial Sector Reforms

The main objective of financial sector reforms in India initiated in the early 1990s was to create an efficient, competitive and stable financial sector that could then contribute in greater measure to stimulate growth. These reforms refer to steps taken to reform the banking system, capital markets, government debt markets, foreign exchange markets, etc. An efficient financial sector is necessary for the mobilisation of household savings and ensure their proper utilisation in productive sectors. Any sensible growth for India focuses on what we do well. Indian capabilities in skilled manufacturing ranging from pharmaceuticals to auto ancillaries, in services ranging from IT and engineering services to health care is growing. We should focus on the following:

- Allow a greater number of small banks. This will help to provide to loans to small-scale industries. The financial objectives are growth in revenues, growth in earnings and wider profit margins.
- Create and cater for demand at the bottom of the pyramid and at the same time help the poor to become more productive. This can be achieved by providing the financial services the poor need, at a cost they can afford to create markets for not only hundreds of millions in our country but elsewhere in the world like Africa and Latin America.
- Falling costs of international trade in goods and services, spurred by improvements in transportation and communications, provide India an opportunity to leapfrog over the traditional development

process. Instead of working out ways to improve trade from textiles to machinery to electronics to skilled services, we can move directly to providing medical services, legal opinions, financial analysis, or chip designs to the world, through 'Make in India' programmes.

- Focus on manufacturing or growing items, where the bulk of value added is via human capital, that is, impart the desired impetus to 'Skill India'.
- Much of the value in global production is moving to property, that is human capital intensive, unlike capital intensive production. We need to focus on human capital-intensive production through good education, a creative environment to link up with markets.
- The financial sector comprises commercial banks, insurance companies, non-banking financial companies, co-operatives, pension funds, mutual funds and other smaller financial entities. The sources of business finance are retained earnings, equity, term loans, debts, letters of credit, debentures, euro issues, working capital loans, venture funding, etc. The above-mentioned is the concept, that is elucidated in detail in 'Fundamentals of Economics' for commerce students.

Concept of Social Security

India does not yet explicitly recognise a national minimum social security cover. There are two aspects of social security–'protection' and 'promotion'. While the former denotes protection against a fall in living standards and living conditions through ill health and accidents, the latter focuses on enhanced living conditions, helping everyone overcome persistent capability deprivation. It involves any of the measures established by legislation to maintain individual or family income or provide income when some or all sources of income are disrupted or terminated or when exceptionally heavy expenditures must be incurred. Social security falls under the Concurrent List. This means both the Union and State governments can make laws regarding this. The following measures can be undertaken by the centre:

- Need to have a universal 'Social Security' system with an increased expenditure in social security in the budget.
- Need to have a 'National Minimum-Security Package' for unorganised sector workers, social insurance, social assistance for

life and health to cover the aged with benefits to all workers within a period of five years financed by the centre and state governments.

- There is a need to have an unorganised sector identification number for every worker in the unorganised sector with a unique identification number for accessing social schemes.
- We need to enhance our focus on social security concerns with reference to retirement income for workers.

Gross National Happiness Index for India

India ranks 118 in the global happiness ranking as per the UN General Assembly's Annual World Happiness report. Even as India commits itself to move on the fast track of economic growth, it must be mindful of the need to invest in improving its social indicators as well. The key parameters for gross national happiness index include GDP per capital, healthy years of life expectancy, social support, trust, perceived freedom to make life decisions and generosity. We need to prioritise focus on the following:

- **Environmental**. Although the government is committed for development, ordinances like land acquisition casts doubts on intent, and whether government wants to protect or destroy the environment. Ecosystems and biodiversity must be preserved as 'social imperatives'.
- **Physical Wellness and Health**. The government has instituted many schemes like RSBY and Janani Suraksha Yojana; however, not much has been achieved. There has been gross negligence on the part of the executing agency in various states and this weakens the trust in government intent and the machinery.
- **Political and Economic Wellness**. Political wellness has been well articulated; however, in certain areas, especially affected by insurgency, this is restricted. There is a huge economic disparity across the spectrum of society which needs to be reduced. The development process should focus on inclusive growth.
- **Social and Mental**. Mental peace is often intrigued by the helplessness of police forces and the law and order machinery. Social rights have still not reached the last individual down the line.

Criminalisation of Politics

- Amendment of Section 8 of the Representation of the People's Act 1951, to ensure disqualification of a person against whom the competent judicial authority has framed charges that relate to grave and heinous offences and corruption. The criminalisation of politics means the participation of criminals in politics which means that criminals can contest elections and get elected as members of Parliament and State legislatures. It takes place primarily due to the nexus between politicians and criminals.
- The Election Commission of India must take very serious note of criminalisation of politics and if the candidate's credentials and records are blemished, he/she should be debarred from politics for life. Indian courts must now seriously consider banning people accused of serious criminal charges from contesting elections.
- The political criminal is defined as an individual who, motivated by his convictions, commits an unlawful act designed to attack the social structure to bring about a reorganisation of the system. Concomitantly, a political crime is any unlawful act committed by a political criminal. Common political crimes include bribery, treason, sedition, espionage, theft, perjury, human rights violations, and whistle-blowing.
- The reason for criminalisation of politics is attributed to lack of enforcement of laws and judgments, vested interests and ulterior motives of profitability. Publishing of the criminal history of candidates fielded by political parties may not be very effective, as voters tend to vote through a narrow prism of community interests like caste or religion, use of muscle and money power; candidates with serious records seem to do well despite their public image, largely due to their ability to finance their elections and bring substantive resources to their respective parties.

Corruption in Society

The complex and non-transparent system of command and control, monopoly of the government as a service provider, underdeveloped legal framework, lack of information and weak notion of citizens' rights have provided incentives for corruption in India. Empowerment of the 'Lokayukt' and 'Lokpal' strictly enforced and legal actions against defaulters. Corruption affects everyone, especially minority and vulnerable populations. As the biggest obstacle to economic and social development, it harms societies as it undermines democracy and human rights by weakening governments. It diverts funds from public services such as healthcare, education, and sanitation and discourages foreign investment, leading to fewer jobs. The forms of corruption vary but can include bribery, lobbying, extortion, cronyism, nepotism, parochialism, patronage, influence peddling, graft, and embezzlement.

- A totally cleansed society of corruption will be progressive and happy, with bonhomie amongst the citizenry and the economically advanced.
- Anti-corruption youth committees be formed of young generation leaders with strong character, selected by the respective DMs/DCs/SSPs of districts and given a designated charter of duties and responsibilities. They require to be empowered by legal legislation to discharge their tasks diligently with high integrity and probity in life. If necessary, police protection to be provided.
- To stop corruption, we require to expose corrupt activities and risks that may otherwise remain hidden, keep the public sector honest, transparent and accountable, help stop dishonest practices in all areas of life, ensure that public sector employees act in the public interest only.
- The police department plays a vital role in anti-corruption drives in cities and townships, working in synergy with multiple agencies of intelligence, IB, R&AW, CAPFs, military intelligence and apprehending defaulters and proceeding with fast track tribunals to finalise verdicts in time frame related to the court cases.

Electoral Reforms

The Chief Election Commissioner had written to the Law Minister requesting expedited action on the electoral reform proposals pending with the government, including the one which seeks an enhanced two-year jail term for those furnishing incorrect information in their poll affidavits. Enhancing the imprisonment period for those furnishing incorrect details in poll affidavits from the existing six months to two years is a key electoral reform proposal of the Election Commission. A two-year jail term could bar the candidate from contesting elections for six years. A recommendation is made for state funding of the election regime which should be accompanied by strict accounting procedures, with legal action against defaulters. Politicians could have social sciences, or constitution and law degrees as eligibility criteria to stand for elections, enhancing professional knowledge, proficiency in handling complex issues and ushering transformative growth in the states.

- Suggested measures to ensure that electoral reforms are implemented. There must be a ceiling on election expenditure, voting through postal ballot, restriction on exit polls, disqualification on conviction for violating the National Honours Act, 1971, optimised voting through electronic voting machines (EVMs), increase in the number of proposers and security deposit, deputation to Election Commission, lowering of voting age to 18 years, prohibition on sale of liquor, etc.
- The arbiter of success of free and fair elections is the large turnout of people of a democratic society. Any candidate with a blemished record must be debarred from standing for elections in the country.
- There are multiple issues plaguing the electoral process in India, namely, criminalisation of politics and politicisation of criminals, money and muscle power, misuse of government machinery, casteism and communalism, non-serious independent candidates, lack of moral values in politics, etc.

Developing Economy

Economic growth, social inclusion, and environmental conservation are three key components of long-term development. Harmonising them is crucial. Sustainable development requires long-term economic growth, a stable livelihood, living in harmony with nature, and the use of appropriate technology. A sustainable economy is one that is resilient and provides a good quality of life for everybody. India is capable of sustaining an economic growth of 9 per cent for many years. The Economic Advisory Council stated that a high sustained GDP growth rate is the key for the world to achieve the 2030 Sustainable Development Goals (SDGs). India, as a developing country, features a mixed economy in the world. The major characteristics of a developing economy are low per capita income, overpopulation, maximum population below the poverty line, poor infrastructure, agro-based economy and a lower rate of capital formation. It is the world's fourth-largest economy by nominal GDP and the third largest by purchasing power parity (PPP).

- Develop core competencies and strength in the manufacturing sector. Strive for a high income per capita with security guaranteed, excellent healthcare, low unemployment rate, high threshold of science and technology, exports higher than imports, high-end technology import and world-class R&D.
- Focus on easy approval of projects and establishment of friendly free clearance mechanisms. 'Ease of doing business' in India facilitates growth and developmental processes attracting foreign direct investment (FDI).
- Impetus to 'Make in India' concept by incentivised policy of GOI.
- Judicious management or our natural resources and avoiding wastage.
- Massive infrastructure development through designated committees at national and state levels.
- Provide tax concessions to firms who set up units in the country. Focus on novelty, innovation and provide incentives for small and medium sized industries.

National Integration

National integration is the awareness of a common identity amongst the citizens of a country. It means that though individuals belong to different communities, castes, religions, cultures and regions and speak different languages, all of them recognise the fact that they are one.

- It is an incontrovertible fact that ex-servicemen and the veterans fraternity are synonymous to 'National Integration' in a secular democratic country. Towards ensuring a well-knit, cohesive, highly motivated citizenry, there is a requirement to equitably organise and conduct national events in various states on sports, important festivals, exhibitions, education, science & technology, defence technology, cyber security, women empowerment etc. The all religion, caste and creed participation and resultant euphoria under 'Tirangaa' is highly integrating and inspiring for the youth and citizenry, to relentlessly strive towards 'Duty, Honour and Country'.
- It is an incontrovertible fact that ex-servicemen and the veterans fraternity are synonymous to 'National Integration' in a secular

democratic country. Towards ensuring a well-knit, cohesive, highly motivated citizenry, there is a requirement to equitably organise and conduct national events in various states on sports, important festivals, exhibitions, education, science & technology, defence technology, cyber security, women empowerment etc. The all religion, caste and creed participation and resultant euphoria under 'Tirangaa' is highly integrating and inspiring for the youth and citizenry, to relentlessly strive towards 'Duty, Honour and Country'.

- This can be best achieved by common laws, a uniform civil code without discrimination of any religion, inclusive growth, and socio-economic development to include education, sports, and health schemes. Well planned involvement by all ministries with a focused effort and a strategised futuristic plan, conforming to the national development plan of the Niti Aayog, as approved by the Hon'ble PM of India.

Important Elements of National Integration

- A six-month integrated course exposure should be mandatory for all civil services probationers with the armed forces in the remotest of frontiers, contiguous to the borders with adversaries, to acquaint them with the realities of military hardships and shortcomings faced by personnel in hazardous terrain and inclement weather conditions. This would provide a fine perspective of soldiering.
- Integration is a dynamic, multi-actor process of mutual engagement that facilitates effective participation by all members of a diverse society in economic, political, social and cultural life, and fosters a shared sense of belonging at the national and local levels.
- The cultivation of the spirit of national integration should commence at the primary school level and must continue till the end of one's life, with virtuous conduct by a citizen abiding by duty, honour and country.
- The essential elements of Indian democracy are fundamental rights, a unified justice system, secularism, common national emblems, national festivals, etc.

Indian Ocean Region: Strategic Connotations

India's strategic location at the head of the Indian Ocean gives it a great strategic status and helps in maintaining contact with the rest of the world.

It helps India to keep close contact with West Asia, Europe, West Africa from the western coast and Southeast and East Asia from the eastern coast. India is considered a soft power and ostensibly one of the potential superpowers of the world. This potential is attributed to several indicators, the primary ones being its demographic trends and a rapidly expanding economy and military.

Indian Ocean Region

- India is eternally vigilant of China's growing presence in the IOR which postulates a security threat for India. As counter-action to China's 'String of Pearls' strategy, India is actively engaging with Iran for its Chabahar port project. This can provide leverage in the Gulf trade, primarily for its massive energy import from the region. The Asia Africa Growth Corridor (AAGC) is in progress to enhance port connectivity, which must be pushed ahead.
- The Indian Ocean Rim Association (IORA) is the predominant organisation that brings together the Indian Ocean states on a common platform to promote maritime safety. The Security and Growth for All in the Region (SAGAR) is aimed at safeguarding maritime interests of its mainland and islands; it also emphasises the role of IORA as a facilitator of trade and fisheries management. It shall further promote tourism and cultural exchanges and shape the notion of the 'Blue Economy'. The desired ministerial push is required to achieve dividends.
- The Sagarmala project was initiated to emphasise port-led development, to build a robust port infrastructure and modernise them due to their importance in trade and economic development. This project deserves to be prioritised for completion towards export-import trade consolidation.
- To be recognised as a 'net security provider in the IOR' by 2030, it is essential to develop infrastructure in the Andaman and Nicobar Command (ANC) and enhance the strategic potential of the Indian Navy manifold. Two aircraft carriers are mandatory and three would be a strategic necessity, attributed to the threat manifestation from PLAN.
- To gain strategic ascendency over rivals, India must establish a 'Zone of Peace' in the IOR and emerge as a 'natural leader in the IOR'.

Development of Infrastructure in Andaman & Nicobar Command (ANC)

Andaman & Nicobar (A&N) is an important nucleus and off-mainland battle station for the economic strategic cooperation of India. The role of A&N in India's strong ties with East Asian countries and other sea-related countries is very critical under the Act East Policy and this is likely to undergo a paradigm shift, due to the rebalancing of the Indo-Pacific region, and China's expansionist polices and criticality in the South China Sea.

- Additional basing facilities of Sukhoi and MiG-29 class of aircraft/ latest acquisitions of multi-role combat aircraft to be established.
- An ANC joint operations centre, which is the nerve centre for integrated planning for surveillance, conduct of operations and logistic support in the IOR is extremely important for joint war-fighting preparedness of the Indian Armed Forces, in case any adverse strategic manoeuvres are undertaken by forces inimical to Indian security. It also maintains an eye on the sea lanes of communication (SLOCs) used for trade between nations.
- ANC to be developed as the headquarters of the Eastern Fleet of the Indian Navy (IN). The third aircraft carrier should preferably be based in ANC. INS *Chakra* to be based in the IOR for purposes of strategic security.
- Capability enhancement to effectively monitor traffic moving from Malacca, Sunda and the Ombai-Wetar Straits. Capability building to react to any situation/contingency developing in the littorals of the IOR.
- Enter into security alliances with littorals in IOR for tracking terrorism, hybrid threats, CBRN threats, drug smuggling, gun-running and human trafficking, conforming to Indian national interests.
- It is a suggested idea to allocate land in Andaman & Nicobar Isles to ex-servicemen and senior veterans, truly creating a blend of secular society whilst integrating the indigenised community, thereby enhancing national security consciousness. It would be a productive outcome and guarantee better threshold of security index in the isles, epitomised as the 'Far East Bastion of Security of India' in the Indian Ocean Region.
- Lift capability for an amphibious brigade to be established

Amphibious brigade with capability of employment in Out-of-Area Contingencies (OOAC) to be stationed by the CDS for the ANC.

- It is a suggested idea to allocate land in Andaman & Nicobar Isles to ex-servicemen and senior veterans, truly creating a blend of secular society whilst integrating the indigenised community, thereby enhancing national security consciousness. It would be a productive outcome and guarantee better threshold of security index in the isles, epitomised as the 'Far East Bastion of Security of India' in the Indian Ocean Region.

Internal and External Security of India

Internal security is the act of keeping peace within the borders of a sovereign state or other self-governing territories, generally by upholding the national law and defending against internal security threats. External security refers to security against aggression by foreign countries and comes under the Ministry of Defence. An external threat also refers to the risk of somebody from outside an company who attempts to exploit the system's vulnerabilities through the use of malicious software, hacking, sabotage or social engineering.

- Creation of CDS and DMA with detailed instructions on the structuring and appointment of military and civil bureaucrats to be streamlined.
- Establishment of joint structures amongst the intelligence and law-enforcement agencies of all nations to work towards counter-terrorism, and drug and human trafficking to be monitored and reported to the NSA by multi-agencies tasked for the same by the IB and those controlled by the MHA for highly sensitive tasks.
- Finalising the 'National Security Doctrine' and the Integrated Theatre Command for the Armed Forces, given the present VUCA environment.
- Identification of 'sleeper cells' in the country and controlling them by the NIA, as they indulge in anti-national activities, which is deleterious to national security and harmony.
- In view of the prevailing environment, in my perception, the "Study of India's Strategic Culture" is important, encapsulating benchmarked strategies of nations, operational art, inception and culmination of war campaigns, and multidimensional joint

integrated operations. An Indian centre of strategic culture should be established for senior officers of the armed forces cleared for Command and Staff as Theatre Commanders in the tri-services, with civilian counterparts of the level of additional secretaries from the ministries of Defence, Finance, Home Affairs, External Affairs, Information & Broadcasting, Roads & Transport, BRO, Intelligence, and senior officials from NSCS, NSAB, DRDO, ISRO, NTRO, etc., (as recommended by the NSA) to refine the strategic thought process in conformity with the national interests of the country.

- 'Madrasas' to impart education, conforming to the education policy and NEP 2021, promulgated by the Government of India in all states, without exception for growth and development of children.
- Regular joint exercises with all strategically important nations is imperative to improve inter-operability and response to common threat manifestations.
- The coastal security defence matrix must be strengthened, comprising naval operations, as also intelligence, surveillance and reconnaissance (ISR) assets, coast guard, air defence, UAVs, air force early warning detachments, space-based satellites and EW systems.
- Unambiguously, the various organisations in the country dealing with issues of internal and external security of India could introduce a 'pro rata' quota of vacancies for ex-servicemen to be enrolled in respective states to strengthen the characteristic security systems and be the vigilante (Eyes/Ears) of the intelligence agencies, viz RAW, IB, etc.

Humanitarian Assistance & Disaster Relief (HADR)

The National Disaster Management Authority (NDMA), headed by the Prime Minister of India, is the apex body for disaster management in India. The defence forces, because of their unparalleled discipline, organisational cohesiveness, huge capacity in terms of logistics and operational capabilities on land and, water and in the air are considered best suited for Humanitarian assistance & disaster relief (HADR) operations. The disaster management cycle consists of six stages, namely, prevention, mitigation, preparedness, response (rescue and relief), rehabilitation and reconstruction.

- Bringing the artificial intelligence/machine learning community and HADR together for harnessing the cumulative advantages of early warning, preparing and mitigating disaster relief. Modern equipment and vehicles are critical to these operations.

- Establish joint training centres with multi-agencies and practice in all states with organised workshops for creating awareness in the public and not panic about the probability of certain fragile geographical zones in mountainous areas, coastal areas intimidated by regular cyclones and hurricanes, volcanic sensitive areas, flash floods/deluge-prone sectors, etc.
- High-energy lasers by adversaries can trigger avalanches in mountainous areas and cause immense collateral damage to human and infrastructure resources. Careful observation, surveillance and vigilance of certain sensitive strategic locations can be undertaken to prevent flash floods/avalanches and mud slides to devastate properties.
- Joint structures of HADR must include modern early warning systems and infrastructure wherein studies and associated analyses are undertaken of prospective disaster zones in various categories and responders trained to take immediate action when and if necessary.
- The Armed Forces are interlinked with HADR depending on the type of disaster manifestation on land, sea or coastal regions of the country. 'Vacancy based' enrolment of ex-servicemen will further strengthen and constitute the air and mission HADR, ensuring competent responsive systems, viz as first responders to obviate tragedies of any visualised magnitude.

NATIONAL SOCIAL SERVICE PROPOSED 'SWACHH BHARAT' ACTION PLAN

Recommend total cleanliness, by creation of a special task force, namely, 'Night Hawks', in all states/UTs of India, comprising municipal workers assigned for cleaning work to operate from 11 a.m. to 6 p.m., to clean all areas (as per guidelines) in respective cities, townships and villages of the country. To involve young voluntary unemployed workers, providing them with initiatives like employment weightage (for national social service), when they apply for employment/placements. In addition, special dress (uniform), awards and other incentives, namely, attractive salary and perquisites, conforming to a planned motivational action plan to be formulated as a policy.

- A voluntary force organised under a director-general at the state level (retired officer from the uniformed services, namely, military, paramilitary and police force can be designated). Under him a skeleton structure (composite organisation), comprising uniformed (ex-servicemen and civil retired employees) to be created for coordinating seamless, well integrated work at all levels.
- Gathering/collection of garbage from residential colonies in black plastic bags to be performed during the daytime by 10 a.m., as per legislated timings.
- The task force garbage pickups/tipper transport 'Challenger' vehicles can be put into service in all states of the country. All the corporate houses can be encouraged to acquire these vehicles in bulk, as part of their CSR contribution, with the corporate's name displayed prominently on the vehicles, given to the municipal corporations, to execute the responsibility as part of this noble mission.
- The task force is recommended to consist of two vehicles and seven persons, namely, task force commander in the first 'Challenger' vehicle, driver with two cleaners (safai karamcharis) equipped with brooms and durable buckets. Second, follow up tipper truck comprises driver and two cleaners (safai karamcharis) with similar equipment wearing overalls, masks, caps, gum boots and gloves. Both vehicles to move together as part of one task force.
- The task force will clean all common utility areas near parks, bus stands, railway stations, schools, markets and places near religious sites and all other public utility and public gathering places.

Encroachments and all other unauthorised and illegal occupation in public places to be removed through the civil administration. This will be done systematically after all encroachers are informed. Small shops in a shopping complex and low-cost housing schemes for these people can be provided at appropriate places within or outside the cities (suburbs), through well-planned schemes and sanctioned plans prepared by the responsible ministries.

Slum areas, including legal occupation with pattas, can be removed and rehabilitation done with proper low-cost housing schemes in suburbs of cities and townships with detailed planning done by ministries and the civil administration.

All water storage tanks, canals, wells, check dams, and lakes are to be periodically cleaned through contract services. Potable water for residents and recycled water for floriculture and toilets. Water conservation, rainwater harvesting, and water recycling methods must be made mandatory in all townships and cities by the municipalities.

Ergonomically-designed bio toilets (gents/ladies) (made in India) and with 24/7 water supply and enough sanitary workers (safai aramcharis) must be established in all states/UTs throughout the country, especially in rural areas, and all temporary gathering, like fairs, sammelans, rallies, etc. Fines can be imposed on offenders not using toilets and spoiling the environment.

There should be labour-saving devices/modern machines (part of 'Make in India') to handle toxic waste like electronic goods, and wastage from hospitals and factories. Solid waste and wastewater treatment effluents from factories must be treated before discharged and made mandatory as per rules/regulations.

Special factories are to be established for recycling plastic waste. The recycled material can be mixed with asphalt and used in road construction. Recycling plants must be established at one per cluster of three townships by the responsible ministry.

All walls of structures throughout the country to be cleaned, with no sticking of bills, hanging banners, etc. Designated areas will be earmarked for campaign banners, bills, etc by the municipalities.

All institutions and public state departments to be responsible to clean and clear debris in respective areas on a daily basis or pay heavy fines levied by municipalities.

All gardens and children's parks, amusement centres to be well maintained by the municipality and/or by corporate houses/NGOs with adequate lighting, floriculture, bio-toilet facilities, garbage bins, etc, catering for the comfort of the people.

It is envisaged in perspective that the ex-servicemen and veterans could suitably be appointed (as volunteers) for this specific responsible job, especially being more disciplined as also being highly conscious of clean environment as obtained in all cantonments and military stations. The incentivisation, police coordination, supportive administration, logistical equipment, human resource provisioning and recognition by mayors, higher authorities and political hierarchy is mandatory for its success. It must be legislative requirement for all township, cities, large villages and should be the prime responsibility of DC/DM and chief minsters of respective states/UTs.

Conclusion

Transforming India into a developed nation implies that every citizen of the country must live well above the poverty line; that education and health are of a high standard; national security is assured; and core competences in certain major areas will enable the production of quality goods for home consumption and for exports, competitively; and, above all, that there will be prosperity for all citizens. While we are now a trillion-dollar-plus economy, with 550 million youth, we must deal with the fact that we have more people living in poverty, more children to bring quality nourishment to, more people to provide with clean drinking water and more people who need to be made literate than any other nation. These are our fundamental challenges for the twenty-first century.

Rural development is not at all a loss-making proposition. What is loss-making is poor implementation. The only thing which is lacking is, perhaps, an integration of efforts to meet with well-defined and measurable objectives in a mission-mode striving towards prosperity. India is still predominantly rural, over 70 per cent of its people living in villages. As of 2011, of the total population of 1.2 billion, the urban population has increased to 377 million but an overwhelming majority of 833 million is still in villages, big and small. India, it has been said, lives in her mid-sized villages, with as many as 485 million people living in villages with a population ranging between 1,000 and 5,000. Additionally, 103 million people live in villages of 500-1,000 population, and 47 million people in villages of less than 500 people.

The priority for the societal transformation of India is accelerated rural development. The key here is that all developmental actions must be sustainable and should be activated in 600,000 villages which have missed both the Industrial Revolution and Information Technology Revolution and, in fact, even the first Green Revolution in many of the states.

Every village in the nation should have basic infrastructural facilities, productivity, and opportunities of an urban setting with rural ambience with the environment preserved. It is difficult to motivate professionals–doctors, engineers and teachers–to live in rural regions due to the lack of good living conditions and facilities and capacity-building and capacity-utilising assets. The next challenge is to make these models of rural development financially sustainable and eco-friendly. For them to succeed, it is necessary to make them available to all in terms of economy, quality assurance and physical accessibility.

It is possible to connect clusters of villages by annular roads or other transport mechanisms, with well-designed traffic to facilitate movement from one village to the next. This will enable agro-industries, service and even high-tech knowledge industries to relocate in the villages, supported by the movement of some government offices and the provision of necessary incentive structures. Each of the clusters has to be managed in an entrepreneurial and innovative manner involving local panchayats, professionals, the administration, business concerns and key local human resources. The clusters will also have to consider the issue of preserving the cultural heritage, human values and environmental assets present within them.

To bring sustainable development and prosperity to rural areas, we need to establish 7,000 self-reliant village clusters by Rural Area Planned Integrated Development (RAPID), under a public-private partnership model in the next six years. It would be a new and innovative cooperative model to bring about sustainable development to villages and would entail establishing physical, electronic and knowledge connectivity between villages. The focus would be on growth-oriented development in an integrated manner. Thrust areas under this mission would include providing clear drinking water, generating power through renewable energy sources, bringing down infant and maternal mortality rates, increasing the literacy rate, and improving the functional literacy of self-help groups and unemployed youth. It would also lay emphasis on enhancing villagers' access to technology, legal recourse, communication, internet, quality healthcare services, education, sanitation and a pollution-free environment.

Further, India's neighbourhood abounds with Islamic fundamentalist regimes, a rising communist superpower and military dictatorship. The authoritarian regimes in this neighbourhood contradict India's multi-cultural democracy. In case India's model succeeds in Asia, the authoritarian models will be under major stress. Thus, there is a constant endeavour to destabilise India. In India, there is a larger youth population today than at any point in history, but this demographic explosion, which has been largely absorbed by the cities, has not been met by a similar growth in economic opportunities for the youth. These high concentrations of unemployed, disenfranchised youth in rapidly growing urban centres may lead to explosive conditions, which might result in social upheaval, political crisis, instability and violence. It is therefore essential to develop cogent strategies to harness the incredible power of youth inventiveness and dynamism to generate economic growth and development. The threat perception is further enhanced by the degenerate functioning of the civil administration and falling apart of policing mechanisms.

A good civil service is necessary but not sufficient for good governance; a bad civil service is sufficient but not necessary for bad governance. Thus, a dilapidated civil service has been a key factor in Africa's economic decline. Conversely, a strong civil service is one of the several reasons why in several east Asian economies, especially Japan, Singapore, and South Korea, authoritarianism has co-existed with excellent economic performance. It can be argued that the link between authoritarianism and economic decline, so evident in Africa, has been inoperative in these Asian countries largely because of their strong civil service. Greater responsiveness and openness can legitimately be demanded of public administrations in many East Asian countries. Clearly, civil service systems in most East Asian countries cannot be considered a problem; they are, rather, an important part of the solution to their other problems.[9]

The situation in many Indian states that are responsible for achieving the Millennium Development Goals is different. A vast gap exists between the stated and unstated objectives. On paper, the avowed objectives of the government is to provide a clean administration and work for the poor, but lucrative posts are auctioned to the highest bidder. Corruption is rampant. People have unfortunately accepted the position as fait accompli and resigned themselves to their fate. They too tend to seek shortcuts and exploit the system by breaking rules or approaching mafia gangs and politicians for favours. Governance reforms are intractable under a 'kleptocracy' that exploits national wealth for its own benefit and is, by definition, uninterested in transparency and accountability. A pliable and unskilled civil service is actually desirable from its point of view—public employees dependent on the regime's discretionary largesse are forced to become corrupt, cannot quit their jobs, and reluctantly become the regime's accomplices. Providing financial assistance from GOI to such states without linking it with performance and reforms would be a waste of resources. In all other cases, reform is manageable, albeit difficult, complex, and slow. Therefore, considering that the states would need external pressure to improve outcomes, certain control by GOI over the IAS and policy domain in social sector is necessary, till such time that the states show signs of improvement in governance.

There are numerous productive measures that can be taken to improve governance. Focusing on evaluated outcomes, rather than internal procedures would help, as would delegation of responsibilities. Retired officers of the uniformed forces are yet another experienced and highly motivated resource pool available in civil society, within the existing civil structure. Dovetailing them into the planning and monitoring process of various government schemes will pay substantively rich dividends. The officer community, because of its expertise in 'transformational leadership', not only has the ability to perceive and plan things meticulously, but most importantly possesses the capacity to lead from the front. It is often said 'Growth of society will have to come from Society itself'; however, this is rarely implemented.

In its quest to become a regional/global power, India needs to modify its present multi-pronged growth strategy. A nation can only achieve a holistic growth if it addresses two issues; one, in terms of all sectors or segments which need to be brought into the fold of a vibrant economy; and two, in terms of enabling sections of the population, whom the growth process has bypassed, to fully engage themselves in the development process. All those involved in the development of the Indian economy—banks, cooperatives, development finance institutions, NGOs and administrators—will have to rethink their strategies in response to the new emphasis being given to holistic growth. Perhaps, the first step in this direction is to identify that segment of the rural economy, which has so far not attracted adequate attraction of the policymakers, but which deserves focus in the new government strategy.

There's no arguing the fact that India has been able to bring about dramatic changes, both at home and abroad. However, it still has a long and tortuous path to travel before it can achieve its grand hopes of becoming a great power. A host of barriers still lie along the road and it is still unclear if it can overcome them. Given the objective factors in India's favour, India is bound to be one of the leading powers of the world. There is no escaping this. We are the second-largest demographically and by 2050, we will be the largest economy doing very well. Militarily, we are doing well; we have manpower empowered well to propel the country move fast. The reasons for not exercising effective power are internal instability, structural weaknesses, and lack of monitoring of implementation of development projects.

Development is an outcome of efficient institutions rather than the other way around. Focus therefore must be shifted from maximising the quantity of development funding to maximising of development outcomes and effectiveness of public service delivery. Despite good achievement on the growth front, India faces significant challenges and needs to take some difficult political decisions. Concerted policy action is needed to raise the 250 million poor out of poverty, and increasingly concentrate on the poorer states. This requires not so much additional resources as better participation of stakeholders and sound delivery mechanisms. This requires improving the environment in which the three agencies of delivery—civil service, panchayats and society itself comprising responsible citizens including retired uniformed personnel—function, as described in this paper.

Ex-servicemen are 'role models' of ethical leadership with ingrained morals and a value system focused on 'Duty, Honour and Country' contributing to society and nation building in substantial measures with a great sense of commitment towards multifaceted progression and excellence in all spheres of activities. Hence, this thesis concludes with articulation of a need for delegation of responsibilities amongst various stakeholders including ex-servicemen. It also cogitates the feasibility of an alternative rural model, for example, the RAPID Model, necessitated by new rural opportunities and impending need necessitated by systemic deficiencies. Ultimately, it emerges that the need for 'Governance Augmentation and Progression' can be brought about at the grassroots levels by ex-servicemen residing in the villages, who, given their sense of commitment and ability to monitor execution of developmental projects, can mitigate the gravity of challenges faced during attainment of objectives. Thus, the potential of the leadership of ex-servicemen can be synergized in the entire process of governance enhancement, to bring about a national rural socio-economic transformation as has been brought out earlier in the prognosis.

> *"Good governance with good intentions is the hallmark of our Government, Implementation with Integrity is our Core Passion".*
>
> **—Narendra Modi, Prime Minister of India**

NOTES

1. The Confederation of Indian Industry set up a task force under Mr. Naresh Chandra in February 2009 to recommend ways of further improving corporate governance standards and practices both in letter and spirit. The recommendations of the Naresh Chandra Task Force evolved over a series of meetings. The leitmotif of the report is to enunciate additional principles that can improve corporate governance in spirit and in practice. The report enumerates a set of voluntary recommendations with an objective to establish higher standards of probity and corporate governance in the country.
2. Aadhaar is a 12-digit individual identification number issued by the Unique Identification Authority of India on behalf of the Government of India. The number serves as proof of identity and address, anywhere in India.
3. The Mahatma Gandhi National Rural Employment Guarantee Act 2005 or MNREGA, earlier known as the National Rural Employment Guarantee Act or NREGA, is an Indian labour law and social security measure that aims to guarantee the 'right to work'. This Act was passed in 23 August 2005 under the UPA government of Prime Minister Manmohan Singh following tabling of the bill in Parliament by the Minister for Rural Development, Raghuvansh Prasad Singh. It aims to enhance livelihood security in rural areas by providing at least 100 days of wage employment in a financial year to at least one member of every household whose adult members volunteer to do unskilled manual work.
4. The Union Government has launched a new scheme, named **'Bharat Nirman Yojana'** on December 16, 2005. This scheme aims at developing the rural infrastructure. This yojana is governed by the *Ministry of Rural Development*. The duration of implementing this scheme has been determined for four years with the expected expenditure of Rs. 1,74,000 crore. The major six sectors and their targets for the next

four years are Roads, Water, Power, Irrigation, Telecommunications and Housing.

5. The blue economy is the phrase used for sustainable use of ocean, sea and coast resources for economic growth, improved livelihoods, and jobs while preserving the health of the ocean ecosystem. Blue economy includes economic benefits that may not be marketed, such as carbon storage, coastal protection, cultural values and biodiversity.
6. The concept of Sagarmala was approved by the Union Cabinet on 25 March 2015. As part of the programme, a National Perspective Plan (NPP) for the comprehensive development of India's 7,500 km coastline, 14,500 km of potentially navigable waterways and the maritime sector has been prepared which was released by the Hon'ble Prime Minister on 14 April, 2016 at the Maritime India Summit 2016.
7. The Government of India launched the National e-Governance Plan (NeGP) in 2006 in which 31 mission mode projects covering various domains were initiated. Despite the successful implementation of many e-governance projects across the country, e-governance as a whole has not been able to make the desired impact and fulfil all its objectives. It has been felt that a lot more thrust is required to ensure e-governance in the country to promote inclusive growth that covers electronic services, products, devices and job opportunities. Moreover, electronic manufacturing in the country needs to be strengthened. In order to transform the entire ecosystem of public services through the use of information technology, the Government of India has launched the **Digital India programme** with the vision to transform India into a digitally empowered society and knowledge economy.
8. In 2015, the Indian government introduced the 'Beti Bachao, Beti Padhao' (BBBP) scheme to address concerns of gender discrimination and women empowerment in the country. The name 'Beti Bachao, Beti Padhao' translates to 'Save the girl child, educate the girl child'. The scheme aims to educate citizens against gender bias and improve the efficacy of welfare services for girls. It was launched with an initial funding of Rs. 100 crore (US$ 13.5 million).
9. P. K. Singh, Y. K. Gera, and Sandeep Dewan. *'Comprehensive National Power: A Model for India'*, New Delhi, India, Vij Books India Private Limited, 2013, pp. 230-235.

BIBLIOGRAPHY

Primary Sources

Annual Reports

ASER Centre. ASER 2014: Annual Status of Rural Education Report, New Delhi: ASER, 2015.

Gujarat. Surat Municipal Corporation, Project Overview, Surat: 2009.

India, Ministry of Defence, IHQ of MoD (Army), Directorate-General Resettlement, Data collected on Ex-serviceman. New Delhi: 2015.

India. Ministry of Rural Development, Final Report of Working Group, New Delhi: 2013.

India. Ministry of Rural Development, Annual Report on PURA Implementation, New Delhi: 2015.

India. Ministry of Statistics and Programme Implementation, NSS Report No. 522 (62/10/01) Employment and Unemployment Situation in India, New Delhi: 2005–2006.

India. Planning Commission Report of the Task Force on Employment Opportunities. Planning Commission, New Delhi: 2000.

India. Ministry of Statistics and Programme Implementation, Sixth Economic Census, New Delhi: Central Statistics Office, 2014.

United Nations. Human Development Report, New York: United Nations Press, 2004.

United Nations. Human Development Report, New York: United Nations, 2006.

USA. World Bank Report on Leadership & Growth, Washington DC: 2010.

Policy Notes

India, India's urban awakening, building inclusive cities, sustaining economic growth, McKenzie Global Institute, April 2010.

India, Ministry of Statistics and Programme Implementation, Press Note on Results of Sixth Economic Census Government of India, New Delhi: 2014.

Mukherjee, A. and Zhang, X. 'Rural Nonfarm Development in China and India: The Role of Policies and Institutions.' Development Strategy and Governance Division, International Food Policy Research Institute, New Delhi: 2005.

Scott Alister, Gibert Alana and Gelan, Ayele. The Urban-Rural Divide: Myth or Reality, Macaulay: Macaulay Land Use Research Institute, London: 2007.

Tamil Nadu, Policy Notes 2013-14 of Industrial Department, Government of Tamil Nadu, Chennai: 2014.

Tamil Nadu, Policy Note 2013-14, MSME Department, Government of Tamil Nadu, Chennai: 2014.

Tamil Nadu, Policy Note 2013-14, Energy Department, Government of Tamil Nadu, Chennai: 2014.

Tamil Nadu, Policy Note 2013-14 on Health, Social Welfare, Social Education, Adi-Dravidar Department, Government of Tamil Nadu, Chennai: 2014.

Tamil Nadu, Policy Note 2013-14 on Health, Social Welfare, School Education, Adi-Dravidar Department, Civil Supplies Department, Government of Tamil Nadu, Chennai: 2014.

Tamil Nadu, Policy Note 2013-14 on School Education, Government of Tamil Nadu, Chennai: 2014.

Tamil Nadu, Policy Note 2013-14 on Public, Home Departments. Government of Tamil Nadu, Chennai: 2014.

USA, World Bank policy on Increasing Governance Capacity, New York: World Bank Press, 1997.

Secondary Sources

Books

Agrawal, K. M. *Kautilya on Crime and Punishment*, Almora: Shree Almora Book Depot, 1990.

Anttiroka, V. and Bailey, S. J.. *Innovations in Public Governance*, New York: IOS Press, 2011.

Bah Mahmoud. *"Rural-Urban Transformations."* New Delhi: IIED Publishers, 2003.

Basile, Elisabetta and Ishita, Mukhopadhyay. *Changing Identity of Rural India: A Socio-Historic Analysis*, London: Anthem Press, 2009.

Bhagwati, Jagdish and Panagariya, Arvind. *India's Tryst with Destiny – Debunking Myths: Undermining Progress & Addressing New Challenges*, Noida: Collins Business, 2012.

Bhatnagar, Subhash. *E-Government - From Vision to Implementations: A Practical Guide with Case Studies*, New Delhi: Sage, 2004.

Bunce, Micheal. *Rural Settlement in an Urban World*, Cambridge: Taylor & Francis Publishers, 1982.

Bhattacharya, Bimalendu. *Urban Development in India: Since Pre-Historic Times*, New Delhi: Shree Publication House, 2009.

Chandler, Clay. *Reimagining India: Unlocking the Potential of Asia's Next Superpower*, New York: Simon & Schuster, 2013.

Clinton, Bill. *Giving: How Each of Us Can Change the World*, New Delhi: Arrow Books, 2008.

Chadha, G.K. *Rural Nonfarm Sector in the Indian Economy: Growth, Challenges and Future Direction*. Washington D.C: International Food Policy Research Institute, 2003.

Dalal, Clayton and Bass, D. B.. *Sustainable Development Strategies: A Resource Book*, Canada: Earth Scan, 2002.

Darshini, Mahadevia. *Growth or Development—Which Way is Gujarat Going*, New Delhi: Oxford Press, 2014.

Dev, S. Mahendra. *Inclusive Growth in India: Agriculture, Poverty and Human Development*, New Delhi: Oxford University Press, 2008.

Dreze, Jean and Sen, Amartya. *India: Development and Participation*, New Delhi: Oxford University Press, 2002.

Debroy, Bibek, Tellis, Ashley J. and Trevor Reece. *Getting India Back on Track: An Action Agenda for Reform*, New Delhi: Random House India, 2014.

Debroy, Bibek. *Gujarat: Governance for Growth and Development*, Gurgaon: Academic Foundation, 2012.

Das, Gurcharan. *India Unbound*, New Delhi: Viking Publisher, 2000.

Friedman, Thomas L. *That Used to Be Us: What Went Wrong With America & How It Can Come Back*, London: Little Brown, 2011.

Gant, George F. *The Concept of Development Administration,* New Delhi: Emerald Group Publishing Limited, 2006.

Gariyalli, C.K., Vettivel, S.K. and Vetri. *AMMA Model of Development in Tamil Nadu,* New Delhi: Vetri Publishers, 2014.

Gupta, K. R. *Rural Development in India,* New Delhi: Atlantic Publishers and Distributers, 2004.

Hirway, Indira and Shah, Amita. *Growth or Development: Which Way is Gujarat Going?* New Delhi: Oxford University Press, 2014.

Islam, R. *Rural Industrialisation and Employment in Asia, Programme,* New Delhi: ILO Asian Employment, 1986.

Jumani, Usha. *Empowering Society: An Analysis of Business, Government and Social Development Approaches to Empowerment,* New Delhi: Foundation Books, 2006.

Kalam, Abdul A. P. J. and Rajan, Y. S. *India 2020: A Vision for the New Millennium,* New Delhi: Penguin, 1998.

Kalam, Abdul A. P. J. and Singh, Srijan Pal. *Target 3 billion: PURA Innovate Solutions Towards Sustainable Development,* New Delhi: Penguin Books, 2011.

Kalam, Abdul A. P. J. and Pillai, Sivathanu. *Thoughts for Change: We Can Do It,* New Delhi: Pentagon Press, 2013.

Kalam, Abdul A. P. J. and Ponraj V. *Manifesto for Change: A Sequence to India 2020,* Noida: Harper Collins, 2014.

Kennedy, Paul. *Preparing for the Twenty-First Century,* London: Harper Collins, 1993.

Kishore, Satyendra. *Re-settlement of Ex-servicemen in India,* New Delhi: Concept Publishing, 1991.

Kumaraswamy, V. *Making Growth Happen In India: A Road Map for Policy Success,* New Delhi: Sage Publications India, 2014.

Karashima, Noboru. *A Concise History of South India: Issues and Interpretations,* New Delhi: Oxford University Press, 2014.

Keuning Wyte. *Ashoka: The Great,* New Delhi: Rupa Publications, 2011.

Mahurkar, Uday. *Centrestage: Inside the Narendra Modi Model of Governance,* Gurgaon: Random House, 2014.

Majumdar, N. A. Inclusive Growth Development Perspectives in Indian Economy, New Delhi: Academic Foundation, 2004.

Marino, Andy. *Narendra Modi: Political Biography,* Noida: Harper Collins, 2014.

Mehta, Prayag. *Psychological Strategy: Alternative Human Development*, New Delhi: Sage Publications, 1998.

Michael and Brady, David W. *Leadership and Growth*, New York: World Bank, 2010.

Maheshwari, Shriram. *Rural Development in India: A Public Policy Approach*, New Delhi: Sage Publications, 1995.

Munshi, K. and Rosenzweig, M. *Why is Mobility in India so Low? Social Insurance, Inequality, and Growth*, USA: Brown University, 2009.

Narula, Uma. *Dynamics of Indian Rural Economy*, Delhi: Atlantic Publishers, 2010.

Patel, Aashu. *Narendra Modi: Visionary Prime Minister*, New Delhi: Penguin Books, 2014.

Murthy, Narayana N. R. *Better India Better World*, New Delhi: Allen Lane, 2009.

Mandal, R. B. and Mittal, Ashok Kumar. *Introduction to Rural Settlements*, New Delhi: Concept Publishing Company, 2001.

Mookerji, Radhakumund. *The Ashoka*, Banaras: Banarsidas Publishers Pvt. Ltd., 2007.

Morris, Sebastian. *A Comparative Analysis of Gujarat's Economic Growth, Growth or Development: Which Way is Gujarat Going*. New Delhi: Oxford University Press, 2014.

Nehra, Surinder Singh and Athawale Sanhita. *Globalization Social Security & Indian Armed Forces*, New Delhi: GB Books, 2015.

Osbome, D.P. and Gaebler, T. *Reinventing Government: How the Entrepreneurial Spirit is Transforming the Public Sector*, New Delhi: Prentice-Hall, 1992.

Nye, Joseph S. Jr. *Future of Power*, New York: Public Affairs, 2011.

Pinto, Brian. *How Does My Country Grow? Economic Advice through Story Telling*, London: Oxford University Press, 2014.

Prasad, K.N. India's Rural Problem, California: Concept Publishing Company, 1991.

Patnaik, U. *The Long Transition: Essays on Political Economy*, New Delhi: Tulika Books, 1999.

Panagariya Arvind. *India: The Emerging Giant*, New Delhi: Oxford University Press, 2011.

Qureshi, Ishtiaq Husain. *Administration of the Mughal Empire*, Mumbai: Majestic Books, 2004.

Sastri, K. A. and Nilakanta. *Life and Culture of the Indian People: Historical Survey*, Bombay: Allied Publishers, 1974.

Sastri, K. A. and Nilakanta. *Age of the Nandas and Mauryas*, Banarsidass Publishers, 1952.

Saxena, M. *Non-farm Employment Opportunities in Rural Areas in Asia*, Tokyo: Asian Productivity Organization, 2000.

Saraswathi, S. *Government, Politics and People: Linkage Politics of Tamil Nadu*, Delhi: Manak Publications, 1995.

Sen, Amartya. *Development as Freedom*, New York: Alfred A. Knopf, 1999.

Shourie, Arun. *Governance and the Sclerosis that has Set In*, New Delhi: Rupa & Co, 2007.

Silam, R. *Rural Industrialisation and Employment in Asia*, New Delhi: ILO Asian Employment Programme, 2012.

Singh, Hoshiar. *Public Administration in India: Theory and Practice*, New Delhi: Sterling, 1989.

Singh, P. K. and Deewan, Sandeep. *Comprehensive National Power: A Model for India*, New Delhi: Vij Books, 2013.

Saith, A. *The Rural Non-Farm Economy: Processes and Policies*, Geneva: International Labour Force, 1992.

Singh, Surat and Singh, Mohinder. *Rural Development Administration in the 21st century: A Multi-Dimensional Study*, New Delhi: Deep & Deep Publications, 2007.

Singha, Komol. *Rural Development in India: Retrospect and Prospects*, Delhi: Concept Publishing Company, 2010.

Singh, Awadesh, K. *Rural Marketing: Indian Perspective*, New Delhi: New Age International, 2005.

Shah, Amita and Pattnaik, Itishree. *High Growth Agriculture in Gujarat: An Enquiry into Inclusiveness and Sustainability*. New Delhi: Oxford University Press, 2014.

Subbarayalu, Y. *South India under the Cholas*, New Delhi: Oxford University Press, 2011.

Tharoor, Shashi. *India's Future is Now: The Vision and Road Map for the Country by her Young Parliamentarians*, New Delhi: Wisdom Tree, 2013.

Toffler, Alvin and Toffler, Heidi. *Revolutionary Wealth*, New York: Alfred A. Knopf, 2006.

Toffler, Alvin and Toffler, Heidi. *War and Anti-War: Survival of the Dawn of the 21st Century*, New York: Little Brown, 1993.

Turner, Mark and Hulme, David. *Governance, Administration and Development*, London: MacMillan Press, 1997.

Venugopal, Dharmalingam. *Indian Banking Reforms and after: A Bank Economist's Take*, Chennai: Forum for Inclusive Development, 2012.

Viswanathan, P.K. and Pathak, Jharna. *Economic Growth and the State of Natural Resources and the Environment in Gujarat: A Critical Assessment', Growth or Development—Which Way is Gujarat Going*. New Delhi: Oxford University Press, 2014.

Journals

Athawale, Yogesh B. "Image of the Armed Forces—Arresting Negative Trends", *USI Journal*, Vol. CXXXVI, No. 564, April-June 2006.

Alagh, Y.K. "Gujarat: Sifting Fact from Fiction," *Mint Opinion*. August 11, 2013.

Anttiroiko, A. and Bailey, S. J. *"Innovations in Public Governance"*, IOS Press, May 2011.

Balaram, K. "Department for Welfare of Ex-Servicemen Proposal", *USI Journal*, Vol. CXX1, 1999.

Banerjee, A. and T. Piketty. "Are the rich growing richer: Evidence from Indian tax data Working papers," MIT and *CEPREMAP*, 2001.

Chakravarty, Anjan, "The Evolving Scope of Rural India." *Advances in Economics and Business*, 3(7), 2015.

Dass, Gurucharan. "The Indian Model", *Foreign Affairs*, Vol. 85, No. 4, July / August 2006.

Dutta, Rakesh. "Ameliorating Ex-Servicemen Conditions, Suggestions and Alternatives", *Indian Defence Review*, 2No. 7, July 1994.

Goel, S.L. "Public Administration", *The Indian Journal of Public Administration*, July-September 2008.

Harmut, Schinder. "Participatory Governance for Poverty Reduction", *Journal of International Development*, 1999.

Jagannathan, R. "Is the Gujarat growth story for real? Apparently, yes." *First Post. Economy*, October 8, 2012.

Kumar, Sampath. "Welfare, Battle Casualties (Part I)", *USI Journal*, Vol. CXXXI, No. 544, April-June 2001.

Kumar, Sampath. "Welfare, Battle Casualties (Part II)", *USI Journal*, Vol. CXXXI, No. 545, 2001.

Kotlyar, I. and Karakowsky, L."Falling Over Ourselves to Follow the Leader", *Journal of Leadership & Organisational Studies*, Vol. 14. 2007.

Mondal, Puja. "Brief Essay on Rural Poverty." *Article Library*, February 2014.

Mondal, Puja. "Rural Reconstruction in India", *Article Library*, May 2014.

Mondal, Puja. "Panchayati Raj System in India", *Article Library*, May 2014.

Mukul, Asher G. "For good statistics and links on Gujarat development and budget, etc, 'Gujarat's budget reflects sound development strategy." *East Asia Forum*, April 3, 2012.

Peters, B. Guy. "Government Reorganization: A Theoretical Analysis", *International Political Social Review*, No. 13 (2), April 1992.

Singh, Jasjit. "Younger Fighting Forces for Greater, Combat Effectiveness", *Indian Defence Review*, Vol. 18, No. 1, January–March 2003.

Singh, Satyindra. "Ex-Servicemen, Tinkering with the Problem", *Indian Defence Review*, No. 1, January 1989.

Singh, Satyindra. "Ex-Servicemen as an Instrument of National Development." *Indian Defence Review*, January 1989.

S. Aijaz. "Uneducated India: Learning at the rural juncture." *Yojana*, February 20, 2015.

Schneider, Harmut. "Participatory Governance for Poverty Reduction." *Journal of International Development*, 1999.

Sanjay, Sethi. "Initiatives for Exploiting the Potential of Ex-Servicemen." *CLAWS*, April, 2015.

Shah, Tushaar and Verma, Shilp. "Real-time Co-management of Electricity and Groundwater: An Assessment of Gujarat's Pioneering "Jyotigram" Scheme." International Water Management Institute, 2007.

Vas, E.A. "Armed Forces, A State's Obligation to Ex-Servicemen", *Indian Defence Review*, No. 2, July 1989.

Yogima, Plan and Sharma, Seth. "Report on Gujarat's 'Rurban Model' to Replace UPA's 'Providing Urban Amenities in Rural Areas", ET Bureau, July 15, 2014.

Magazines

Debroy, Bibek. "Moral of the Gujarat Story." *India Today*, December 21, 2012.

"India's Electricity Reforms: A Power Shortage May Thwart India's Rush to Modernity." *Economist*, September 22, 2005.

Jaitley, Arun. "Corporate should utilise Ex-servicemen in Workforce", *Business Standard*, August 19, 2014.

Poromesh, Acharya. "Education: Panchayat and Decentralisation, Myths & Reality." *Economic and Political Weekly*, February 2002.

Shah et al. "Secret of Gujarat's Agrarian Miracle after 2000." *Economic and Political Weekly*, December 26, 2009.

Newspapers

Agarwala, Ramgopal. "Developing Modern Village Clusters", *The Hindu*, September 18, 2014.

Goswami, Priyankan, "Indian Democracy, Where Anna Hazare Failed", *Times of Assam*, December 13, 2011.

"Indian bureaucracy rated worst in Asia, says a Political & Economic Risk Consultancy report", *The Economic Times*, January 11, 2012.

Jha, Amarendra. "From plain ugly to khub-surat." *The Times of India*, July 31, 2005.

Web References

http://www.naandi.org/Safewater/default.asp, Accessed on 21-02-2016.

http://www.fig.net/pub/morocco/proceedings/PS1/PS1_1_okpala.pdf, Accessed on 02-04-2016.

http://lanic.utexas.edu/project/etext/llilas/cpa/spring06/welfare/corbridge.pdf, Accessed on 07-05-2016.

http://guj-epd.gov.in/epd jyotiyojna.htm. Energy & Petrochemicals Department, Accessed on 02-08-16.

http://economics.ouls.ox.ac.uk/9480/, Accessed on 07-06-2016.

https://sites.google.com/site/errajanikantissuediscussion/policy/pura.Indra, Rajni Kant. PURA, Information & Analysis, Accessed on 04-09-2016.

http://www.unescap.org/pdd/prs/Project Activities/Ongoing/Rural-Urban%20 Linkages/Rural-Urban%20Linkages-policyimp.pdf, Accessed on 09-07-2016.

INDEX